ENVIRONMENTAL JUSTICE, POPULAR STRUGGLE AND COMMUNITY DEVELOPMENT

RETHINKING COMMUNITY DEVELOPMENT SERIES

Series editors: Mae Shaw, University of Edinburgh, Rosie R. Meade, University College Cork and Sarah Banks, University of Durham

The Rethinking Community Development Series is an international book series that offers the opportunity for a critical re-evaluation of community development. Rethinking what community development means in theory as well as in practice, it aims to draw together a broad range of international, cross-disciplinary and cross-generational perspectives.

Each book in the series:

- provides an international perspective on community development;
- theorises issues and practices in a way that encourages diverse audiences to consider the potentiality and future directions of community development;
- encourages practitioners to engage more critically with their work.

Also available:

Politics, power and community development

Class, inequality and community development

Funding, power and community development

Ethics, equity and community development

Information on all titles is available on our website:

https://policy.bristoluniversitypress.co.uk/rethinking-community-development

Rethinking Community Development

ENVIRONMENTAL JUSTICE, POPULAR STRUGGLE AND COMMUNITY DEVELOPMENT

Edited by
Anne Harley and Eurig Scandrett

First published in Great Britain in 2019 by

Policy Press
University of Bristol
1-9 Old Park Hill
Bristol
BS2 8BB
UK
t: +44 (0)117 954 5940
pp-info@bristol.ac.uk
www.policypress.co.uk

North America office:
Policy Press
c/o The University of Chicago Press
1427 East 60th Street
Chicago, IL 60637, USA
t: +1 773 702 7700
f: +1 773-702-9756
sales@press.uchicago.edu
www.press.uchicago.edu

© Policy Press 2019

British Library Cataloguing in Publication Data
A catalogue record for this book is available from the British Library

Library of Congress Cataloging-in-Publication Data
A catalog record for this book has been requested

978-1-4473-5083-5 hardback
978-1-4473-5085-9 paperback
978-1-4473-5084-2 ePdf
978-1-4473-5086-6 ePub
978-1-4473-5087-3 Mobi

The rights of Anne Harley and Eurig Scandrett to be identified as editors of this work has been asserted by them in accordance with the Copyright, Designs and Patents Act 1988.

All rights reserved: no part of this publication may be reproduced, stored in a retrieval system, or transmitted in any form or by any means, electronic, mechanical, photocopying, recording, or otherwise without the prior permission of Policy Press.

The statements and opinions contained within this publication are solely those of the author and not of the University of Bristol or Policy Press. The University of Bristol and Policy Press disclaim responsibility for any injury to persons or property resulting from any material published in this publication.

Policy Press works to counter discrimination on grounds of gender, race, disability, age and sexuality.

Cover design by Liam Roberts
Front cover image: Ian Martin
Printed and bound in Great Britain by CMP, Poole
Policy Press uses environmentally responsible print partners

We dedicate this collection to Temistocles Machado, a community activist in Buenaventura, Colombia who played an important role in the Civic Strike to Live with Dignity, discussed in this book, and who was assassinated on 27 January 2018 while it was being prepared; and to all of those killed in the various environmental justice struggles included in the book and beyond, in recognition of their suffering and sacrifice. Aluta continua.

Contents

List of figures — ix
Series editors' preface — xi
Preface — xiii
Acknowledgements — xv
Notes on contributors — xvii
Abbreviations — xxiii

One	Community, development and popular struggles for environmental justice *Anne Harley and Eurig Scandrett*	1
Two	Resisting Shell in Ireland: making and remaking alliances between communities, movements and activists *Hilary Darcy and Laurence Cox*	15
Three	'No tenemos armas pero tenemos dignidad': learning from the civic strike in Buenaventura, Colombia *Patrick Kane with Berenice Celeyta*	29
Four	No pollution and no Roma in my backyard: class and race in framing local activism in Laborov, eastern Slovakia *Richard Filčák and Daniel Škobla*	53
Five	Tackling waste in Scotland: incineration, business and politics vs community activism *Jennifer Mackay*	69
Six	An unfractured line: an academic tale of self-reflective social movement learning in the Nova Scotia anti-fracking movement *Jonathan Langdon*	83
Seven	'Mines come to bring poverty': extractive industry in the life of the people in KwaZulu-Natal, South Africa *Mark Butler*	101
Eight	Ecological justice for Palestine *Simon I. Awad*	117
Nine	Learning and teaching: reflections on an environmental justice school for activists in South Africa *Bobby Peek and Jeanne Prinsloo*	135
Ten	The environment as a site of struggle against settler-colonisation in Palestine *Abeer al-Butmeh, Zayneb al-Shalalfeh and Mahmoud Zwahre with Eurig Scandrett*	153

Eleven	Communities resisting environmental injustice in India: philanthrocapitalism and incorporation of people's movements	173
	Eurig Scandrett, Dharmesh Shah and Shweta Narayan	
Twelve	Grassroots struggles to protect occupational and environmental health	189
	Kathy Jenkins and Sara Marsden	

Conclusion 211
Anne Harley and Eurig Scandrett

Index 219

List of figures

1.1	Locations of specific environmental justice struggles discussed in the book	11
3.1	Map of Colombia, showing strategic position of Buenaventura	31
3.2	Clashes between police and community members at the *punto de encuentro* in the Isla de la Paz neighbourhood	41
3.3	The historic march of 21 May 2017 with an estimated 200,000 people	43
3.4	Women's march, 3 June 2017	48
4.1	Map showing location of power plant project, town centre with residential areas and Roma settlement	55
4.2	(a) One of the three containers serving the community only one day after it was emptied; and (b) an anti-flood channel in which waste piled up	64
4.3	A billboard from the campaign for a new underground waste storage system	65
8.1	Map showing Palestinian loss of land, 1917–2012	119
9.1	Externalisation	137
9.2	Enclosure	138
9.3	Exclusion	139

SERIES EDITORS' PREFACE

Rethinking Community Development

Communities are a continuing focus of public policy and citizen action worldwide. The purposes and functions of work with communities of place, interest and identity vary between and within contexts and change over time. Nevertheless, community development – as both an occupation and as a democratic practice concerned with the demands and aspirations of people in communities – has been extraordinarily enduring.

This book series aims to provide a critical re-evaluation of community development in theory and practice, in the light of new challenges posed by the complex interplay of emancipatory, democratic, self-help and managerial imperatives in different parts of the world. Through a series of edited and authored volumes, *Rethinking Community Development* will draw together international, cross-generational and cross-disciplinary perspectives, using contextual specificity as a lens through which to explore the localised consequences of global processes. Each text in the series will:

- *promote critical thinking*, through examining the contradictory position of community development, including the tensions between policy imperatives and the interests and demands of communities.
- *include a range of international examples*, in order to explore the localised consequences of global processes.
- *include contributions from established and up-and-coming new voices*, from a range of geographical contexts.
- *offer topical and timely perspectives*, drawing on historical and theoretical resources in a generative and enlivening way.
- *inform and engage a new generation of practitioners*, bringing new and established voices together to stimulate diverse and innovative perspectives on community development.

If you have a broad or particular interest in community development that could be expanded into an authored or edited collection for this book series, contact:

Mae Shaw	Rosie R. Meade	Sarah Banks
mae.shaw@ed.ac.uk	r.meade@ucc.ie	s.j.banks@durham.ac.uk

Preface

This book was born some years ago, when the series editors suggested to Eurig, a committed lifelong activist in the environmental justice field as well as an academic, that a collection on environmental justice and community development might make a useful contribution to the series *Rethinking Community Development*. During a conference of the Popular Education Network, Eurig approached Anne, an academic who has been involved in environmental justice issues in a different context, to co-edit the collection.

The process of producing the book has been a joy, although not without its difficulties. The contributors are all engaged in some way with struggles against the exploitations of neoliberalism, some as activists, some as academics, many as both. Activists constantly operate to time-scales determined by the situation in which we and our comrades find ourselves. Academics in all parts of the world also face the sustained imposition of neoliberal practices on their working conditions. Writing the stories of the very different struggles included in this book has thus not always been easy, but the book has allowed a valuable space for engagement and reflection, as well as, hopefully, providing important insights and lessons to other activists and academics and activist-academics involved in struggles around the world. It has truly been a privilege to work with such a range of committed activists and scholars.

Many of the chapters have been co-produced, a process that has been a generator of new insights. Many of the chapters began as dialogues between two or more of those involved in a struggle, or acting in solidarity. Thus, even when the name of only one author appears, the chapter is usually the result of some kind of collective process, although one person has taken on the work of writing and the views expressed are those of the author. Where more than one author's name appears, in most cases they are given in alphabetical order, except when the contributors themselves have chosen to deviate from that. Where joint authors have decided, collectively, that one person has taken on most of the work, that person's name is cited first, or we have used 'with' to indicate a division of labour between the writing work, content and argument in developing the chapter.

The chapters reflect on struggles related to environmental justice at a micro/community level, as well as struggles at a more macro level. What is striking across the chapters is the 'generative themes' of solidarity and agency; the very things Bhattacharyya (2004) argues to be the foundation of community development. The stories show that often, 'development' as it is currently constructed is in fact about the opposite. The accounts of micro-level struggles, and those taking place on a more macro level, identify tensions around how particular struggles relate to each other or the ways in which activists from outside the communities directly affected by environmental injustice (as is the case for many environmental activists and activist-academics) engage with those who are. A number of the chapters thus speak to potential or actual fault-lines or fractures in struggles at micro or macro level. What is clear from the stories, then, is that solidarity involves work, and especially by those of us who have been privileged – in however compromised and conflictual ways – by the eroding forces of capital accumulation and hegemonic patriarchy. It also requires from us a deep reflection on the ways in which, as activists, academics, academic-activists or any other permutations, we assume the thinking and agency of those engaged in struggle, and act to build this.

Anne Harley *Eurig Scandrett*
Pietermaritzburg *Edinburgh*
July 2018 *July 2018*

Acknowledgements

We would like to thank all of the contributors to this book for their commitment to the project, and for providing their chapters under often difficult conditions.

We would also like to thank the series editors, Sarah Banks, Rosie Meade and Mae Shaw, for approaching us to work on this book and providing really useful feedback on our initial proposal. In particular, we would like to thank Mae Shaw, who has encouraged this project from the beginning and given helpful advice whenever we asked for it.

The editors and contributors would like to acknowledge all those involved in the environmental justice struggles described in this book.

Notes on contributors

Abeer al-Butmeh is the Coordinator of Palestinian Environmental NGOs Network – Friends of Earth Palestine. She obtained her BA and Master's degree from Ber Zeit University, specialising in water and environmental engineering. She has worked in this field since 2006. She has participated in local and international conferences related to water and environment, and in many environmental research studies locally. She has also participated in many environmental activities and events locally and internationally.

Zayneb al-Shalalfeh is a Palestinian woman with an MSc degree in Water Security and International Development from the University of East Anglia, UK. She has over nine years of progressive experience and several publications in Water, Sanitation, Hygiene (WASH) and Food Security. She has worked in both development and humanitarian projects, with several international and Palestinian organisations.

Simon I. Awad is the Executive Director of the Environmental Education Center (EEC) of the Evangelical Lutheran Church in Jordan and the Holy Land (ELCJHL). The EEC, based in Palestine, works in the fields of education, advocacy, protection of biodiversity and climate change. A key element of his work is providing education in an attempt to protect and restore ecosystems in Palestine. Simon has authored and co-authored several books and is an activist in eco-justice issues and human rights, undertakes voluntary work in these areas and is an ornithologist. In charge of running several local development institutions in Palestine, Simon has also represented the EEC in many local, regional and international forums.

Mark Butler has spent a lifetime trying to learn from, and support, emancipatory and popular militancy. At the moment he does this mainly through work with the Church Land Programme, a small, independent non-profit organisation based in KwaZulu-Natal province, South Africa. He is still learning but was largely responsible for typing up his chapter (as part of a larger project on struggles around extractive industries). However, the central section, and the leading insights, ideas and politics, are simply an honest attempt to capture the thinking and the words of people on the ground where these developments are going down – as well as the extraordinary work of mutual encouragement and reflection that these militants do with his colleagues at the Church Land Programme.

Berenice Celeyta is a human rights activist with over 30 years of experience of working in defence of communities and vulnerable sectors all over Colombia, investigating and documenting abuses and building the capacity of communities to prevent and resist violations. She advises the Buenaventura civic strike executive committee on human rights issues. In 1998 she was awarded the prestigious Robert F. Kennedy Human Rights Award.

Laurence Cox has been active in social movements for over 30 years. He co-edited *Silence Would Be Treason*, Ken Saro-Wiwa's last writings before his execution by the Nigerian military dictatorship for opposing Shell. He is Senior Lecturer in Sociology at the National University of Ireland Maynooth.

Hilary Darcy is a Dublin-based educator and researcher interested in globalisation, the state and social movements. After successfully campaigning to Repeal the 8th (Amendment), she has returned to finish her PhD at Maynooth University Department of Sociology on the policing of social conflict, based on her fieldwork in Erris, Co Mayo.

Richard Filčák is Deputy Director at the Centre of Social and Psychological Sciences and acting Head of Forecasting Institute, Slovak Academy of Sciences. His work and research interests are mainly in environmental and social policy development in the transitional countries of Central and Eastern Europe – with particular attention to social and territorial exclusion leading to exposure to environmental risks; access to resources; and vulnerability of people. He has worked as a consultant and lead/senior expert for the Slovak government, UNDP, UNEP, World Bank, European Commission and various NGOs.

Anne Harley is Lecturer in Adult Education and Education and Development at the University of KwaZulu-Natal, in Pietermaritzburg, South Africa. Previously, she undertook research for the National Land Committee and the Black Sash. Anne also heads up the Paulo Freire project in the Adult Education discipline, which runs a variety of popular education events, including those related to environmental justice, in collaboration with civil society organisations. Her key area of interest is informal learning in struggle.

Kathy Jenkins has been involved in Workplace Health and Safety, professionally through public health, health promotion and university teaching, and also through active involvement in the trade union movement, for the last 25 years. She has been active in Scottish Hazards, which campaigns for improved working conditions in Scotland, since 1992 and is currently its secretary and one of its trustees. Kathy has also been actively involved in the European Work Hazards Network and is currently a member of its Steering Group. She is a trustee of Trade Union Friends of Bhopal and of the Bhopal Medical Appeal. She is a member of Unite the Union and a Health and Safety Branch officer.

Patrick Kane has been involved in solidarity activism supporting social movements and trade unions in Colombia for over a decade. At the time of writing, he was based in Colombia on fieldwork as part of a broader research project into social movement learning and knowledge production funded by the UK's Economic and Social Research Council.

Jonathan Langdon has been working with social movements in Ghana since 2001. At the same time he has worked closely with renewable energy movements/groups in Nova Scotia, such as Responsible Energy Action in Antigonish, as well as sitting on the steering committee of the Nova Scotia Fracking Resource Action Coalition (NOFRAC). Langdon's award-winning work (David Jones award, 2013 and 2017) has been published in prominent international and Canadian development, participatory research and adult education journals. He is the editor of *Indigenous Knowledges, Development and Education* (Sense 2009). He is Canada Research Chair for Sustainability and Social Change Leadership at St Francis Xavier University, in Mi'kma'ki/Nova Scotia, Canada.

Jennifer Mackay is a social/environmental activist and waste campaigner and researcher. Jennifer is currently doing her PhD at Queen Margaret University, Scotland, focusing on Community Waste in Scotland and in India, and has also studied gender and intersectionality. She has worked for the Scottish Environment Protection Agency, Community Recycling Network Scotland and Scottish Education and Action for Development. She has conducted studies in ecological economics and environmental justice and community activism against climate change. Jennifer has also worked on toxic chemicals and waste campaigns with Friends of the Earth Scotland, Friends of the Earth Europe, Greenpeace UK and Global Anti-Incinerator Alliance.

Sara Marsden began her career with seven years as a UK government health and safety inspector (working for the Health and Safety Executive), and then worked as the national health and safety coordinator for a large UK trade union, bringing her into contact with the Hazards movement and other advocacy/activist groups. Her subsequent professional work included private sector and government regulation in a number of areas closely related to health risk, latterly broadening to a public health perspective and MSc training in public health policy research. She is currently working as an independent researcher (including for the Trade Union Friends of Bhopal) and is active in the Hazards movement, the People's Health Movement (Scotland) and Common Weal (a Scottish 'think and do' tank).

Shweta Narayan is a researcher and an environmental justice activist who advises the Community Environmental Monitoring (CEM) programme for The Other Media. She has also been associated as a volunteer for the campaign for justice for the survivors of the Bhopal Gas Tragedy since 2002.

Bobby Peek is the co-founder of groundWork, a South African environmental justice NGO that was started in 1999. His 25 years of environmental justice activism were fuelled by living on the fenceline of an oil refinery in apartheid South Africa. He works in and supports local and global actions for environmental justice.

Jeanne Prinsloo has designed and coordinates the groundWork Environmental Justice School for Activists. She teaches and researches in the field of cultural studies, with a focus on representation and identities.

Eurig Scandrett is an environmental activist, Senior Lecturer in Public Sociology at Queen Margaret University, Scotland and a trade union representative with the University and College Union. He previously worked in environmental biology, community work and adult education and was Head of Community Action at Friends of the Earth Scotland.

Dharmesh Shah is a researcher and environmental activist associated with citizens' science initiatives in India. He is interested in the anthropology of waste and understanding the role of plastics in the anthropocene. He also works on issues related to environmental health, toxics, mining and animal rights.

Daniel Škobla is a senior researcher at the Institute for Ethnology and Social Anthropology of the Slovak Academy of Science in Bratislava. He graduated in Sociology from the Central European University (CEU) and obtained a PhD from the Polish Academy of Sciences in Warsaw. He worked as a Poverty Reduction Officer with the United Nations Development Program and carried out research on the living conditions of the Roma population in Central Europe. He provided technical assistance for the Slovak government regarding the Decade of Roma Inclusion 2005–2015 and the EU Framework for National Roma Integration Strategies 2020. He has also been involved in Roma advocacy on an international level, participating in numerous meetings throughout Europe. He has also cooperated with the non-governmental organisations European Roma Rights Centre, Amnesty International and the Open Society Institute. He has written for academic journals such as *Slovak Sociological Review*, *Polish Sociological Review* and *Ethnic and Racial Studies*.

Mahmoud Soliman Zwahre is a Palestinian activist and one of the 2009 founders of the Popular Struggle Coordination Committee, as an umbrella for non-violent resistance in occupied Palestinian land. He is also the coordinator of the popular committee against the segregation wall and illegal Israeli settlement in Al-Ma'sara village, south of Bethlehem. Mahmoud is a PhD candidate at Coventry University. His research is on the mobilisation and demobilisation of Palestinian society towards unarmed popular resistance from 2004 to 2014.

Abbreviations

AMRC	Asia Monitor Resource Centre
ANC	African National Congress
ANROAV	Asian Network for Rights of Occupational and Accident Victims
ANROEV	Asian Network for the Rights of Occupational and Environmental Victims
CLEAN	Community Labor Environmental Action Network
CLP	Church Land Programme
COSH	National Council for Occupational Safety and Health
CRNS	Community Recycling Network for Scotland
CSR	corporate social responsibility
EEC	Environmental Education Center
EIA	Environmental Impact Assessment
EJS	Environmental Justice School
EQA	Environmental Quality Authority
ESMAD	Escuadrón Móvil Antidisturbios (Mobile Anti-Disturbance Squadron)
EU	European Union
EWHN	European Work Hazards Network
FACK	Families Against Corporate Killers
FCRA	Foreign Contributions (Regulation) Act
GAINS	Green Alternatives to Incineration in Scotland
GP	general practitioner
HIA	Health Impact Assessment
ILO	International Labour Organization
ITUC	International Trade Union Confederation
JNF	Jewish National Fund
KZN	KwaZulu-Natal
NAPM	National Alliance of People's Movements
NEP	New Economic Programme
NGO	non-governmental organisation
NOFRAC	Nova Scotia Fracking Research and Advocacy Coalition
OHS	Occupational Health and Safety
PAS	Publicly Available Specification
PCN	Proceso de Comunidades Negras (Black Communities Process)

PCPIR	Petroleum, Chemicals and Petrochemicals Investment Region
REA	Responsible Energy Action
RÚVZ	Regional Public Health Authority
SAC	Special Area of Conservation
SEPA	Scottish Environment Protection Agency
SML	social movement learning
TTIP	Transatlantic Trade and Investment Partnership
UK	United Kingdom
UN	United Nations
UNCED	United Nations Conference on Environment and Development
UNDP	United Nations Development Programme
US	United States (of America)

ONE

Community, development and popular struggles for environmental justice

Anne Harley and Eurig Scandrett

Introduction

'The environment' comprises many aspects of the world: the complex ecosystems and biological and chemical cycles on which all life on the planet depends; the resources exploited by human societies throughout history in structures of production and consumption to meet needs and desires; the spaces in which both production and its waste stream are located and in which human non-productive, reproductive, creative and recreational activity occurs; and the physical structures of habitation that shape our horizons and our personalities. In the conditions of late capitalism, the environment is a site for capital accumulation, a source of raw materials, a place to locate productive industry, a space to be traversed in the distribution of commodities to markets and a sink for the depositing of the wastes of production and consumption. Increasingly, capital finds new ways to commodify the environment itself, as 'second nature'. Alongside this, environments are gendered and racialised as nature and social structures are shaped and reshaped to favour the interests of powerful social groups. These activities, of powerful classes and groups extending their interests, are often referred to as 'development'.

The social structuring of environments and their dispossession in the interests of capital are made possible in regimes of colonialism. Recent scholarship has emphasised the significance of different modes of colonialism and their impacts on resource dispossession and construction. It is perhaps significant that many of the chapters in this collection are located in settler-colonial societies in different stages of 'development' – Canada, Palestine, South Africa – as well as in postcolonial Ireland, India and Colombia. Significant for our purposes are the different social relations of accumulation in these modes of colonisation – in the former resource dispossession follows a logic of population expulsion, whereas in the latter it is accompanied by proletarianisation and exploitation of labour power.

At the same time, environments are structured through gender regimes. In different contexts, the gendered division of labour has tended to allocate women's (free, unpaid) labour to the means of reproduction, including for community environmental maintenance and responsibility for different environments from those of men – at times bringing women and men into conflict over environmental spaces. Men have often been allocated to extractive and manufacturing labour, leading to gendered constructions of environmental risk. As well as privileging men in a patriarchal gender order, these processes of gendering the environment have also served the purposes of capital accumulation.

This political economy of the environment does not go unchallenged. The activities of such 'movements from above' are met and constantly forced to adapt through the agency of environmental justice movements from below. Such movements and their constituents provide stubborn resistance to their environments being commodified or recreated in the image of the powerful. They mobilise to defend and extend the environments in which subaltern groups survive, thrive, cherish or deem sacred. From environmental non-governmental organisations (NGOs) to urban community action groups, from indigenous and peasant anti-colonial movements to radical scientists, the interests of the environment – and the embedded material interests of the actors – stop, extract concessions from and occasionally overturn the interests of power. Moreover, the classes and social groups engaged in this conflict, both dominant and subaltern, form more or less stable alliances on the basis of shared or accommodated interests, and even generalised interests built from the particularities of struggle. The environment, in all its complexity, is therefore a product of social and political struggle over access, definition and evaluation.

It is in this constant dynamic process of clashes between interests, between alliances of movements from above and below, of wars of position and manoeuvre, in which the environment is forged, that activities that may be classed as 'community development' take place. The purpose of this book therefore is to attempt to analyse some of these struggles, by inviting those engaged in these activities and their allies to elucidate the roles of the different actors, their interests and power, and to discern strategies for alternative forms of development. In so doing, the contributors and we ourselves draw on shared analytical tools derived from Marxism, social ecology, feminism, anti-colonialism and other emancipatory traditions. These analytical approaches have proved to be powerfully robust in emancipatory work around gender, 'race', anti-colonialism and political ecology as well as class and capital. They have also provided invaluable insights for the practices of community development, popular education and social movement mobilisation.

Whilst environmental justice struggles and 'environmentalism of the poor' were largely unrecognised by western social theory, the two dominant western traditions of environmentalism – ecocentric and technocentric – emerged from concerns about the environmental impacts of 19th and early 20th-century capitalist expansions, and proposed either protectionist or managed solutions (Guha, 2000; Martínez-Alier, 2002). Ultimately, both traditions have found ways of accommodating to capital accumulation.

Hegemony and sustainable development

In 1992, partially as a result of pressure from western environmentalism, the United Nations Conference on Environment and Development (UNCED, or 'Earth Summit') published *Agenda 21: A global plan of action for sustainable development*. This concept of sustainable development was presented as a solution to the conflicting demands of industrial development and environmental limitations.

The struggle for hegemony around sustainable development provides an insight into the wider conflicts of the period. The accelerated environmental devastation that accompanied both postwar/postcolonial organised capitalism and centrally planned economies; the exposure, by OPEC's price fixing, of the dependence of western capitalism on oil (hydrocarbon capitalism) and thus vulnerability; the explicit toxicity of capitalist cost shifting made tragically clear by the Bhopal (1984), Chernobyl (1986) and Karin B (1988) disasters and exposing at the same time the myriad smaller toxic tragedies occurring daily; and the scientific exposure and increased public awareness of long-standing ecological damage in the forms of biodiversity loss, acid rain, ozone depletion and global warming, all created a series of fronts on which the environment became central to the war of position with capital. By the time that the pressure on governments from the increasingly organised and effective environmental movement had led to the UNCED, the mechanisms of state-managed capital accumulation with concessions to the more powerful sectors of the working class and formerly colonised peoples were collapsing.

Nonetheless, this is the model adopted in Agenda 21, ostensibly an agreement between states to involve all sectors of society, privileging key disempowered groups (women, youth, indigenous people, workers and so on) as they lead progress towards a social democratic reading of sustainable development. Meanwhile, the global economy had become neoliberal, driven by the violent experiments of South American military regimes; the Thatcher and Reagan governments of the United Kingdom (UK) and United States of America (US); the growth of the Pacific tiger economies; the post-communist dash for assets in the former Soviet Union; structural adjustments in indebted postcolonial countries, principally in Africa; the emergence of post-import substitutionist new economic policies in South America and Asia; and the soon-to-be-opened-for-post-Apartheid-business South Africa.

In this phase of capital accumulation and class redistribution of assets, the environmental movement provided a challenge, both politically (opening up a new front since the labour movement was in retreat) and materially (environmental damage provided a genuine limit to capitalist growth). The mechanisms for incorporating both the environment and the movement into the interests of capital accumulation had not yet been developed. Lesley Sklair (2001) examines the process through which the sustainable development historical bloc developed at a global level, in which the transnational capitalist class built alliances with the transnational environmental elite in order to capture the environmental movement for global capital. This served to neutralise or marginalise radical environmentalism's threat to the capitalist class's economic interests, causing divisions in the environmental movement (see Doherty and Doyle, 2013) and generating new oppositional strategies (Seel et al, 2000).

A parallel process occurred at local levels through the interface with community development (Scandrett, 2000), although it played out in diverse ways in different socio-political contexts. Local Agenda 21 advocated that local authorities should enter into a dialogue with citizens, local organisations and private enterprises to adopt 'a local Agenda 21' (UNCED, 1993).

For some community workers working 'in and against' the local state, this provided legitimacy for the radical work of engaging with community struggles and working to build a participatory democracy by placing public services, development planning and local production under the control of locally organised citizens. Eurig worked for Friends of the Earth Scotland at this time to develop community action for environmental justice (Agents for Environmental Justice and

Scandrett, 2003). Anne became deeply involved in Earthlife Africa (ELA), an environmental justice organisation that emerged in South Africa in the late 1980s, and co-chaired ELA's 1992 conference, 'What does it mean to be green in South Africa', which drew on Agenda 21. Local Agenda 21 provided a Trojan horse for the promotion of participatory democracy in a range of public services as well as in environmental campaigning.

At the same time, the discourse of participation, consultation and stakeholder involvement was manipulated to obfuscate power relations and give a semblance of participation while key decisions were made elsewhere. Business interests also mobilised to incorporate local communities and implement 'dispossession through participation' (Collins, 2006). Participatory methods, which were proliferating, became marketing opportunities for branded techniques, and a focus on methods helped to depoliticise environmental community work, hiding questions of politics: participation in what, on whose terms and for whose benefit? As neoliberal reforms privatised services, cut local state budgets and centralised decision making, participatory processes were employed to manage cuts to public services and deliver what many activists referred to as the 'hidden agenda 21'.

By the time of the next Earth Summit, in Johannesburg in 2002, sustainable development had become the preserve of the transnational corporations through initiatives such as 'type 2 agreements'. In contrast to the state-led (type 1) framework of Agenda 21, type 2 agreements are those between private sector and (selected) civil society, bypassing any vestiges of a social interventionist state, legitimising privatisation of state services and excluding any radical environmentalist and social movement actors not acting in the interests of capital.

Environmental justice movements

Meanwhile a parallel process was occurring in populations outside these debates. In the US, the environmental justice movement emerged from among African American, Hispanic, poor white and Native American communities. This alternative strand of environmentalism challenged both the discriminatory practices of federal environmental protection and the elite understanding of 'environment' of mainstream environmentalism. To some commentators (Faber and McCarthy, 2003), this movement showed the potential emergence of a new hegemonic bloc of subaltern actors challenging racialised capital accumulation in its most advanced country as, in Cox and Nilsen's (2014) terms, local militant particularist struggles emerged into national and international campaigns and social movements. Others pointed out that 'materialist environmentalism' (Guha and Martínez-Alier, 1997) or 'environmentalism of the poor' (Martínez-Alier, 2002) constitutes an ongoing current of social challenge to economic cost shifting. As the US environmental justice movement achieved some concessions within a dominant neoliberal paradigm, focus shifted to more reformist agendas, initially optimistically through alliances with mainstream NGOs in a frame of 'just sustainability', and latterly as a complete incorporation into neoliberal conditions. Carter (2016) has documented how elements of the US environmental justice movement (in the Los Angeles Latino communities) have been transformed through neoliberalism to what he calls EJ 2.0:

> This shift in EJ movement politics is shaped by broader political-economic changes, including the shift from post-Fordist to neoliberal and now green economy models of urban development; the influence of neoliberal multiculturalism in urban politics; and the increasingly prominent role of Latinos in city, state and national politics. (Carter, 2016: 21)

While Agenda 21 has largely gone the way of its raison d'être 'sustainable development' as a historic bloc, incorporating, neutralising and policing any radical components of the environmental movement while achieving some concessions, the struggles over environmental community development continue. 'The community' remains a locus for outside intervention for both incorporation into development and mobilisation against development. 'Development' largely operates to destroy community and to dump onto the environment, to engender division, to fragment and marginalise, to seek out the most efficient means of shifting costs and maximising productivity. Communities may be 'part of' the environment from which value may be extracted, or else used as a sink for dumping waste and pollution. Community resources are expropriated and communities expelled, with fractions forming migrant waves or settling, mistrusted, among people in neglected urban environments. The entire development process damages communities and their environments, from investment decisions, through production and distribution of goods and services, to the eventual decline and neglect as investments are re-orientated more profitably. When forms of development are created that do not correspond with the interests of capital accumulation or geopolitical imperial influence, an attempt is made to crush these.

Nonetheless, 'community' has demonstrated considerable resilience, whether as communities of migrants, of resistance, of struggle, of the 'imagined communities' of national self-determination and subaltern ethnicities. Those tasked with community development, whether professionally or as activists, engage with neighbourhoods, workers, indigenous peoples, those subject to diverse exploitation.

The logic of development by movements from above in neoliberal times has produced diverse structures of exploitation and subsequently fragmented communities whose subjectivities are forged from this. Harvey (2006) has analysed the fragmentation of oppressions and oppositions that neoliberalism generates through different dimensions of 'accumulation by dispossession' alongside the labour process exploitation that dominated earlier phases of capitalist development. Any attempt to practise environmental community development needs to be mindful of this context and seek to address the particular disjunctures that it throws up: residential communities, sink communities, migrant communities, workplace communities, communities of interest whose subjective knowledge of these interests is obfuscated through the practices of labour fragmentation, casualisation and migration controls. The chapters of this book seek to explore these themes.

The state, civil society and popular struggle

Those who engage in community work as professionals, activists, representatives or educators are caught between incorporation and attempting to resist 'development' and promote alternatives, all with diminishing or zero resources. While academic literature continues to generate critical analysis of neoliberal development and its impact on environments, communities and classes, largely drawn from varieties of Marxism or anarchist theory, the practical and professional guides for community workers remain largely impervious to this theory. Some activists produce their own analysis, often driven by the imperative of the next campaign or reflecting on the failure of the last one, sometimes laced with burn-out. Much of this analysis occurs informally in spaces of critical reflection in homes, communities, workplaces, campaigns. Some of it is published online and forms a literature in parallel to, and interacting with, the material generated by academics (many of whom are also activists), and often read and commented on by other activists within 'echo-chambers' of small self-referencing groups. All these literatures have value – the suggestions for practical action, the academic analysis and the reflexivity from the front-line. What this book seeks to do is draw on all these in order to assist those engaged in struggles for environmental justice – as community workers or social activists, environmentalists or community mobilisers – to address the difficult questions about praxis in the face of the neoliberal onslaught.

We are mindful of a significant risk in compiling this volume. The literature is full of examples of academics presuming a superior analysis to those engaged in struggle, seeking to interpret the situation on behalf of the 'ordinary people' who, it is implied, lack the intellectual resources, or because of false consciousness, ideology or not enough (political) education are unable to develop a sophisticated analysis until the arrival of the 'professional' intellectuals. Vanguardism can be a particular disease of the Left, and in the world of NGOs who feel that they are required to 'lead the people' (and often do so back into neoliberal capital). For Anne, the methodology of Jacques Rancière provides an antidote to this tendency, with his 'axiom of equality' (axiom because we have to postulate it, since we can't prove it):

> Basically, there is at the outset an egalitarian maxim that has a certain number of consequences and they are all there at the outset, including in the frustrating form that means that, when people ask you what needs to be done, you answer that it's up to them to work out what they want to do. (Rancière, 2016: 91)

This fits with our understanding of Gramsci, and his requirement that we accord to ordinary people both agency and thought: 'all men are intellectuals'. Fortunately, as it turns out, the agency and intelligence of the dominated does not require the left intellectual to 'discover' it, since it is ontological. As Cabral (1979: 31) says, 'struggle is a normal condition of all living creatures of the world. All are in struggle, all struggle'. We believe, within a Gramscian frame, in the actual struggle of ordinary people to change the world from where they are and work and move.

The environment is a key battleground and potential location for struggle, as economic decision making in the interests of capital accumulation leads to cost shifting onto the environments of those with least economic or political leverage. While the impact of, and resistance to, this environmental-economic dumping is not new, in the current stage of neoliberalism it has become increasingly acute and systematic, and has generated new waves of self-reflective community action and social movement. Analytically this has been explored through the discipline of political ecology. The state is largely playing an important role as midwife of neoliberal implementation, as security for the agents of dispossession, as conduit for incorporating civil society, yet remains a site of struggle in which the war of position is played out. That applies also to the institutions of civil society, including the universities where we and many of the contributors are located.

Resistance emerges from a range of actors in which 'the community' and the complex and contradictory ways in which it understands 'the environment' are at the centre. The book addresses this problematic from a range of angles. It also addresses the range of tactics and methods that constitute part of the community development repertoire, which may be used – and incorporated – in diverse ways.

A role for community development?

The *Rethinking Community Development* series aims to help practitioners to question what community development means in theory and practice in current times, providing international, cross-generational and cross-disciplinary perspectives and using contextual specificity as a lens to look at localised consequences of wider, global processes.

But why is it necessary to 'rethink' community development?

Geoghegan and Powell (2008) argue that there are currently three different discernible kinds of community development – *of* neoliberalism, *alongside* neoliberalism and *against* neoliberalism. Much of contemporary community development is a central instrument in consolidating neoliberalism (Popple, 2006; Geoghegan and Powell, 2008). However, there needs also to be a recognition that in our current context the main opposition to neoliberalism includes a protectionist and viciously xenophobic imagined community. There is thus currently a very real struggle for the soul of community development.

However, it is not simply the current context, and its effects on the practice of community development, that requires us to pause and 'rethink' – it is also the conceptual difficulties associated with community development per se. To a great extent, this is because the concepts of both community and development are, and have always been, highly contested (Bhattacharyya, 2004; Matarrita-Cascante and Brennan, 2012; Kenny, 2016).

How, then, can a contribution to the series focusing on environmental justice help? Kenny (2016: 24) specifically identifies 'developing appropriate responses to environmental degradation and climate change, the latter becoming increasingly urgent' as a key current challenge for community development practice and theory today. As Matarrita-Cascante and Brennan (2012) argue, resources, including natural resources, are a critical component of community development; and as these resources become increasingly limited or compromised, the question of what community development, for whom, becomes increasingly fraught. Hopefully, this book makes a useful contribution. However, we would argue that an environmental justice lens has an even more profound strength in 'rethinking' community development.

According to Bhattacharyya (2004), the core purposes of community development are *solidarity* and *agency*. Solidarity and agency are key aspects of environmental justice struggles; the contributors to this collection are working in very different contexts, across the globe, but all are seeking to build solidarity and agency. The environmental justice movement has also been perhaps one of the most successful in bridging the macro–micro gap, and the chapters in this book consider these linkages. Looking at local environmental struggles – the contextual specificity that this series emphasises – allows us to explore this notion of community development as solidarity and agency, while also problematising it. How can we build solidarity in an age of rampant, competitive individualism, in a context of competition over scarce resources? How can we recognise the inherent agency of people to resist, and build this, in an age where the power of neoliberal capital appears so great, as the first book in this series, *Politics, power and community development*, explored? 'How is it possible to strengthen and combine both the small resistances and general challenges to neoliberalism in ways that can lead to transformative change?' (Carpenter, Emejulu and Taylor, 2016: 3).

Structure of the book

To help us understand the micro–macro connection, the remaining chapters are organised crudely from those that focus on very localised struggles to those which consider macro, global links (Figure 1.1).

In Chapter Two, Hilary Darcy and Laurence Cox analyse an iconic environmental justice struggle against the Shell gas pipeline in western Ireland in terms of community-led processes and collective self-education in the face of economic might, state corruption, police brutality and postcolonial political division. In Chapter Three, Patrick Kane writing with Berenice Celeyta documents a remarkable popular uprising in the Colombian port city of Buenaventura from

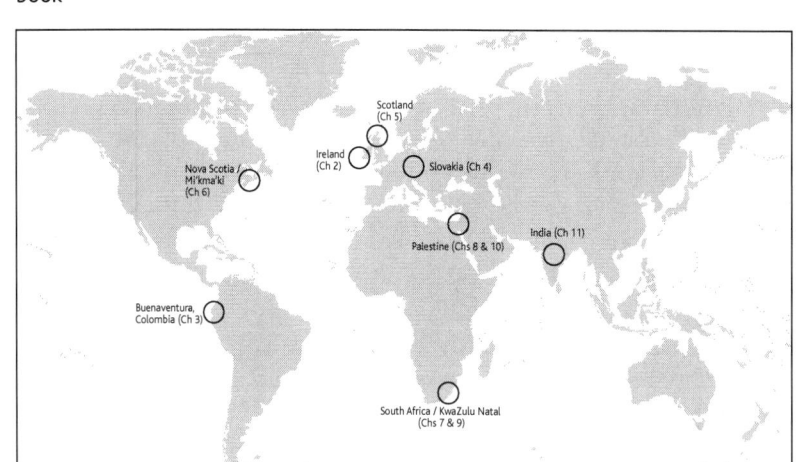

Figure 1.1: Locations of specific environmental justice struggles discussed in the book

Patrick's experience of working closely with human rights activists during the civic strike. Not a typical environmental justice struggle, the strike is rooted in both a human ecology of some of the most excluded populations of Colombia and a massively accelerated level of exploitation centred on the port utilised for export by the neoliberal expansion of extractive industries. In the current context of growing right-wing xenophobia, in which tools of 'community development' can be employed to exclude as well as unite, Richard Filčák and Daniel Škobla's Chapter Four explores how ethnic divisions between Roma and non-Roma populations in Slovakia undermine class solidarity in struggles for environmental justice.

A number of chapters reflect on inter-connections between micro and macro struggles as communities take tentative steps to 'join the dots by joining hands'. In Chapter Five, dealing specifically with waste management in the neoliberal context, Jennifer Mackay draws on her experience in the development of community recycling initiatives in Scotland, which were undermined by the interests of capital and state environmental policy. Subsequent waves of incinerator developments mobilised communities in opposition, and were again defeated by sustained movements from above. In Chapter Six Jonathan Langdon describes a successful campaign against fracking in Nova Scotia/ Mi'kma'ki, Canada, analysing his experience of learning *to*, *through* and *in* struggle (Foley, 1999) through alliances between First Nation and Settler communities. The communities directly affected by coal mining in KwaZulu-Natal in South Africa are foregrounded by

Mark Butler, who cautions in Chapter Seven against the tendency for activists and NGOs to 'speak for' those whose analysis is grounded in their experience of resistance.

Simon I. Awad provides an overview of the environmental history of Palestine and the impact of Zionist/Israeli settler-colonialism in Chapter Eight. In the context of the current military occupation of the West Bank, he discusses how the Environmental Education Center is able to promote resilience and resistance through a range of environmental community development initiatives. Addressing in particular the dialectic between local struggles and wider movements through educational praxis, in Chapter Nine Bobby Peek and Jeanne Prinsloo examine an innovative environmental justice school for community and social movement activists from across South Africa, run by the NGO groundWork.

Continuing the theme of settler-colonialism, in Chapter Ten Abeer al-Butmeh, Zayneb al-Shalalfeh and Mahmoud Zwahre collaborate with Eurig Scandrett to draw on a range of grassroots struggles in the context of an active and aggressive process of settler-colonisation in Palestine. The contributors are engaged in a range of struggles and come together to make the connections between community development, environmental justice and popular struggle as anti-colonial praxis.

Some of the contradictions of working in solidarity with peoples' movements in a context of neoliberalism and ultra-right wing communalism are highlighted in Chapter Eleven by Dharmesh Shah and Shweta Narayan, co-produced with Eurig Scandrett. They reflect on the very real dilemmas that community workers and activists are facing in India in the front-line of Narendra Modi's radical deregulation, along with state repression and Hindutva violence. In such a context, philanthrocapitalism is providing a vehicle for the neoliberal incorporation of grassroots environmental justice movements, closing down opportunities for resistance to accumulation by dispossession.

Chapter Twelve, the penultimate macro-level chapter, by Kathy Jenkins and Sara Marsden, addresses the under-researched area of the interface between the community and the workplace in relation to environmental justice, and especially in the forms of struggles for occupational and environmental health, drawing on discussions with a wide range of community-based, trade union, anti-toxics and environmentalist groups across Asia, North America and Europe.

In the concluding chapter, we reflect on the key themes that emerge from the collection, as well as on the process of production of the book.

References

Agents for Environmental Justice and Scandrett, E. (2003) *Voices from the grassroots*, Redressing the balance Handbook series (4), Edinburgh: Friends of the Earth Scotland.

Bhattacharyya, J. (2004) 'Theorizing community development', *Journal of the Community Development Society*, 34(2): 5–34.

Cabral, A. (1979) *Unity and struggle: Speeches and writings*, New York: Monthly Review Press.

Carpenter, M., Emejulu, A. and Taylor, M. (2016) 'Editorial introduction: What's new and old in community development? Reflecting on 50 years of CDJ', *Community Development Journal*, 51(1): 1–7.

Carter, E.D. (2016) 'Environmental Justice 2.0: New Latino environmentalism in Los Angeles', *Local Environment*, 21(1): 3–23.

Collins, C. (2006) '"The Scottish Executive is open for business": The New Regeneration Statement, The Royal Bank of Scotland and the Community Voices Network', *Variant*, 26, www.variant.org.uk.

Cox, L. and Nilsen, A.G. (2014) *We make our own history: Marxism, social movements and the crisis of neoliberalism*, London: Pluto Press.

Doherty, B.J.A. and Doyle, T. (2013) *Environmentalism, resistance and solidarity: The politics of Friends of the Earth International*, London: Palgrave Macmillan.

Faber, D.R. and McCarthy, D. (2003) 'Neo-liberalism, globalisation and the struggle for ecological democracy: Linking sustainability and environmental justice', in J. Agyeman, R.D. Bullard and B. Evans (eds) *Just sustainabilities: Development in an unequal world*, London: Earthscan, pp 38–63.

Foley, G. (1999) *Learning in social action: A contribution to understanding informal education*, Chicago: University of Chicago Press.

Geoghegan, M. and Powell, F. (2008) 'Community development and the contested politics of the late modern agora: Of, alongside or against neoliberalism?', *Community Development Journal*, 44(4): 430–47.

Guha, R. (2000) *Environmentalism: A global history*, New York: Longman.

Guha, R. and Martínez-Alier, J. (1997) *Varieties of environmentalism: Essays north and south*, London: Earthscan.

Harvey, D. (2006) *Spaces of global capitalism: Towards a theory of uneven geographical development*, Oxford: Oxford University Press.

Kenny, S. (2016) 'Community development today: Engaging challenges through cosmopolitanism?', *Community Development Journal*, 51(1): 23–41.

Martínez-Alier, J. (2002) *The environmentalism of the poor: A study of ecological conflicts and valuation*, Cheltenham: Edward Elgar.

Matarrita-Cascante, D. and Brennan, M.A. (2012) 'Conceptualising community development in the twenty-first century', *Community Development*, 43(3): 293–305.

Popple, K. (2006) 'Critical commentary: Community development in the 21st century: a case of conditional development', *British Journal of Social Work*, 36: 333–40.

Rancière, J. (2016) *The method of equality. Interviews with Laurent Jeanpierre and Dork Zabunyan*, Cambridge: Polity Press.

Scandrett, E. (2000) 'Community work, sustainable development and environmental justice', *Scottish Journal of Community Work and Development*, 6: 7–13.

Seel, B., Paterson, M. and Doherty, B. (2000) *Direct action in British environmentalism*, London: Routledge.

Sklair, L. (2001) *The transnational capitalist class*, Oxford: Blackwell.

United National Conference on Environment and Development (UNCED) (1993) *Agenda 21*, New York: United Nations, https://sustainabledevelopment.un.org/content/documents/Agenda21.pdf.

TWO

Resisting Shell in Ireland: making and remaking alliances between communities, movements and activists

Hilary Darcy and Laurence Cox

What happened in Erris?

In April 2000 an announcement in the parish newspaper informed residents of Erris that a new gas pipeline was proposed to run through the area to bring gas from the offshore Corrib field to a new refinery to be built at Bellanaboy. Erris is a strikingly beautiful, isolated and thinly populated part of County Mayo in north-west Ireland, surviving mostly on fishing, small-scale farming and tourism. A small number of villages, including Rossport and Pullathomas on opposite sides of Broadhaven Bay, were connected by quiet and narrow roads, which the state would soon upgrade for the benefit of the oil companies. Broadhaven Bay is protected as a European Union (EU) Special Area of Conservation (SAC). Initial responses in Erris, like those in Mayo generally, were positive about the boost to local employment and the prospect of children being able to stay and find work locally. It took time for residents' questions and doubts to clarify into a realisation that this was an experimental, high-pressure gas pipeline that, in the case of an accident, would destroy many of the homes located close to the planned route. Consultation was limited, and the 2002 decision by An Bord Pleanála (the Irish Planning Board) to refuse planning permission for the project was overridden in 2004 through the intervening influence of Taoiseach (Prime Minister) Bertie Ahern. Four years later, Ahern would be forced to resign after a corruption inquiry. Construction of the pipeline and refinery continued without consent from the community and without official permissions.

Those interested in the area, including trade unionists who had worked on the Kinsale offshore gas field, noted that Ireland's oil and gas regime had been changed in 1987 by energy minister Ray Burke, and again in 1992 by the then finance minister Bertie Ahern, from an approach inspired by Norway's successful gas and oil industry, giving the state a 50% stake in any commercial find and applying a 50% corporation tax, to a regime that abolished any state participation in the development and provided for a 100% tax write-off. Burke, who made this decision while meeting alone with the oil companies against his civil servants' advice, remains to this day the most senior minister, in a notoriously corrupt polity, to have done prison time (for tax fraud).

Matters came to a head in the winter of 2005, when members of the local community refused to allow Shell access to their land for preparatory work on the pipeline. Rather unwisely, the company pursued proceedings for contempt, with the result that five of those involved – three landowners and two figures in the community known to be influential in the emerging campaign, all men, Shell choosing to ignore opposition from female landowners – were sent to Dublin's Mountjoy prison indefinitely. Under Irish law they would have to remain there until they 'purged their contempt' and agreed not to interfere with the construction of the pipeline. This proved to be a double-edged sword for Shell, as those involved had no intention of doing so.

The company had managed to create martyrs out of five people who looked and sounded like the western farmers and fishermen who for many symbolise the true spirit of Irishness. Even more damagingly, Mayo is an area where the Land War – a series of evictions, boycotts, mass meetings and other conflicts that led to a poor peasantry becoming landowning farmers and the end of the Anglo-Irish aristocracy – saw some of its sharpest conflicts (including that directed at Captain Boycott). Imprisoning such people for defending their land, on foot of legislation that granted compulsory purchase powers to private corporations for the first time, was not exactly a masterstroke. Mass mobilisations in the small town of Belmullet were followed by large-scale marches in the capital city, and at this stage the media were happy to run with the story. The 'Rossport Five' had become national figures. After the five had spent 94 days in prison, Shell dropped the injunction and they were released, in a victory for direct action. However, the community-led campaign, learning from the experiences of the Munster-based community campaign against Dow Chemical, understood the need to pursue a multipronged approach and continued to engage with official planning processes to redirect the project to sea.

As often in Ireland, opposition parties – initially particularly Greens and Labour – as well as mainstream trade unions, offered verbal support. Green Party leaders held photo opportunities with local activists – and shortly afterwards took part in a government that used the military against the campaign. Laurence was present at a meeting with the then Labour Party President Michael D. Higgins, who promised support for the campaign; once he was successful in being elected President of Ireland, nothing more was heard from him on the subject. A local parliamentary deputy and community general practitioner (GP), Gerry Crowley, elected on a ticket of defending local hospital services, sought to ensure that the campaign followed his line of approach. Meanwhile, the community and campaign struggled to develop an understanding and approach that placed local people at the centre of decision making, as opposed to the traditional brokers who seek to lead and claim credit for most campaigns in Ireland.

Solidarity came from Irish direct action campaigners, the product of more than a decade of collaboration between radical ecologists and anarchist activism; from British and European activists of a similar bent; from student groups; from the unorthodox republicans of Éirigi; from some development, human rights and civil liberties organisations and individuals; from international opposition to the oil industry and Shell in particular; and from Norwegian trade unions critical of Statoil's involvement.

We have documented changing police and activist strategies elsewhere (Cox and Ni Dhorchaigh, 2011). For the purposes of this piece we can start by noting the damage done to Shell's image – particularly in Norway, where its partner Statoil was ultimately state owned – by film of police breaking the community picket outside gates to the proposed refinery by baton-charging local protestors. This marked the beginning of an explicit 'no arrest' strategy – observed and experienced by Hilary, who was living at the solidarity camp during this period – the practical implication of which was a large amount of intimidation (in an isolated rural community where numbers of tooled-up police and private security often outnumbered inhabitants, campaigners were followed by police, under daily surveillance by private security, their wives threatened with sexual violence, police cars parked outside their houses and so on), kettling, confiscation of cameras and off-screen violence (beatings, breakings of fingers, people thrown into ditches and onto barbed wire). At least one British undercover police officer is known to have infiltrated the community-led campaign.

As resistance became more intense and direct action more effective at blockading construction work, so too did repression. Private security, often recruited from far right milieux in Eastern Europe, wore badges with skulls celebrating 'battles' against unarmed locals. A leading campaigner had his fishing boat boarded and scuttled by masked men; another was assaulted by masked men inside a Shell compound and hospitalised as a result. Frontline Defenders, Amnesty International and a UN Special Rapporteur carried out investigations highly critical of state and corporate violence and breaches of the law (Barrington, 2010); meanwhile, the relatively new police ombudsman found itself powerless to act on the hundreds of complaints of police violence. Repeated calls from government ministers, criminologists, lawyers and human rights NGOs for a public inquiry into the police operation were ignored. In 2011 an accidental recording of police joking about raping and deporting protestors drew national attention; after over 700,000 viewings on YouTube it was eventually covered by national television and a disgracefully bad investigation was carried out that targeted the activists concerned more than the police (Dublin Shell to Sea, nd).

The self-inflicted poor image of corporate and state behaviour forced the partial concession of a redrawn pipeline, further away from houses but still crossing a SAC and running under an area prone to landslides. Local concerns about the health and safety of the project were validated by repeated acts of negligence, including one tragic incident in which an employee died during the underwater part of the construction. In 2016 the pipeline and refinery finally entered production.

It is important to note the complex, changeful nature of gas and oil ownership during this campaign: the Corrib gas field was discovered in 1996 by Enterprise Oil, who continued as co-venturers on the Corrib project with Statoil and Marathon until Royal Dutch Shell purchased their majority stake in 2002. Shell, Statoil and the Canadian group Vermilion, who bought out Marathon in 2009, continue as stakeholders, with Shell E&P as the operator and main shareholder on the project. The community-led campaign understood early on the importance of selecting a clear target, given the corporate context of buy-outs, merging and rebranding. In the wake of nationwide boycotting and picketing of Shell-owned petrol stations, in solidarity with the community struggle, Shell was forced to sell its entire retail and commercial business in Ireland to Topaz.

This chapter draws on discussions with activists in the campaign and seeks to draw out useful lessons for comparable campaigns elsewhere.

Assessment

The campaign's 15 years of resistance to one of the world's biggest oil companies, backed up by the full force of the state, marks out the 'Rossport' struggle as well beyond the ordinary. The wonder is not that the pipeline was built, but that resistance lasted so long: costs were more than quadrupled (from €800 million to €3.2 billion), massively raising the bar for any future developments of this nature. As an indirect effect, resistance to fracking in neighbouring regions marked notable successes, with an initial refusal from many local authorities being parlayed at a later point into legislation banning fracking in the Republic. Most recently, all opposition parties – including those otherwise supporting a minority government – supported a bill banning all offshore oil and gas exploration in Ireland.

More broadly, the campaign transformed the way radical politics was done in Ireland. During the extended period of 'social partnership' up to the 2007–8 crash, the vast bulk of most movements remained willing to accept access to policy makers and funding for service-delivery activities following state priorities in return for operating within institutional channels, accepting the broad framework of state policy and acting in isolation from other movements. Broad-based alliances against neoliberalism and direct action forms of resistance were confined to the radical wings operating within the anti-capitalist 'movement of movements' (Cox, 2006). Rossport saw the coming together of this approach with community-based struggles and extensive popular learning in a decisive way as the recession saw the state withdraw from partnership. The practices of grassroots solidarity politics advanced during the campaign would feed into a range of campaigns including opposition to water charges (Cox, 2017), abortion rights, housing, migrant and sex-worker rights.

Rossport continues as a reference point for a way of doing politics that doesn't privilege the state or the party but instead places those most affected by the issue at the centre of decision-making processes. It became a strategic and symbolic site for resistance to corporate and state power, shaped by an alliance of a community-based environmental justice struggle with the long-term involvement of a range of Irish social movements of the Left and the intensive commitment of a substantial number of primarily international ecological activists.

All this was achieved by a tiny and disadvantaged rural community facing extensive economic pressure (corporate money given to local projects in return for political support; local politicians and business interests scenting benefits from the pipeline); extensive state violence;

exhausting legal processes from planning appeals to criminal trials; and media demonisation of participants as directed by shadowy republican terrorists. Internally, family and local loyalties were often torn when personal connections had accepted corporate money or those hostile to the project disagreed on how to develop resistance (at times, as with the award-winning film *The Pipe*, in the glare of video cameras). Local community members disagreed with activists from national organisations, while Irish and English activists fell out. Those who did not object to gas extraction per se but had health and safety concerns or prioritised benefits to the local community, or the national tax take, disagreed with ecologists whose concern was to 'keep it in the ground'. Political parties, both mainstream (Labour and Greens) and radical (Sinn Féin and Socialist Workers Party) adopted instrumentalising and at times manipulative attitudes, while trade unions also proved less than reliable allies at times.

Success, then, is not about an absence of disagreement and divergence – normal in even relatively homogeneous communities. It is about the ability to work together despite these. Given the inevitability of internal conflict for community-led campaigns, we must ask ourselves, as grassroots and community-oriented activists, how we can help to transform conflict into a productive force. The eventual building of the pipeline had far more to do with the balance of forces against the campaign than with internal difficulties.

Structural factors

Before moving to focus on the community education dimension of the campaign, we might ask how community-based campaigns can maintain broad cohesion despite these internal differences and external pressures.

In the Irish context, the early and symbolic imprisonment of five local men was important in preventing other actors (local notables, mainstream parties or NGOs, urban radicals) from dominating the campaign. Following established traditions, it was agreed at the outset of their three-month imprisonment that decisions would have to be made by the families of those imprisoned, and this community-centric power remained after their release. The nature of the interests at play – the vast profits involved in oil and gas production and the state's openness both to direct corruption and to wider 'national interest' concerns – removed most of the more opportunistic supporters who might have successfully placed themselves at the head of a campaign that threatened such interests less.

At the same time, the derisory consultation, ignoring of planning process and health and safety concerns, the scale of violence and intimidation and the hostility and downright lies from state and corporate media enabled a much faster learning process among locals who might otherwise have placed more faith in established institutions' goodwill and the scope for easy resolution of the issues. The local community, and their radical supporters, thus had a clearer field for developing a genuinely community-led radical campaign than might otherwise have been the case.

'Unofficial' environmental justice movements – often centred not so much on outright opposition to 'development' as on the contestation of who will actually benefit from a particular development strategy – have a long history in Ireland (Allen and Jones, 1990). Such campaigns, rooted in rural communities, often take time to build a broad consensus and avoid permanent breakdowns of interpersonal relations – but, once started, have an immense capacity for resistance and a strong capacity to resist violence and vilification.

Particularly interesting in this campaign were the prior relationships built between anarchist and other urban, class-oriented activists, focused on issues of social justice and distribution, and ecological activists, whose primary concern was preventing environmental destruction. The long trust built up between these movements stood the campaign in good stead when it came to both recruiting and educating ecological activists from overseas into the importance of economic survival for rural communities – and the need to take the lead from community decision-making processes. Such activists brought a significant range of practical skills relevant to non-violent direct action; website development, media and research; grassroots organising and facilitation practices and permaculture.

Environmental justice and community (self-)education

One fruitful way of tracing the campaign's developing self-confidence and capacity to constitute an effective collective actor is to name the multiple dimensions of self-education that local activists went through in the process of the campaign. Shell to Sea started with two campaign goals, moving to three in the course of the campaign's own learning:

1. any exploitation of the Corrib gas field to be done in a safe way that would not expose the local community in Erris to unnecessary health, safety and environmental risks;

2. to renegotiate the terms of the Great Oil and Gas Giveaway, which saw Ireland's 10 billion barrels of oil equivalent off the West Coast go directly to the oil companies, with the Irish State retaining a 0% share, no energy security of supply and only 25% tax on profits against which all costs could be deducted;
3. to seek justice for the human rights abuses suffered by Shell to Sea campaigners due to their opposition to Shell's proposed inland refinery. (Shell to Sea, nd)

When translated into campaigning knowledge, these goals involved the development of counter-expertise around health, safety, environmental and planning issues; radical self-education around economic and power-political interests; and a critical engagement with policing and the courts.

Counter-expertise

Eyerman and Jamison (1991), starting from the environmental movement, highlight the extent to which social movements involve the development of counter-expertise, the capacity to credibly challenge the perspectives presented by official experts. From campaigns against pollution and the nuclear industry on, campaigners typically find themselves faced in planning, court and media contexts by official expertise co-constituted by the industry, the state, academia and journalists and that they have to be able to stand up to if they are to convince others.

In the case of the pipeline project, the initial counter-expertise required had to do with the untested and experimental nature of the pipeline. It involved identifying the health and safety risks, in particular to households located close to the pipeline route. Campaigners had to become experts on environmental issues, not only those to do with fossil fuels and climate change in general, but also those tied to, for example, fisheries in Broadhaven Bay, the SAC designation, the history of landslides in particular areas, the relationship between Carrowmore lake and water supply for the region, contamination of drinking water. They also had to develop the necessary procedural expertise to negotiate the planning and appeals process – to say nothing of the skills involved in engaging with the courts, media, politicians, NGOs and so on.

Radical self-education

The oil industry is extremely complex and operates on a scale far beyond most of our experience as everyday social actors. Grasping what it means in practice is no easy task. This can run from understanding how few local jobs are actually likely to be created long term from a pipeline and refinery project to uncovering the ways in which the Irish State had dismantled its own royalty and tax regime vis-à-vis the oil multinationals.

So too with the operations of this kind of power politics, whether grounded in the corruption of individual politicians or in the state's ruthless pursuit of what it conceives of as its strategic interests. One obvious example has to do with relationships with politicians. Rural and urban Irish property-owners, however small, are used to seeking the intervention of county councillors and local parliamentary deputies to resolve 'problems' ranging from securing planning permission for a new house to evicting travellers, seeking roadworks, health provision or investment in community projects, and presiding over the opening of sports, school and other facilities. It can be a slow and difficult process to realise that the scale of the money involved in the oil industry, and the fundamental nature of the interests involved, mean that the friendly local politician will not be your friend in these contexts.

There are some parallels here to Alf Nilsen's (2010) work on the limits of 'citizenship' knowledge in the Narmada anti-dam campaign in western India: indigenous populations that had transformed local power relationships through successfully asserting their legal rights as citizens found that legally oriented strategies resisting displacement by dam construction were ineffective, as they challenged the very same interests that had been happy to support the enforcement of other forms of legality against minor abuses by petty local officials.

Policing and the courts

Erris is very much the sort of region from which gardaí (Irish police) are recruited. Elderly locals normally experience the police (if not always the courts) as their allies against a variety of threats and inconveniences, and are rarely exposed to the kind of aggression and intimidation that marks police engagements with urban working-class youth, travellers or republicans. The 'moral shock' of seeing once-trusted police beat, threaten and lie about oneself, one's family and neighbours is not to be over-estimated, particularly given the importance of the sense of belonging to a 'national community' excluding such groups.

It is thus a strong indicator of the learning involved in the campaign that it extended its original goals (1 and 2, discussed previously) to include an uncompromisingly phrased demand for 'justice for human rights abuses' suffered by campaigners.

More generally

The first part of this chapter questioned simplistic notions of unity and success and restated the importance of sustained popular mobilisation, learning through action and alliance formation as key elements of the potential needed to bring about a better world. The second part explored *diverse* forms of subaltern knowledge and organisation in this context. Here we can refer in particular to Gramsci's distinction between common sense and good sense; from a community education point of view this implies that a confident community, actively constituting its own political capacity rather than seeking reliance on an established political broker (in effect the negotiation of common sense) is a self-educating agent (Mayo, 1999; Ytterstad, 2014).

In the late 1970s and 1980s, rural communities in the southern Irish province of Munster, facing greenfield site projects for chemical plants for US multinationals, eventually developed sophisticated mechanisms of knowledge transfer, so that the immediate announcement of impending development was followed immediately by locals from a neighbouring town able to explain in comprehensible and realistic detail what this would mean in practice.

Something similar developed in Erris: the No Consent project (Anon, nd) interviewed local activists about what they had learned from the campaign that could be shared with similar communities facing the oil and gas industry elsewhere. Turned into a very readable booklet and (even more importantly) a portable exhibition of photographs and quotes, this was brought to several communities facing fracking in the 2010s, to great effect. Other networking processes helped to put local activists together with those in similar, disadvantaged rural communities encountering fracking, sharing expertise and developing solidarity.

The state's retreat, marked by the passing of anti-fracking legislation and the scale of support for anti-drilling legislation, is indicative of how effective the Erris community has been – through its self-development as an autonomous political actor, its painstaking self-education and its concern for knowledge transfer to related communities elsewhere, sharing what had been learned from Nigeria and Norway.

Community-based environmental justice despite the professionals

Paid professionals, in the campaign against Shell, were mostly prominent by their absence – with the exception of one or two NGOs who used the issue to pursue legal cases of their own and abandoned the campaign once these had been concluded. This of course parallels the actions of party politicians noted earlier.

A couple of honourable exceptions can be noted. The small and radical development group AfrI (Action from Ireland) retained a genuine connection to the campaign throughout. Returned development worker Sister Majella McCarron, with a history of involvement in the Ogoni campaign against Shell's operations in the Niger Delta, was a consistent ally. Some of the 'outside activists' involved in the campaign were trained or employed as community workers of various kinds, although their actions in Erris were not carried out on this basis.

There were specific Irish contexts to this. 'Social partnership' has already been mentioned: the involvement since 1987 of trade unions, farmers and employers in corporatist decision making, extended in the 1990s to include community, environmental and most other social movements – or at least their formal and funded manifestations – meant that by 2005 most community groups were structured around state funding and involvement in 'consultation', in return for abandoning direct confrontation with the state and not directly criticising state policies. Similar situations obtained for environmental groups, who consistently avoided mentioning the Rossport campaign within Ireland. While not identical with the US reliance on private foundation money, criticised by INCITE! (2007), the net outcome is the same.

We can also highlight an even longer-standing distinction in Ireland between 'consensual' forms of community development in rural areas, geared to advancing local claims around the distribution of mainstream rewards, and 'oppositional' community development – largely in urban working-class and traveller contexts (Curtin and Varley, 1995). In a 'consensual' context, it was easy for Shell to distribute small amounts of money to 'community' projects and the state to remind existing groups of favours owed and salaries still being paid. Such relationships place strong limits on what community workers can advance politically.

In No Consent, some local campaigners did feel in retrospect that some of those whom they had condemned as being 'bought off' by Shell money would have been better understood as slow learners, who could have been won to the campaign in time and should not have been written off entirely. However, it has to be said that few if any such individuals managed this learning curve from their own side, so these reflections may rather represent common feelings of regret at ruptures within small-scale communities.

Leaving Irish specifics aside, when the state understands its core interests as being at stake – as has been the case for the last 100 years when the oil industry is in question – it will always be hard for those whose professional position and organisations depend on state funding to seriously oppose it. Criminalising movements is particularly effective in detaching this layer of professionals. Such professionals as were able to engage *as professionals* in the area were rather a handful of journalists, trade unionists and academics.

This does not, however, mean that professionals *employed by the community* rather than by the state might not have contributed more strongly to the campaign if such people had existed. One line of critique, then, challenges professionals as such and seeks to restore the central role of unpaid local community activists; another asks whether and under what circumstances it might be possible for community organisations with their own staff to become independent from state and corporate money.

Conclusion

However, none of this means that solidarity and agency are absent. Solidarity was very widely expressed both nationally and internationally, in important practical ways. The development of popular agency – as opposed to relying on official processes, corporate consultation, elected representatives or NGOs and professionals – was central to the actual learning process involved.

In many ways this represents a return to some of the foundational approaches in community development, which are about asserting the development of popular agency rather than the insertion of paid professionals as a goal in its own right. This is perhaps particularly significant where the issues at stake are such as to pit what the state perceives as its core interests against very different perspectives on the part of the community. Rossport stands as one of the key reference points of contemporary grassroots community-led campaigning in Ireland today. Its lessons and practices ripple outwards and onwards into the development practices of residential, cultural and issue-based communities.

Finally, it is worth considering how far we are now within the dying days of the fossil fuel industry, with renewables taking the lead in many countries on economic as well as ecological grounds, and support for extraction in new and vulnerable areas (tar sands, Arctic exploration, fracking) now the prerogative of hard conservative governments such as the UK, US and Australia. In this context, environmental justice activism in disadvantaged rural communities raises new kinds of issues, of what will constitute a viable future survival strategy in the context of peak oil and climate change.

References

Allen, R. and Jones, T. (1990) *Guests of the nation: People of Ireland vs the Multinationals*, London: Earthscan.

Anon (nd) *No consent: Experiences of challenging the Corrib Gas Project*. A resource for community campaigns. Self-published.

Barrington, B. (2010) 'Breakdown in trust: A report on the Corrib Gas dispute', for Front Line Human Rights Defenders.

Cox, L. (2006) 'News from nowhere: the movement of movements in Ireland', in L. Connolly and N. Hourigan (eds) *Social movements and Ireland*, Manchester: Manchester University Press, pp 210–29.

Cox, L. (2017) 'The Irish water charges movement', *Interface*, 9(1): 161–203.

Cox, L. and Ní Dhorchaigh, E. (Darcy, H.) (2011) 'When is an assembly riotous, and who decides? The success and failure of police attempts to criminalise protest', in W. Sheehan and M. Cronin (eds) *Riotous assemblies: Riots, rebels and revolts in Ireland*, Cork: Mercier, pp 241–61.

Curtin, C. and Varley, T. (1995) 'Community action and the state', in P. Clancy et al (eds) *Irish society*, Dublin: Institute for Public Administration, pp 379–409.

Dublin Shell to Sea (nd) '"Give me your name and address or I'll rape you": the reality of Corrib policing', https://vimeo.com/21952231.

Eyerman, R. and Jamison, A. (1991) *Social movements: A cognitive approach*, Cambridge: Polity.

Hederman, W. (2012) 'Masterclass in spin', *Village Magazine* (March edition).

INCITE! (2007) *The revolution will not be funded*, Boston: South End.

Mayo, P. (1999) *Gramsci, Freire and adult education*, London: Zed.

Nilsen, A. (2010) *Dispossession and resistance in India: The river and rage*, London: Routledge.

Shell to Sea (nd) 'Campaign Aims', http://www.shelltosea.com.

Ytterstad, A. (2014) 'Good sense on global warming', *International Socialism*, 144, http://isj.org.uk/good-sense-on-global-warming/

THREE

'No tenemos armas pero tenemos dignidad': learning from the civic strike in Buenaventura, Colombia

Patrick Kane with Berenice Celeyta

Introduction

From 16 May to 6 June 2017, the Colombian Pacific port city of Buenaventura bore witness to one of the country's most important social struggles of the 21st century. For 22 days, the majority Afro-Colombian and indigenous population engaged in a civic strike that paralysed the city, and with it the country's most important port: virtually all businesses were closed; all public transport suspended; up to 70 community roadblocks shut down traffic within the city, including halting the transit of more than 2,600 trucks that carry goods into and out of the city's port every day. The demands of the 'Civic Strike to Live with Dignity in Buenaventura' were centred upon improving living conditions through basic public services and infrastructure for the city's population, and increasing popular participation in decisions over the city's territory and environment that have been increasingly affected by corporate infrastructure projects and the expansion of the port. Participation in the strike snowballed, and within two days had effectively become a generalised, joy-filled uprising, involving people from all demographics and all neighbourhoods across the city and rural communities lining the main highway out of the city. In the days that followed, the population would come face to face with the brutal tactics of the Colombian state in its attempts to generate terror and quell the strike, and remain steadfast in the face of live bullets, tear gas and riot vans.

As sites of struggles for social transformations, and as spaces often characterised by alternative, oppositional norms and value practices, social movements produce unique types of knowledge, often overlooked by academia. Reflecting on social movement praxis, then, is an inherently useful undertaking. This chapter thus reflects on the

Buenaventura strike. Both authors were members of the Buenaventura civic strike human rights monitoring committee, and witnessed at first hand everything from the state violence (including tear gas and use of live ammunition) to negotiations with government and meetings of the strike committee. In our reflections we use an approach developed by Mathers and Novelli (2007) specifically for the purpose of studying social movement 'strategies and practices'. Rather than an intervention into the activist world from the standpoint of the academic world, the approach seeks to 'transverse both worlds through the development of roles such as "activist-researcher"' (Mathers and Novelli, 2007: 230). This type of research, based upon solidarity and direct engagement between the social scientist and social movement, can produce knowledge that is genuinely relevant and useful to social movements and critical social scientists.

However, the Buenaventura civic strike was one of those rare, awe-inspiring examples of a social mobilisation that transcended the historic struggles of black and indigenous communities, social movements, activists and trade unions, and became a generalised mass uprising in which the majority of the population participated in some way. Our reflection thus extends beyond social movement. Through six in-depth interviews with protagonists in the strike, from members of the strike executive committee to neighbourhood-level organisers, as well as the first-hand experience of the authors, this chapter seeks to unpick some of the processes, dynamics and important factors in the strike as identified by the protagonists themselves. It foregrounds their voices as much as possible to consider a series of interrelated questions: What lessons did the strike's protagonists learn from their involvement? What were the unseen political decisions, organising strategies and oppositional forces? And what lessons can activists or academics seeking broader social transformations learn from the Buenaventura civic strike?

Origins of the strike: Buenaventura and Colombian 'development'

The strike took many by surprise. Having suffered generations of structural racism and state abandonment in the post-slavery period, and more recently the intense militarisation of civic life and horrific levels of systematic violence against the civilian population, few believed that Buenaventura could be the site of one of the most historic popular uprisings in Colombia's history. Few, that is, aside from a disparate but collective group of committed activists and social leaders belonging to a handful of civil society organisations including trade unions, campaign groups, NGOs and social movements. Indeed, the civic strike in Buenaventura was by no means a spontaneous uprising: it was the result of years of tireless organising and strategising to bring civil society sectors together and develop a common agenda that would mobilise Buenaventura's urban and rural populations, and ultimately shift the balance of power in the city and deal a blow to transnational capital and the Colombian government's neoliberal development model.

To begin to understand the Buenaventura civic strike, it is important to grasp the city's role as the geographical point at which two very different dynamics collide (Figure 3.1): on the one hand, the increasingly globalised Colombian national economy and the violent implementation of a neoliberal development model based upon free trade, extractivism and expansion of infrastructure; and on the other, the ways of life and cultures of the ethnic indigenous and

Figure 3.1: Map of Colombia, showing strategic position of Buenaventura

Afro-descendent (Afro-Colombian) communities who inhabit the Pacific region and its vast rainforests, mangrove swamps, coastlines and river communities. This dynamic has involved the genocidal, uninterrupted violent subjection and exploitation of ethnic peoples and natural resources, albeit in constantly altering forms, since the immediate aftermath of the Spanish invasion until the current time.

The rainforests of the Colombian Pacific region have been characterised as one of the most biodiverse and water-rich ecosystems on the entire planet, as well as being abundant in economically valuable minerals including gold (Escobar, 2008). Of the roughly one million who live in the Pacific region, it is estimated that around 90% are of Afro-Colombian origin, and around 50,000 belong to the various indigenous ethnicities that inhabit the region (Centro Nacional de Memoria Historica, 2015: 26). These different communities have unique cultures, cosmovisions and traditions, but that on the whole are based upon a harmonious relationship with their environment or territory, and more collective and collaborative approaches to land tenure and agriculture production. Afro-descendent populations, forcibly brought from Africa as enslaved peoples and forced to work on haciendas, plantations and mines, made the region their home as they won their freedom, many as maroons who escaped and set up *'palenques'* or independent settlements, and others who gradually won their freedom following the 1851 manumission law. They have forged their communities and life-styles around fishing, hunting and small-scale agriculture and mining along the rivers and coasts of the Pacific (Escobar, 2008).

The city of Buenaventura is crucial to the economic model implemented by successive Colombian governments, in which increased international trade is a key aspect. It is Colombia's principal port on the Pacific Ocean, the point at which the country's numerous free trade agreements stop being abstract contracts and negotiation and become the abject material reality of commercial goods packed into shipping containers. It has been estimated that more than 60% of Colombian imports and exports pass through the various port facilities in Buenaventura (Taula Catalana por los Derechos Humanos en Colombia, 2016: 6). In the early 1990s, driven by neoliberal policies, the privatisation of the port and mass lay-offs and casualisation of the workforce worsened the already precarious social conditions for the local population. Today, the world-class port facilities sit in stark contrast to the conditions of communities living in their shadow: the city has only primary-level care facilities (no hospital with facilities for treating conditions of any complexity), and poor sewerage and drainage and running water (particularly absurd, given the abundance of water in this region). The unemployment rate according to state institutions is around 64% (compared to a national average of about 10%), while the same proportion of urban households live in poverty (it is much higher in rural areas – about 92%) (Centro de Memoria Historica, 2015: 59), making it one of the poorest municipalities in Colombia.

Buenaventura's population, both urban and rural, has suffered horrific violence and mass human rights violations over the past two decades since the beginning of the new century, in particular by paramilitary groups, which have created a permanent humanitarian crisis for the local population. According to government figures, over 196,000 people in Buenaventura, or 47% of the total population, have been victims of the political violence in some way (El Tiempo newspaper, 2017). Over 100,000 people have been forcibly displaced from the city. In 2014, Human Rights Watch released a report that documented how paramilitary groups routinely 'forcibly disappeared' and dismembered their victims and enforced strict military control over vast areas of the city (Human Rights Watch, 2014). This violence takes place in one of Colombia's most militarised cities, with a huge police and military presence.

Social movements and civil society organisations in Buenaventura argue that the urban violence is linked to the planned port expansion and large infrastructure projects, which in turn are linked to the raft of free trade agreements that Colombian governments have signed with countries and blocks including the US, the EU, Canada and Israel. This point was made forcefully throughout the civic strike, as one leader argues:

> 'One fundamental point which we wanted to demonstrate with the strike ... is that these private port expansion projects appeared and there began a whole phenomenon of forced displacements, evictions, and murders focused in the areas where these mega-projects were being proposed ... so this had led to the violent situation which we were rejecting.' (Anonymous interviewee, interview with Patrick Kane, 26 October 2017)

Since the early 2000s, as well as the violence, populations living in areas reclaimed from the sea by communities whose culture and livelihoods are inextricably linked to their proximity to the it, have increasingly seen their environment privatised (literally fenced off in some instances) and degraded, impeding in many cases their access to traditional fishing routes in the sea and mangrove swamps. This is as a result of these areas being earmarked for the expansion of port operations and tourism initiatives. According to the government's development strategy, the ongoing long-term programme of mass infrastructure projects in Buenaventura will gradually require the relocation of large swathes of the city's population away from seafront areas, inland to areas in which they will lose their contact with the sea, an important aspect of the economic and cultural identity of these Afro-Colombian communities.

Preparing for the strike: building unity in diversity

The recognition in the 1991 constitution of ethno-territorial collective rights for Afro-Colombian communities, particularly with regard to land tenure and a degree of self-determination, created a wave of political organising in rural black communities across Colombia, led by the Proceso de Comunidades Negras (PCN) (Black Communities Process) (Escobar, 2008). This process was aimed at securing collective land deeds for black communities, but also involved a deeper process of documenting and strengthening elements of Afro-Colombian identity, culture and traditions, with an emphasis on the importance of the concept of territory, understood not just as a piece of land but as based on the recognition that Afro-Colombian and indigenous communities have 'unique ways, rooted in culture, of using the diverse spaces constituted by rivers, forests, mangroves, hills and oceans' (Escobar, 2008: 170). In around 2012, as a response to the levels of violence and the conclusion that the violence was inextricably related to port-related infrastructure projects in order to displace communities and weaken social resistance, the PCN began another, similar organising process, this time targeting urban black communities in Buenaventura. Afro-Colombian identity, and the central importance of territory to this, were developed alongside an analysis that highlighted the link between the development of corporate mega-projects, the violence and the plight of the local population. The initial aim was to strengthen and increase the collective participation of these communities in the decision-making processes related to the development projects; however, the cumulative effect in terms of increasing consciousness and strengthening the organisational processes of these communities would be seen in the 2017 civic strike.

Another important element identified by interviewees was the prominent role played by the Catholic church from the very beginning of the process. The role of Buenaventura's Archbishop Hector Epalza Quintero, and the church's social arm, the Pastoral Social, was decisive at various moments, in particular during the increase in violence between 2012 and 2014, evoking the legacy of a previous archbishop of Buenaventura, Gerardo Valencia Cano, who was an important figure from the 1960s onwards in the 'liberation theology' tradition based on the notion that the church should take a 'preferential option for the poor' and devote its energy to support the emancipation of marginalised sectors of society, including in a pedagogical and organisational sense. The church remained one of the few voices, alongside a handful of local social movements and human rights organisations, denouncing human rights violations and supporting communities during the years of increased violence in Buenaventura since 2000.

In tracing the background to the strike, it is clear that 2013/14 represents an important moment for social movements in Buenaventura as they organised in response to a new peak in the levels of violence and social control exercised by paramilitary groups against the civilian population, and a resultant increasing anger and rejection of the violence by the city's people:

> 'We began to see a phenomenon in the population: the population began to lose its fear ... People had stopped accompanying the dead because of the fear, which is one of our cultural traditions, but then they killed a shopkeeper, and people broke the fear, over 300 people attended the wake ... (later) they killed a boy who went into a neighbourhood to sell raffle tickets, they killed him for that, so what did the people do? I have to highlight that it was mainly the women and youths, they took the boy's corpse, lifted him onto their shoulders ... and took him to the mayor's office to show what was happening.' (Anonymous interviewee, interview with Patrick Kane, 26 October 2017)

On the back of these remarkable occurrences, a small group of organisations, including community groups, human rights organisations, the PCN and the Pastoral Social, decided to organise a march *para enterrar la violencia* (to bury the violence) on 19 February 2014, in order to highlight the ongoing human rights crisis in the city. "We were expecting 5,000 people to march, because in Buenaventura it isn't easy to get people to protest ... but in reality around 50,000 came out, the march totally surpassed everyone's expectations"

(Anonymous interviewee, interview with Patrick Kane, 10 November 2017).

On the back of this historic march, this core group of organisations took a historic decision: they would join forces and begin to work together on structural civic issues affecting Buenaventura:

> 'Each of us was fighting to change Buenaventura, but each on our own issues. Then when we came together we understood that everything we were doing was to transform Buenaventura.' (Anonymous interviewee, interview with Patrick Kane, 26 October 2017)

The group started holding weekly meetings that provided a space for political debate and discussions around issues affecting the city, and the opportunity for a deeper analysis and understanding of the problems facing Buenaventura. From early on, the discussions led to a consensus that the urgency of the situation required the organisations to mobilise for structural solutions, as well as the realisation that such fundamental issues as water or health could unite heterogeneous sectors of Buenaventura's civil society across economic, social and political divides:

> 'Imagine, nobody can live without a hospital, nobody can live without water, nobody can live without a job … eventually people understood that and it facilitated our coming together because it was a reality that nobody could deny … it didn't matter if you had the nicest house in Buenaventura but no water, what good is that to you?' (Anonymous interviewee, interview with Patrick Kane, 18 September 2017)

The small group of organisations began to reach out, sector by sector, to other civil society organisations in Buenaventura:

> '[We made] a list of all of the organisations in Buenaventura, social organisations, also the trade unions from different labour sectors, transport etc., all sectors including small businesses … we made a programme for visits and began to go and tell them we were planning a strike … and to convince them to join us, sector by sector.' (Anonymous interviewee, interview with Patrick Kane, 26 October 2017)

As well as providing the weekly meeting space, the local diocese also put organising resources into the strike committee, using church services and its community engagement work to garner support for the strike and educate churchgoers on the central causes and demands of the strike: "We called people to join the strike in the church services, during masses we managed to bring people together, to motivate people and explain the process" (Anonymous interviewee, interview with Patrick Kane, 10 November 2017). The participation of the Catholic church in an organising sense also helped with the process of unifying sectors that otherwise might not have come together:

> 'The church was like the umbrella ... the meeting point, so the business sector says "if the church is there then we will join", the political sectors say "we'll work with the church", the community says "if the church is there then let's go" ... There is a respect from all of the sectors.' (Anonymous interviewee, interview with Patrick Kane, 18 September 2017)

By the time the civic strike was declared, 85 disparate civil society organisations had announced their participation in the strike; this number would grow to 120 during the strike's first days.

The 'Civic Strike to Live with Dignity'

The civil society organisations of Buenaventura finally decided to go ahead with the civic strike on 16 May 2017, after three years of unfulfilled commitments from the Colombian government with regard to an 'emergency plan' that had been agreed following the march in February 2014. The emergency plan had promised to resolve the city's multiple crises, in particular in relation to healthcare, drinking water and basic sanitation. The spirit of the list of demands was based upon the protection of life (and dignified living conditions), the environment and territory.

The puntos de encuentro

From the beginning, 11 *puntos de encuentro* (roadblocks) were planned at strategic points across the city to stop the circulation of traffic (other than that granted exemptions, such as security forces and essential services):

> 'Initially, when we said "ok how are we going to do the civic strike", we were clear that the population had to be on the streets all over the city, because if we concentrated in just one point it would be easy for them to come and disperse us, so we said we needed *puntos de encuentro*, and the population should go and pass time there, sing, tell stories, and to keep updated with the situation, and we gave different themes to each of the points ... they were spaces of communication, organising, pedagogy, culture and analysis.' (Anonymous interviewee, interview with Patrick Kane, 26 October 2017)

However, as participation snowballed over the first days of the strike, the number of *puntos* rapidly grew (the total number is contested, but is generally put at between 40 as 70), in neighbourhoods all across the city:

> 'We started to see a phenomenon, new *puntos* would pop up all over, we had named 11 points but spontaneously people started to create their own *puntos* ... in the end somebody told us there were 70 *puntos* ... So the people really took over the strike.'

As the strike went on, the number of *puntos* would vary depending on the progress of negotiations between the strike organisers and the city – when progress stalled or obstacles were encountered, *puntos* would spring up and traffic would be blocked, while the disruption of traffic became more focused on halting the circulation of lorries into and out of the port. Crucially, rather than being centrally organised and directed, the *puntos* took on their own dynamics, and were used for everything from music concerts to football matches, political debates and information centres for updating the population on developments and relaying messages from the central organising committee.

The *puntos* allowed street- and neighbourhood-level organising of the strike, and proved to be the heartbeat of the strike; permanent physical spaces for the local population to participate, with people taking shifts to ensure that the points were covered 24 hours per day:

> 'Every day more people came, we started off on our point with about ten people but we ended up being a very strong *punto*, we had lots of young people involved, and we were very united ... We went to the shops giving pedagogical

talks to the people, and also asking for support, as we didn't have food at the *punto de encuentro* we needed them to help and they would give us bread, and people would come past and leave money to support the effort.' (Anonymous interviewee, interview with Patrick Kane, 29 October 2017)

The *puntos* showed the all-encompassing demographic of those participating, which became a feature of the strike as whole: the civic strike crossed class, gender, racial and generational lines:

'Here us women are always involved in everything, we were there and we couldn't believe it, the youth would arrive to take over the night shift, the oldest of them was only 25 years old, they were the ones who were there from midnight until eight in the morning, steadfast and prepared.' (Woman neighbourhood leader, interview with Patrick Kane, 29 October 2017)

It was also the first time that indigenous communities in the rural areas of Buenaventura had joined forces and mobilised with the Afro-descendent population, another point highlighted by interviewees as significant in understanding the broad-based, almost generalised levels of participation and support in the strike.

The *puntos* effectively shut down the city for 22 days, and throughout its duration the civic strike dominated the lives of the entire population and consumed the existence of the city. Virtually all workplaces and businesses, universities and schools, were shut; public services, including all buses and taxis, were halted; the flow of traffic around the city was halted, leaving the roads virtually empty of traffic and turning the city into a giant pedestrianised zone; basic food staples were carefully rationed. Solidarity and kinship became even more important in communities across the city as people relied on families and neighbours for information, support and basic necessities. Daily mobilisations and activities were called by the strike committee and were widely publicised and shared through social media as well as at the neighbourhood-level *puntos*. The atmosphere during the first three days of the strike was at times carnival like, filled with a joyous sense of catharsis: the population of Buenaventura had risen up and taken control of their city. People of all demographics gathered on the streets, children played football on the roads, adults everywhere excitedly debated the latest developments and rumours. At the same time there was a sense of nervous anticipation: everybody knew that it was a question of time before the government would send the dreaded Escuadrón Móvil Antidisturbios (ESMAD) (Mobile Anti-Disturbance Squadron), the Colombian police anti-disturbance unit, and rumours about the imminent arrival of the ESMAD abounded at the *puntos*, in several cases spread by the police themselves.

The state strikes back

During the first three days, the police maintained a visible yet generally non-confrontational presence. However, the situation changed dramatically on the fourth day of the strike, Friday 19 May 2017, when a massive military-style operation was launched and ESMAD riot squad operatives arrived by air, land and sea, accompanied by plain-clothes police officers using live firearms against unarmed protestors. The operation was mounted simultaneously on multiple *puntos de encuentro*, both urban and rural, beginning with the rural communities blocking the only highway that connects Buenaventura with the rest of the country. From this moment, for the remainder of the strike, the *puntos* would become the focal point of confrontations between security forces and the community (Figure 3.2).

> 'We would go around the streets with a megaphone to call the community, and to tell them what was happening, that the ESMAD was coming and attacking the community, and to please come and support us ... we arrived at a strategy, we have a bridge and the bars are metal, so each time the police were coming we would hit the bridge, and the community would hear the noise and come out, many people would come out ... this filled us with strength, it showed unity, and unity breeds strength.' (Anonymous interviewee, interview with Patrick Kane, 29 October 2017)

As the confrontations of 19 May continued through the afternoon and into the evening, reports began to spread of looting of several shops and supermarkets around the city. The looting would become a major source of contention, with strike leaders convinced that it was orchestrated by the police in order to justify the imposition of a military curfew across the city:

> 'What we don't understand is how from around 5pm the police suddenly all disappeared, they took all the police

Figure 3.2: Clashes between police and community members at the *punto de encuentro* in the Isla de la Paz neighbourhood

Photo by Patrick Kane

> away, so the question is why did the police disappear for four or five hours and in that time the looting took place. We are convinced it was planned and organised by them step by step ... fortunately the looting had a positive repercussion, because we went to a supermarket where lots of kids were looting, and we said "guys, you can't do this, this isn't the strike", and we made a human chain, and the local radio stations transmitted it all live. This had a very big psychological effect, because they wanted to blame us strike leaders for the looting ... but this pierced the government's arguments and gave confidence to the population.' (Anonymous interviewee, interview with Patrick Kane, 26 October 2017)

The military curfew that was announced in response to the looting banned public meetings and mobilisations, ordered the population to be indoors from 6pm until 6am and saw the deployment of army troops to patrol the streets of the city. These events changed the dynamics of the strike, and, rather than breaking the resolve of the population, served to create an even stronger sense of injustice and antipathy towards the government and security forces, and therefore to deepen the conviction and resolve of the civic strike.

The strike executive committee had called for a mass march to take place on Saturday 20 May 2017. However, in response to the level of police aggression on 19 May, and the imposition of a military curfew in the city explicitly prohibiting public gatherings, the executive committee decided to cancel the march because of concerns of a further escalation in violence. One of the executive committee members describes what he experienced when he was delegated by the committee to go and announce the cancellation of the march and dissuade people from marching:

> 'I saw there was very few people, so I was speaking to them when I began to hear a rumbling noise coming from far away ... I went to the curve in the road to look, and what I saw left me completely [shakes head in exasperation] ... The people were marching on both sides of the road, marching compact and firm, as if marching to war like soldiers. When I saw that I rang a *compañera* and said there is huge number of people coming and nothing, nothing that can stop them ... around 15,000 people arrived to the city centre ... I have a photo of the march in which you can see the indignation and determination on the people's faces ... one policeman was so afraid that he wet himself ... I always say that one of the slogans of the strike took on its real meaning that day: *el pueblo no se rinde carajo* (the people doesn't give up, dammit!). That day the slogan became literal, the people we didn't give up, and at a key moment which could have broken the strike that march revived the strike and it demonstrated to the government that the strike wasn't over.' (Anonymous interviewee, interview with Patrick Kane, 26 October 2017)

As a result of this remarkable act of defiance, the strike executive committee decided to call a mass march (Figure 3.3) for the following day, Sunday 21 May 2017, a day that would make history as the largest mass march in the city's history:

> 'We believe that on the march there was at least one person from every household in the city ... where else in the world in a city of 395,000 people, 200,000 go out to march: that's half of the population marching and it definitely filled us

Figure 3.3: The historic march of 21 May 2017 with an estimated 200,000 people

Photo by Patrick Kane

> with … the people were waiting for what we would say, where to next? As the strike committee, we had won an amazing authority, just remembering it I get emotional … There are some writers who have said that when the people decides, there is nothing which can stand in its way, that's why the revolutions happen when the people decide.' (Anonymous interviewee, interview with Patrick Kane, 26 October 2017)

Meanwhile, the *puntos* held, despite ongoing attempts to move convoys of lorries into and out of port facilities accompanied by ESMAD riot police and plain-clothes police officers carrying live firearms, usually sometime between 10pm and 6am. These daily skirmishes became a symbolic defining feature of the strike as communities (particularly young people) organised in order to resist the passage of the convoys, unarmed protestors facing live bullets as the government gave the clearest possible message that the port's economic function was a more important matter than the lives of the local population. The *puntos* thus became even more important to the organising process, as the communities resisted the aggression of the security forces. The night-time operations caused panic and traumatised communities, as tear gas was fired indiscriminately (often from helicopters) into streets where families were sleeping, causing houses to fill with gas and many children to be hospitalised, and many protestors as well as bystanders were shot with live ammunition. In total, state human rights ombudsmen institutions documented 716 cases of human rights violations by security forces during the strike, including 38 cases of people shot with live bullets or tear gas canisters (Defensoria del Pueblo, August 2017). One student was killed during the violence of 19 May. Many community members reported racist abuse by police officers towards them, including one incident in which an officer threw a piece of bread at some female protestors and shouted "here, have some food, we know you're hungry Negros". Holding the *puntos* thus came at considerable cost:

> 'Many children had to go to hospital because they shot the gases towards the houses, and the houses are wooden so the tear gas enters and you can't escape it ... They shot a tear gas canister through the window of my house and the glass cut my mother and niece ... everyone was screaming ... another time me and my seven-year-old daughter got caught in the middle of a confrontation with the ESMAD, we had to hide under the bridge with me on top of her to protect her, risking my own life to protect her ... it is these experiences which mark the kids ... I feared for our lives, because there were bullets, we saw with our own eyes they were shooting bullets, any of us could have died.' (Woman community leader, interview with Patrick Kane, 26 October 2017)

Negotiations

Negotiations between strike representatives and the national government began very early in the strike; however, progress would prove to be very slow, particularly after the violence began and the state of emergency was declared on 19 May. For negotiations with the national government, ten separate technical commissions (including many professionals from the city with technical knowledge and local information) were set up on the following themes:

1. territory, housing and infrastructure;
2. healthcare;

3. productivity and employment;
4. environment;
5. water and basic sanitation;
6. education;
7. culture, recreation and sport;
8. access to justice, protection and victims;
9. human rights, protection and guarantees; and
10. mechanisms for financing and implementation of the final agreement.

Through the negotiations, the strike committee was able to demonstrate how state policies have historically had disastrous social, economic and ecological consequences in Buenaventura. For example, despite the city's being nourished by nine rivers in its surroundings, the population of the city does not have access to drinking water, with inevitable consequences for the health and quality of life of the majority black and indigenous population.

The key sticking point throughout negotiations was the question of how to overcome the strike committee's concerns that the strike agreements would not be fulfilled by the national government or its successors, as has been the case with so many agreements signed in the wake of mobilisations in Colombia; or that the fund would be overseen by the notoriously corrupt local administration in Buenaventura.

An agreement was struck to suspend the strike on 6 June 2017, after a unique and innovative funding formula was found: a law would be passed to establish a special fund, to run for ten years, for the 'comprehensive development of Buenaventura'. It obliges national government to set aside money in the national budget for the works agreed to as a result of the strike, covering all of the thematic areas listed above. The fund will be implemented and overseen by an executive committee that will include representatives of the civic strike committee, as well as the national and local government, and will have independent observation by UN and national ombudsmen organisations.

The law was passed in the national Parliament on 15 December 2017, sparking widespread celebration and optimism. This optimism has waned somewhat since then, as the setting up of the fund and the fund's executive committee has been painstakingly slow. Furthermore, the process now faces the test of the change of national government administration: the election in June 2018 of Ivan Duque marks the return of the ultra-right-wing political party, Centro Democratico, led by controversial ex-President Alvaro Uribe who led a brutal neofascist regime between 2002 and 2010.

Learning from the strike

From the most experienced of the strike leaders, to the children who lived the process, nobody who lived through the civic strike will ever forget the experience. The strike in many ways represented a steep learning curve for all involved, not least the strike leadership:

> 'Nobody can prepare you for that ... for me it is like doing a master's, during the strike and also since the strike, I feel like I'm having a huge education ... it's learning in the process of doing, but at the same time teaching others to learn while doing by showing them the example.' (Anonymous interviewee, interview with Patrick Kane, 10 August 2017)

Others spoke of the sense of unity and solidarity that has prevailed in the months since the strike ended, and the deep friendship bonds formed as a result of the shared experience of resisting on the *puntos de encuentro* together, as described by one neighbourhood-level organiser:

> 'People really showed that they love Buenaventura and that they want to contribute to resolve the problems ... I see people now who I never used to speak to but since we were together on the *punto de encuentro*, as if they were old friends, because what we went through in those days ... made us brothers and sisters, "what they do to you they do to me".' (Anonymous interviewee, interview with Patrick Kane, 26 October 2017)

This intangible sense of raised individual and collective consciousness, while impossible to measure, points to a key argument within social movement learning literature. The learning experiences of unarmed communities who stood together and resisted tear gas and bullets, fired at them by state security forces seeking nothing more urgent than to escort lorries packed with commercial goods to and from the Buenaventura port, simply cannot be reproduced. Beyond the practical knowledge gained in such circumstances, around organising and acting collectively, such an experience also creates a unique type of oppositional consciousness, created by being exposed to the deadly force and aggression of the very institutions responsible for the protection of the community. This oppositional consciousness is imbibed with a sense of unity and solidarity with those who also find themselves exposed to the same situation. These learning experiences are formative and deep, just like the new friendship bonds formed on the barricades of the *puntos*. While a number of (interrelated) learnings emerge, some of the most critical involve learning about mobilising and organising, and sustaining solidarity; about the nature of leadership, and the relationship between 'leaders' and 'followers'; and about the nature of the state.

Learning about mobilising, organising and sustaining solidarity

A critical learning cited by one of the strike leaders was the importance of the oft-unseen, thankless effort that goes into organising processes:

> 'One thing which we learned in the committee was the importance of persevering, for years and years we had been pushing and pushing, sometimes only three of us would come, sometimes 30 or 40, but we carried on meeting every week, patiently organising towards the strike, and the people learned this too, you can't try and do something and expect it to be done the next day … in the social movement and in questions of building the consciousness of the people, if you don't persist then you won't get anywhere.' (Anonymous interviewee, interview with Patrick Kane, 26 October 2017)

As discussed previously, this long, patient process resulted in a remarkable level of support and participation beyond simply those organisations directly involved. Leading up to and during the strike, local radio and television media gave widespread, sympathetic coverage to the civic strike, and several well-known local celebrities gave vocal support. The civic strike inspired a frenzy of production from the thriving Buenaventura cultural scene, with local Hip Hop artists in particular leading the way and recording a multitude of songs that provided the soundtrack to the daily mobilisations and activities at the *puntos*. Famous salsa and Hip Hop artists from the city also participated actively in the mobilisations, and even on one occasion organised a spontaneous *marcha de los artistas*, in which an estimated 10,000 people participated.

The civic strike thus achieved something extraordinary: it created a situation of hegemonic support among Buenaventura's civil society

Figure 3.4: Women's march, 3 June 2017

Photo by Patrick Kane

spheres for the collectively constructed demands of the strike. In part this was due to the almost irrefutable nature of the central demands of the strike, which were centred on basic human rights that were being denied to the entire population (such as the demands for a hospital and running, clean water) and hence even government negotiators and conservative commentators could not publicly oppose them. But it is also testament to the painstaking months and years of organising and preparation that went into convincing diverse sectors of the city of the need for drastic action to bring real change for all bonaverenses. This remarkable sense of solidarity allowed resistance to be maintained, even in the face of state brutality.

Learning about the nature of leadership, and the relationship between 'leaders' and 'followers'

The scale of the civic strike raises the important question of the nature and dynamics of the relationship between the strike leadership (the executive committee and the plenary of around 120 civil society organisations) and the mass of the population. As previously discussed, through the experience of the mass march the strike leadership learned that it was the people who controlled the ebb and flow of the strike, not them. The general population played a determining role as an autonomous actor able to drive forward and embolden the strike committee, something that was replicated in other important moments. As one strike leader commented, "I had never truly seen the sovereignty of the people before then, true democracy... when the community is so engaged in the strike that when the leaders get overwhelmed or weakened, the community picks them up and whoosh, pulls them out of it" (Anonymous interviewee, interview with Patrick Kane, 26 October 2017). As a result, leaders need to ensure that they understand what the grassroots is thinking: "we've learned to gauge the community's state of mind, it's almost like a science, but between us in the strike committee we have learned to read the indicators of what is going on in the community". The strike leadership also learned that in order to retain legitimacy, absolute transparency in the conduct of the strike and the negotiations needed to be maintained.

In the negotiation period the strike committee's success was reliant upon the ongoing level of participation in and support for the strike and the strike leaders. The decision to televise the initial phases of the negotiations (until the thematic commissions were formed) added to this sense of shared purpose and struggle, and hugely raised the popularity of and confidence in the strike committee's leaders as they went toe to toe with government negotiators and demonstrated an ability to match their discourse and posturing with a profound understanding of the issues affecting Buenaventura, backed up with hard facts and figures:

> 'To transmit the negotiations was fundamental ... it was what catapulted us, it meant people could see what was going on and it filled them with pride, they could see how well prepared we were, we had all the arguments and we knew the issues so well, we ran rings around the government, they had no reply ... this gave us the initiative because we got the recognition, everybody was watching and supporting.' (Strike leader, interview with Patrick Kane, 29 October 2017)

The televised debates engaged the focus of the entire city and became the subject of endless analysis and debate on every corner and in every home. This ensured the accountability of the strike leaders to the grassroots.

Learning about the nature of the state

In the months following the strike, one prominent strike leader said that she felt that the scale of the state violence and repression of the strike, linked so clearly and symbolically to powerful economic interests by the brutal violence employed in order to guarantee the passage of the convoys carrying goods into and out of the port, provided the population of Buenaventura with an invaluable political lesson about the true nature of the state and the interests that it represents. In the face of the violence, the population was forced to unite and develop strategies of collective resistance against the daily attacks by the very state security forces that many had previously seen as their protectors. As has been previously argued by Choudry, encounters with the repressive security machinery of the state can be deeply politicising experiences for individuals in the developing of alternative political subjectivities (Choudry, 2015).

Conclusion

At the time of writing, a year after the civic strike in Buenaventura, not much has changed, yet everything has changed. Not much has changed in that the population of Buenaventura have yet to see the concrete materialisation of most of the concessions that they achieved, such as new hospitals, schools, drainage and safe, clean water services. However, the civic strike irreversibly altered the political and social landscape of Buenaventura. Today, the executive committee of the civic strike has become established as a political actor that is, in some respects, arguably more powerful in the city than the local government led by the mayor. The members of the civic committee enjoy huge public recognition and support; regular meetings are held between national government officials and work commissions from the civic strike committee about the implementation of the various aspects of the strike agreements. While it would be premature to argue that power has shifted away from traditional political and commercial elites that have dominated Buenaventura for so long, these developments certainly represent a blow to their previous hegemony and signal a political earthquake with huge implications:

> 'Everybody got to the point where we just wanted to be treated with dignity, and that is why in the end the people rose up, and the history of Buenaventura was divided in two, before and after: the people of Buenaventura are different

now, there is no going back to what we were before the strike, it is a different community, a community with an antecedent of collective struggle, of collective strength ... and this force is going to accompany us in future struggles.' (Anonymous interviewee, interview with Patrick Kane, 18 September 2017)

The violence, however, continues. According to government figures, between January 2016 and July 2018, 326 activists and social leaders were assassinated in Colombia, including human rights and environmental defenders (El Espectador newspaper, 2018). The popular community leader Temistocles Machado, who played an important role in the strike, was murdered by presumed paramilitaries on 27 January 2018. Aside from the murder of Temistocles, several members of the strike executive committee have also suffered threats, surveillance and harassment. With the election of a president who represents a party with well-documented historical links to paramilitary organisations that have terrorised social movements for decades, the outlook is not promising for the situation of repression and human rights violations in Buenaventura and across Colombia. At the time of writing there is much concern within the social movements involved in Buenaventura's civic strike over the future security of activists in the city.

Ultimately, the implementation of the historic gains won by the people of Buenaventura will depend upon the ability of the strike's civil society leadership to retain and mobilise public support when necessary. To this end, one shortcoming at the time of writing, recognised by local leaders, is the lack of a city-wide pedagogical and organising campaign, in order to increase the masses' appropriation of the struggle's gains and consolidate the increase in consciousness generated in the city by the collective experience of the civic strike.

The Buenaventura civic strike demonstrated the capacity of populations who for multiple generations have been subjected to the ravages of colonialism and racialised global capitalism to leverage political power and target a strategic weakness of the free trade-based economy: the necessity for the constant physical circulation of commercial goods in containers on the back of trucks flowing constantly into and out of major ports. By shutting this down, the population dealt a blow to powerful international economic interests and took a stand against an economic development model that in Buenaventura has placed absolute priority on profits, while subjecting the local population to horrifying levels of violence, poverty, environmental degradation and increasing displacement from their territories. They showed that the global capitalist system is sometimes most vulnerable at the points where it seems most impenetrable or invincible.

References

Centro Nacional de Memoria Historica (2015) *Buenaventura: Un Puerto sin Comunidad*, Bogota: Centro Nacional de Memoria Historica.

Choudry, A. (2015) *Learning activism: The intellectual life of contemporary social movements*, Toronto: University of Toronto Press.

Defensoria del Pueblo (2017) 'Informe de Derechos Humanos Paro Civico Buenaventura', http://www.defensoria.gov.co/es/nube/noticias/6555/INFORME-DE-DERECHOS-HUMANOS-PARO-CIVICO---BUENAVENTURA-2017.htm.

El Espectador newspaper (2018) '"De 326 lideres asesinados, 81 serian del Cauca": Defensoria del Pueblo', https://www.elespectador.com/noticias/judicial/de-326-lideres-asesinados-81-serian-de-cauca-defensoria-del-pueblo-articulo-801007.

El Tiempo newspaper (2017) 'La mitad de Buenaventura en condicion de victima', http://www.eltiempo.com/colombia/cali/la-mitad-de-buenaventura-en-condicion-de-victima-126252.

Escobar, A. (2008) *Territories of difference: Place, movements, life, redes*, Durham, NC: Duke University Press.

Human Rights Watch (2014) 'The crisis in Buenaventura: Disappearances, dismemberment and displacement in Colombia's main Pacific port'.

Mathers, A. and Novelli, N. (2007) 'Researching resistance to neoliberal globalization: Engaged ethnography as solidarity and praxis', *Globalizations*, 4(2): 229–49.

Taula Catalana per la Pau I els Drets Humans a Colombia (2016) 'Asedio a las comunidades: Los impactos de una empresa catalana, GRUP TCB, en Buenaventura, Colombia', informe.

FOUR

No pollution and no Roma in my backyard: class and race in framing local activism in Laborov, eastern Slovakia

Richard Filčák and Daniel Škobla

Introduction

It was the bleak December of 2007. Petitioners were walking door to door to collect signatures. Ultimately, almost 9,000 people decided to sign and stand up against the planned construction of a massive coal-burning power plant. It was a rather good achievement in the eastern Slovakian district of Laborov, comprising 100,000 inhabitants. There were also people who did not sign up. Some had hopes of new jobs in the power plant, some declined because of fear and some simply had no particular interest. There were also those who were not asked to sign up local Roma living in segregated neighbourhoods on the outskirts of the town, a community of around 3,500 people. Legally, they were inhabitants of the town, but in everyday life they were unwanted and overlooked by local decision makers and the majority of ethnic Slovaks. Being the subject of long-lasting institutional discrimination and prejudice, they are considered by some to be almost an 'environmental burden', a kind of 'pollution' on the 'pure body' of the town, producing nothing more than waste and problems.

Care for the environment and the fight against pollution have been serious agendas in public policy making in Laborov and have revolved around two main issues. Firstly, air pollution linked to a highly controversial plan to build a coal-burning power plant in the immediate vicinity of the town centre (culminating in years 2006–10). Secondly, the issue of waste management in the town, which came to be increasingly presented in the public debate. While the former could be considered an example of short-term popular mobilisation and community resistance to environmentally irresponsible big capital investment, the latter is an instance of a managerial problem recategorised into an ethnic issue and example of racialisation and reproduction of prejudices and discrimination against local Roma. Thus, this chapter can be seen as a case study of the racialisation and class division of an environmental justice struggle and a contest of framing between 'environmental justice' and racial oppression, in which the Roma are cast as no more than equivalent to environmental pollution.

Our study, the fieldwork for which was undertaken in March 2017 and January 2018, is based on available written records (media and documents), interviews and observational research, involving fieldwork in Laborov. The intention was to determine the facts on the ground following the campaign against the power plant history and the living conditions and positionality of local Roma in relation to those who organised the struggle and who later became representatives of the town. Extensive literature on inequalities, social/environmental justice and class divisions in society guide our approach and analysis. We also pay special attention to Pierre Bourdieu's concept of 'embodied social structures', which are the cognitive structures that social agents internalise and implement in their practical knowledge of the social world (Bourdieu, 1984). Another source of inspiration was Loïc Wacquant's (2008) theorising regarding segregated ghettos as an instrument of ethno-racial closure and control. A factual record of what actually happened in the town was elaborated during the fieldwork, together with gathering insights into the situation of marginalised Roma in Laborov. Unless otherwise stated, all statements and testimonies were gained directly from our respondents, who included representatives of civic association, the town office and local Roma.

A tale of a coal-burning power plant

Laborov is a town located in the south-eastern part of the Slovak Republic. Lacking precious natural resources, and away from important industrial hubs, the region has traditionally and predominantly depended on agriculture. However, after the Second World War several processing industries were built from scratch or rebuilt and extended under socialist industrialisation. Located almost directly in the town centre, after a massive reconstruction in 1984, the biggest employer for the town became a sugar-processing factory. The low-skilled jobs in agriculture and the factory provided employment opportunities for sedentary Roma who settled in the region for several decades.

Restructuring of the economy in the 1990s based on the privatisation of state-owned factories, which consequently became victims of market liberalisation, led to the collapse of the sugar-processing industry. Technology, engines and valuable assets were sold, and iron from construction was disposed of as scrap metal. What remains in Laborov today is an abandoned factory site, a reminder of the past.

In 2006, surprising news spread throughout Laborov. Unknown private developers, called the Czechoslovak Energy Company, intended to build a new, modern coal-burning power plant in the location of the former sugar mill, no more than 200 metres from blocks of flats, family houses and a school (Figure 4.1). Events unfolded rapidly. In May 2006 the mayor of Laborov sent a letter to the investor in support of the project; no later than November of the same year the investor submitted project documents to the Ministry of Environment for approval. Why was the town of Laborov chosen for this investment, given that there were no coal deposits in the area, and no history of large energy projects? According to the official investor's explanation, it was because of the railway track connecting Ukraine and the US steel plant in Košice. For historical reasons there are a different-gauge railway tracks into eastern and western Europe; thus, when iron or coal is transported, one has to unload the materials from Ukrainian waggons at the border and reload them into Slovak ones. To avoid this problem and decrease costs, a special railway track was constructed in eastern Slovakia during socialism, connecting Krivoj Rog (coal and

Figure 4.1: Map showing location of power plant project, town centre with residential areas and Roma settlement

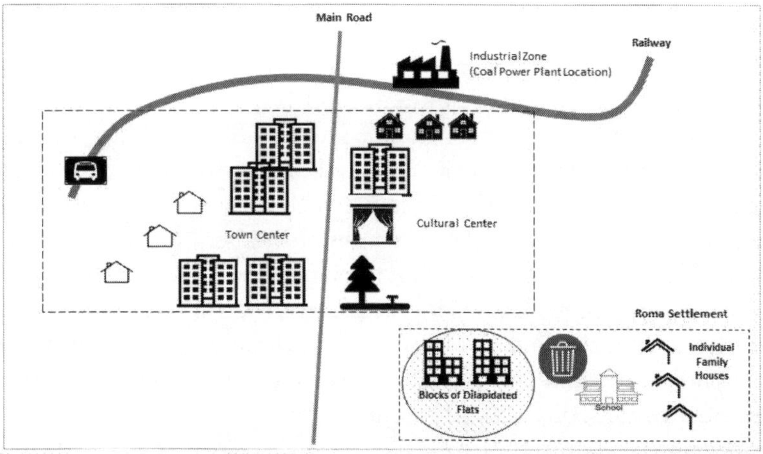

Source: Richard Filčák and Daniel Škobla

iron mining area in Ukraine) and the Košice steel plant. The price of building plots in Laborov was low, unemployment was high and municipalities seemed to be prepared to accept any investment that brought in at least some jobs and revenue.

The project idea stemmed from an investor with a rather unclear background. As pointed out by one of the NGO experts interviewed: "The whole set-up was weird. We were not able to find out who was behind it. The investor, the one who was the face of the project, was definitely too small a fish. The project was professionally prepared, and we had suspicions that it was backed by one of the big players on the energy market, but were not able to find evidence." Under current law, it is extremely difficult to trace ownership. The Czechoslovak Energy Company was virtually unknown among experts and the business community, having a small office with limited staff and no history of projects of this size. There were also rumours that the company was a front for politically connected investors; according to activists: "We did not have the feeling it was coming from the political top … most likely, it was the idea of private investors affiliated with one of the smaller coalition parties in those times, seeking to profit through political connections … you know, they had a minister and the Ministry of the Environment under their political control."

The mere idea seemed ridiculous at first glance: burning coal at the edge of the district town, in an agricultural region and in a country that had no immediate demand for electricity production. With two new blocks of the Mochovce Nuclear Power Plant under construction and an increasing share of renewable energy, Slovakia is close to a balanced energy production and consumption pattern. The very idea also contradicted the official energy policy goals and all related governmental strategies. Last but not least, in the context of EU climate change targets it contradicted goals to phase out coal from the energy mix. Even though the power plant would be, according to technical documentation, built with state-of-the-art technology, the anticipated emissions of carbon dioxide would increase total Slovakian emissions by an estimated 8%. State-of-the-art technology also means automation and a very limited number of low-skilled and menial jobs. Moreover, since the developer was registered outside of the county, they would pay local property tax, but the profits from electricity sales would not remain there. It was assumed that the obligatory Environmental Impact Assessment (EIA) report, submitted by the investor to the Ministry in June 2007, would reveal all of these concerns.

The EIA report and its outcomes were perhaps the main breakthrough in generating public resistance to the project. Contrary to expectations, it gave the project a green light. A civic platform, Laborov First, was established that immediately turned to NGOs with experience in environmental campaigns and advocacy. There are not many of them in Slovakia and the first choice was the highly visible and well-known organisation Greenpeace. Later, the initiative also contracted a legal firm that specialised in protecting public interests. Using advice from Greenpeace, Laborov First built its resistance on negative health impacts as its main talking point, while using legal obstructions combined with popular protests. The initiative was advised to mobilise public opinion. When asked about success factors, representatives of the initiative emphasised several times their professional managerial skills and, last but not least, solvency: "The campaign, legal documentation – it all costs money … we often see on TV some activists fighting against something. They do not have a chance; you need organisation and experience managing people and money." Resistance to the power plant, however, followed the general pattern of divisions organised along ethnic lines, typical for Slovakia. There was no Romani participation in the Laborov First initiative, nor was the petition against the plant distributed among the Roma in the settlement. As one of the respondents put it: "We were not interested in getting the Gypsy in. They live in waste. What do they know about clean air?"

From the investor's perspective, the process started surprisingly well, since elected local municipal representatives were not against the plant's construction. However, on 3 July 2007 the investor, following the requirements of the EIA Act, organised a public hearing in the premises of the municipal town hall. The investor estimated that 600–800 people attended (their opponents say up to 1,000), a remarkable number when considering the total population of the town. The investor described the meeting in its Final Position (a document required under the 24/2006 Slovak Law EIA) in the following way: 'Overall, we may evaluate the public hearing as emotional, chaotic, physically demanding and not professional and it is mainly due to the public' (EIA, 2007: 20). In another place in the document we read about 'persistent resistance of prepared and participating – perhaps manipulated citizens' (p 19). Since Laborov is close to the state border with Hungary, the Hungarian government expressed an interest in using the Espoo Convention on transboundary impacts in order to become part of the EIA process. The outcomes of the public hearing in Metorajaújhely, Hungary were summarised by the investor in the following way: 'Detailed and professional responses were provided to the requests and questions from people participating, yet even so, the public was not satisfied. Around forty people participated in the meeting (towards the end only about thirty); it cannot by any means be considered the broad public' (p 23). Derogatory remarks about public discontent expressed at both hearings indicate that there was massive opposition.

There is long-standing criticism of the EIA process in Slovakia, particularly because the investor must pay for the assessment and thus the companies and experts contracted are inevitably biased; something that a high-ranking representative of the Ministry of Environment conceded in a personal interview in April 2017. The authors of this EIA did their best to demonstrate that the overall impact of a coal-burning power plant in the town, coal transport, gas emissions and waste management were all manageable and harmless. The overall message of the EIA report was that there were strong, scientifically and economically rigorous data on the project's benefits, backed by real experts, while there was manipulated, misleading public opinion, coordinated by a few local protesters and external NGO troublemakers: if only people would listen to investors carefully, they would realise the benefits of the project.

To boost resistance, Laborov First organised the highly successful petition against the plant construction in early December 2007. Yet, on 19 December 2007 the EIA Final Report supported the construction and the Ministry of Economy issued its certificate for the power plant. Laborov First responded by organising public demonstrations in January 2018.

Meanwhile, there were other entities entering the process. Since the EIA study did not indicate possible violations of environmental standards, the Regional Public Health Authority (RÚVZ) in Laborov requested the submission of another specific impact study, the Health Impact Assessment (HIA). A major shortcoming of this HIA study was the exclusion of residents from the immediate vicinity of the proposed power plant. As a result, the RÚVZ rejected the proposed location of the power plant, which thwarted the investment project (Sládek, 2016). This decision marks the turning point in the story. In February 2010 the County Regional Authority dismissed permission for the power plant operation and discontinued the investment plan.

How much does 'class' actually matter?

It is indisputable that many local citizens, regardless of their social positioning, engaged in active opposition towards the plant. However, what was not visible, at first sight, was that what on the surface appeared to be grassroots local activism in Laborov was largely organised and orchestrated by a newly born platform, formally registered as an NGO. Its leading figures were local bourgeoisie who, due to a combination of personal and business interests, felt endangered by the prospective plant. One of the major apprehensions was that the investment would result in a decrease of real estate value and, probably, a diminishing local economy. For example, during a visit to Laborov we found out that the power plant was supposed to be built on land that was in the immediate vicinity of the restaurant owned by one of the Laborov First representatives. The restaurant would then find itself located next to hundreds of waggons transporting coal in and ash out. Here, local business interests evidently clashed with external business interests. Laborov can thus be considered an example of an environmental justice conflict between stronger transnational bourgeoisie and weaker local sections of bourgeoisie, a situation that represents an intra-class conflict. Seen through this lens, the Laborov case was not a typical environmental justice struggle, since the opposition to the plant derived from local business interests and not from poor communities.

Local Roma, who are situated in the lowest ranks in local social hierarchies (as we explain later), happened, in the first stage of this story, to be the object of manipulation on the side of the investor. Aware of the general public opposition to the project, the investor attempted to gain support from the poorest groups, motivating them through false promises of jobs in the new power plant. (We assume that the investor had to be aware that state-of-the-art technology does not create more than a few jobs for the low-skilled segment of the workforce.) The investor even brought a Romani group to the EIA hearing at the town council. However, given their small number (the hearing reported something between 800 and 1,000 participants, while the Romani group consisted of approximately 50 people), it seemed that the investor had wrongly assessed the situation and the group could not influence the discussion. It is difficult to reconstruct what exactly happened during the public hearings, and personal accounts of the locals and external NGOs do not indicate any harsh confrontation, but it is clear that the Romani were discouraged from speaking. As one of the Laborov First representatives recalled: "They [Roma] came in, but there were too few of them and they did not have a clue about what was going on, so they were easily prevented from speaking and, after a while, then simply left." According to the Romani whom we interviewed, regardless of whether individuals were informed of the negative environmental consequences or not, local Roma simply did not consider the health aspects of the investment to be important, taking into account their already miserable living conditions and unhealthy housing. The opinion of the Laborov First representatives was that the Romani involvement in public hearings on the side of the investor was an attempt to manipulate and misuse them in order to counterbalance opposition numerically. Thus, paradoxically, the investor was the only agency in the process who involved Roma in the decision-making process. He did it for the strategical objective of breaking the unity of opposition; and unintentionally further reproduced the racist prejudice that Roma can be easily manipulated and 'bought'.

Laborov First, initially formed as an NGO, after the discontinuation of the investment plans quickly realised its political potential and began to work de facto as a political party under the control of the same people. It decided to run in the local elections in 2010, obtaining the majority of seats in the town hall, and its leader became the mayor of the town. One of the mayor's first steps was to prohibit a prestigious international Gypsy cultural festival in the town, since, according to our Romani informants among the festival organisers, the town's leadership did not like the idea of local Roma from the settlement (located at the edge of town) coming to the centrally located Cultural Centre during the festivities. There appears to be no official or written record of the municipality's decision, in either council session records or the regular bulletins about town events published on the web. This is perhaps illustrative of how Roma are collectively marginalised and excluded, often surreptitiously, by dominant classes.

Another, highly controversial, decision of the mayor and the Laborov First-dominated council was the regulation allowing the police to confiscate trolleys, strollers and bikes belonging to the local Roma, used to collect wooden boards or other waste material for heating or improving their dwellings. This order was executed without legal basis, but in the name of populism and the fight for a 'clean' city. Thus, after Laborov First won the environmental justice battle it quickly positioned local Roma as a primary target of institutional racism and punitive measures. In the first Laborov First bulletin in 2013, these targeted Roma individuals are referred to as 'asocials', avoiding the standard ethnic category but using a highly offensive term unequivocally associated with local Roma in Slovak mainstream discourse. In the subsequent 2014 local elections, although Laborov First narrowly lost the post of mayor it gained most of the seats (13) on the town council. Laborov First claimed that the new mayor was elected only because of 704 votes from the Romani settlement and accused him of 'repaying back these votes by pro-Roma deeds' (Laborov First website, 2016). According to our Romani informant, in fact Roma from the settlement with one accord voted for the Laborov First opponent as a direct result of the confiscation regulation.

Because of Laborov First's domination in the town council since 2010, environmental issues and green topics, especially waste management, have made it into the local and public policy discourse. We have to understand here that this was uncommon in Slovakia, where environmental topics were rarely high on the agenda of municipalities. This apparently successful story, however, also has a bleak side. The political programme of Laborov First, to an important degree, touches upon popular widespread anti-Roma prejudice that blames the Roma for waste management problems. Laborov First did not introduce racism and anti-Gypsyism in the town, but very 'skilfully' and cynically surfed on the wave of negative attitudes towards Roma.

Roma of Laborov

In order to understand the Romani positionality in this story we have to make a brief historical excursion. In the period following the Second World War the Roma in Slovakia, under the enforced official policy of full employment, usually worked as agricultural or industrial labourers. The settlements in which they lived were usually located at the edges of villages and were characterised by dilapidated housing and the absence of basic physical infrastructure. Official policies during state socialism from the 1960s attempted to demolish 'Roma settlements', resettle their inhabitants and provide standard accommodation. However, in social practice these policies, for various reasons including local resistance, have not fully met their declared goals (Scheffel, 2005). The living conditions of Roma dramatically worsened with the neoliberal restructuring in the 1990s, when many Roma lost their jobs in state-owned factories and cooperatives that were either privatised or shut down (Guy, 2001). The settlements thus expanded both because of demographic dynamics of the population and due to widespread evictions from apartments in towns.

The Romani settlement in Laborov is a segregated neighbourhood located at the edge of town. Originally there were just four standard three-storey panel blocks that were intended for workers in food-processing plants. Nowadays it is an area with a population of some 3,500 (around 16% of the town's inhabitants, according to estimates) with extremely poor living conditions, a lack of infrastructure and an absence of water and sewerage. There is not a single playing field for children. At times, epidemic disease outbreaks, such as hepatitis and even syphilis, are reported in the area (Sládek, 2016). Most local Roma face rampant unemployment, and households are heavily indebted and are trapped in unemployment and welfare dependency. Families are living in run-down blocks built by the previous socialist regime, or new social housing (with 'lower' construction standards) or old family houses and shelters built from non-standard materials (UNDP, 2012). An ethnically segregated elementary school constructed with EU funding ten years ago is located directly in the settlement (Škobla and Filčák, 2016). It has around 950 pupils and 65 employees. A gym and playgrounds (usually standard and basic school facilities) were not constructed. As the deputy director puts it, with slight embarrassment, "people [local non-Roma] complain if money goes into the settlement".

Structural changes in the 1990s were among the key factors framing the relationship between the Roma and dominant classes, leading to increasing ghettoisation and spatial segregation. Slovakian Roma as a labour force were no longer an asset (in the production process) but increasingly a liability and burden. While, practically speaking, they were excluded from the labour market and were victims of deindustrialisation, automation and contraction in production and consumption patterns due to structural changes, they are presented nowadays as a kind of free rider in the social benefit system (Filčák and Steger, 2014), as people who intentionally scrounge welfare and avoid work. In reaction to spatial changes that derived from these configurations, they were forced to form a hyper-ghetto, which is a closed structure described by Wacquant (2008: 95) as 'an impermeable social capsule sentencing its stigmatized inhabitants to develop independent forms of social reproduction with little help from the outside and no hope of escape'.

A tale of waste and garbage

From at least the late 1990s, one of the most important challenges for municipalities has been waste management. A growing quantity of waste, and resistance to the construction of new landfills in the proximity of dwellings ('not in my backyard' syndrome), contributed to a situation where waste management becomes discriminatory and disproportionately imposed on social or ethnic groups that occupy a weak position in local hierarchies and lack the social and economic capital to protect their interests (Filčák et al, 2017). Officially, waste management fees began to be collected from residents in accordance with a new law in 2001, but the implementation has encountered difficulties. Residents often were not informed properly about the duty to pay for waste collection. People did not pay their fees, debts were accrued and municipalities meted out high penalties. The highest individual debt for communal waste disposal in Laborov has risen to €4,500. According to the municipality's official website, in 2018 around 1,400 individuals, overwhelmingly from Romani settlements, are indebted in respect of communal waste disposal.

Under these circumstances the inhabitants of the Laborov settlement practically became 'hostages' of the situation because the town hall, using collective indebtedness as a pretext, abandoned the emptying of standard garbage cans and instead installed large-capacity containers that were emptied once a week only (Figures 4.2a–b). Meanwhile, garbage was piling up in and around the containers, littering the surrounding areas. The pervasive disorder surrounding the main access road to the settlement created the impression that local residents were negligent in terms of cleanliness. However, keeping the area clean was virtually impossible, as residents of the settlement were collectively refused the standard waste collection services. The collective 'punishment' of cancelling waste disposal services for the entire residential area is an example of institutional discrimination faced by local Roma.

Waste management, at the same time, has become increasingly costly for municipalities, since central government further increased the cost of landfills in order to push towns and villages to separate and recycle (something that Slovakia has been relatively slow to achieve – while the EU average was 43.5% in 2014, Slovakia achieved only 10.3%). In late 2015 Laborov First, as an attack on the new mayor, claimed that cleaning the shanty town cost as much as €50,000. The municipality collected the waste and disposed of it temporarily (and legally, with the permission of the local environmental authority) at the municipal property on Kpt. Šverma Street. Disposal of the waste immediately sparked a reaction from the majority, with central and regional media reporting widely on the case. Local people told invited TV crews about "waste full of [rodent] carcasses, faeces and parasites of all kinds", that the shanty town was full of "hepatitis, venereal diseases and other diseases" and that they did not want this waste in the town. The

Environmental justice, popular struggle and community development

Figure 4.2: (a) One of the three containers serving the community only one day after it was emptied; and (b) an anti-flood channel in which waste piled up

Photos by Richard Filčák

municipality was subsequently forced to deposit the waste in a distant landfill, at an additional cost of €16,000.

The Romani settlement, in the perception of the dominant class, represents a stain upon the town, with its waste characterised as extremely dangerous and contagious. Garbage and pollution in the settlement were constant topics in local policy debate, stigmatising Roma as 'dirty', 'lazy' and 'incapable' of taking care of their living environment, as reported on Slovak TV in April 2014. One of our respondents literally said that Roma are "children of the garbage". Without standard jobs, the majority of Roma live on petty, informal income derived from garbage collection and utilisation, using well-off non-Romani quarters as the source of material. The most recent step in response is Laborov First's campaign for a new underground waste storage system in order to thwart garbage picking. The idea is in many ways an economically viable and better alternative for town waste management. Yet, in the context of inter-ethnic relations in the town, it further enhances prejudices and escalates the marginalisation of Roma.

A billboard from the campaign for a new underground waste storage system, supporting changes in waste collection, is shown in Figure 4.3. The campaign is against trash collectors, and the slogan 'We support underground waste storage' can be seen at the bottom. Although Roma are not explicitly mentioned, from the context it is obvious.

Figure 4.3: A billboard from the campaign for a new underground waste storage system

Photo by Richard Filčák (March 2017)

The story of waste management presented here is a good illustration of class and ethnic division, structural oppression and the peculiarities of environmental justice in Laborov, at least in three main aspects: firstly, unpaid fees for waste collection become a primary source of an indebtedness trap for most local Romani inhabitants; secondly, waste management policy (implying the purported dirtiness of Roma) becomes a symbolic instrument of Romani stigmatisation; and thirdly, garbage picking, carried out by some impoverished Roma, serves as a pretext for their physical exclusion from the town centre, enclosing them as much as possible in the ghetto.

Conclusion

In this chapter, two tales of Laborov have served us analytically to uncover deeper roots and barriers in addressing environmental justice. However, we cannot understand them without unveiling the collective interests of ruling classes, as well as the context of local social and inter-ethnic relations. Our account is understandable only if we recognise that local Roma, due to profound structural discrimination, are disempowered and have few possibilities to influence local decision making.

This is not to say that we are essentialising Roma and looking at them solely as passive victims. Social reality is much more complicated; many are working hard to improve their lives, making great efforts to achieve meagre material security for themselves and their children (for example, they migrate for labour, work in precarious jobs and so on), and they have their own 'ways' in which to negotiate with local government. Moreover, given their numbers, as an electorate they can play an important role in local elections and support one or another candidate.

On the other hand, through structural lenses local Roma as a group are so deeply disempowered that at present they can hardly influence community development, either collectively or through self-mobilisation. The external assistance in respect of empowerment is meagre. There are three community workers in Laborov (formally employed by the town but funded by the European Social Fund), mediating and assisting in communication with state and municipality institutions, but their work is not aimed at the political empowerment of the group. There is no NGO or church operating in the area. Local self-organising that aims to build capacities to gain or wield more political power is practically non-existent in the fragmented community.

The racialised strategy of the ruling groups lies in effectively reframing Romani problems from a social issue to an ethnic problem and a security issue. The Roma are presented as the undeserving poor who do not want to work and are essentially 'dirty', 'lazy' and 'scrounging' in respect of welfare, carrying cultural predispositions and health risks for the non-Romani population of the town. The disempowerment of Roma and the dynamics of ethnic relations in the town were, cleverly but cynically, identified by the power plant investor in an attempt to exploit the situation and mobilise Roma on his side to gain numerically in order to acquire more ballots for the project during the public hearings.

The relational positionality of local Roma in the social space of Laborov, to a decisive extent, influenced the story of environmental justice mobilisation in the town. Without considering 'the tale of waste and garbage', the environmental justice struggle in Laborov would likely be read as an example of successful activism pursuing its goals. Yet our analysis of structural conditions and social practices reveals patterns of oppression hidden beneath the surface. The Laborov case thus opens an important question of 'framing' environmental justice and how to promote environmental justice in Central and Eastern Europe: can environmental justice be pursued without achieving social justice?

Acknowledgement

The study drawn on in this chapter was supported by the project APVV-17-0141 Analysis of Barriers in Access to Employment for Marginalized Groups of Population funded by The Ministry of Education, Science, Research and Sport of the Slovak Republic.

References

Bourdieu, P. (1984) *Distinctions: A social critique of the judgment of taste*, translated by Richard Nice, Cambridge, MA: Harvard University Press.

Environmental Impact Assessment (EIA) (2007) Environmental Impact Assessment of New Energy Source Laborov (Public Consultations), https://www.enviroportal.sk/sk/eia/detail/novy-energeticky-zdroj-trebisov.

Filčák, R. and Steger, T. (2014) 'Ghettos in Slovakia. The environmental exclusion of the Roma minority', *Analyse & Kritik*, 2: 229–50.

Filčák, R., Szilvasi, M. and Škobla, D. (2017) 'No water for the poor: The Roma ethnic minority and local governance in Slovakia', *Ethnic and Racial Studies*, 41(7): 1390–407, http://dx.doi.org/10.1080/01419870.2017.1291984.

Guy, W. (ed) (2001) *Between past and future: The Roma of Central and Eastern Europe*, Hatfield: University of Hertfordshire Press.

Laborov First website (2016) http://trebisovnahlas.sk/obcasniky/ [Accessed May 21, 2018]

Scheffel, D. (2005) *Svinia in black and white: Slovak Roma and their neighbours*, Toronto: University of Toronto Press.

Škobla, D. and Filčák, R. (2016) 'Infrastructure in marginalised Roma settlements in Slovakia: Towards a typology of unequal outcomes of the EU funded projects', *Sociology/Sociológia*, 48(6): 551–71.

Sládek, J. (2016) *Príbeh verejného zdravotníctva* [Public healthcare story], Trebišov: EXCEL Publishing.

UNDP (United Nations Development Programme) (2012) *Report on the living condition of Roma in Slovakia*, Bratislava: United Nations Development Programme.

Wacquant, L. (2008) *Urban outcasts: A comparative sociology of advanced marginality*, Cambridge: Polity Press.

FIVE

Tackling waste in Scotland: incineration, business and politics vs community activism

Jennifer Mackay

Introduction

Towards the end of the twentieth century, community composting and recycling of waste was thriving. Communities throughout Scotland were developing local services and social enterprises to reuse or recycle increasing amounts of domestic and industrial waste. These initiatives shared expertise through horizontal networks, which also started to campaign against the production of waste by industry. Minimising waste production, combined with community-controlled recycling, was the way forward.

Around the same time, waste industry businesses developed a new generation of waste disposal facilities: Energy From Waste (incinerators that recover the energy released from burning waste) and a number of policy initiatives were directing efforts away from community work and towards industry. The European Commission was planning to reconfigure the waste hierarchy to include Recovery (of energy) over Recycling within the Waste Framework Directive; the Publicly Available Specification (PAS)100 composting legislation was enforced on community composting initiatives; Renewable Order Scotland included burning waste as part of qualifying for renewable credits; and efforts were made to redefine 'zero waste' to include Energy From Waste at the Scottish Parliament level. This chapter analyses how these events started intensifying community struggles against the demise of community waste initiatives.

In their resistance to the environmental injustices of Energy From Waste, communities have used a range of tools, such as good neighbour agreements, international community links with other communities experiencing the same situations, public inquiries, creating a wave of Energy From Waste science knowledge and the emergence of a social economy within community waste initiatives in their defence against the waste industry's domination of waste. However, the waste industry also mobilised as a movement from above, with its own innovative ideas that led to the hijacking of the term 'zero waste'. This is essentially a typical example of a repeated cycle of waves of community activism at loggerheads with big business and politics that leaves communities burned out and with a lack of trust for the system, which is rigged for communities to fail.

One of the guiding principles of the circular economy approach to industrial ecology is that one person's waste is another's resource. An underlying flaw in this is that a political economy overrides the industrial ecology. In a competitive market, waste becomes a resource only if the price is right and the waste cycle, from design, through production, use and disposal, is determined by a financial calculus. Markets for waste, moreover, are never free markets. Public interest in the safe management of waste means that the state and governance regimes are a major component in the political economy of waste. The governance regime is motivated in theory by criteria such as public health and ecological sustainability, but more significantly, in the context of neoliberal economics, in practice by the influence of stakeholders with strong economic interests. The state, while providing a narrative of acting for the public benefit, is driven at the same time by the imperative of those whose profits are affected by particular policy outcomes. Thus, waste policy is driven by the interests of capital, although under pressure from movements from below, while being shrouded in the narrative of public and environmental benefit.

After a long campaign of mobilisation in Scottish civil society, and the final toppling of an unpopular centralising Conservative government in the UK, a referendum delivered to Scotland a devolved Parliament that was elected in 1999. One of the powers gained by the Scottish Parliament is over waste, and an early action was the announcement of the Scottish National Waste Strategy.

Zero waste

When the National Waste Strategy process was announced in 2000 its stated objective was to divert waste from landfill. Landfill was in crisis. Many sites were reaching capacity and local protests over health concerns were becoming a significant feature at existing and potential sites. At the level of the EU, the Landfill Directive of 1999 was in the process of being implemented in member countries through national or regional mechanisms. In Scotland, the process involved

Scottish Environment Protection Agency (SEPA) working with the Scottish local authorities and setting up area strategy groups. These groups initially were made up of local authorities' waste and cleansing department representatives; waste industry and business interests; and community recyclers. In the first instance, the focus was on municipal household waste. Local authorities were leading on the process of changing the future of how waste was dealt with under the EU Landfill Directive.

The process was rife with complex relationships between all parties, but the main conflict was between the waste industry, driven by business, contracts and profit, and the other stakeholders, who were publicly funded. There was competition from the very start and the economic leverage of the industry meant that it would never have been an even playing field. Cost-effectiveness became the big challenge – and not the environment – for most players, and a so-called 'Best Practicable Environmental Option' gave greater weight to financial considerations than to environmental protection.

Local authorities were pressed for space within existing landfill sites and were running out of time before the Landfill Directive came into effect. As they were running out of time and space, waste business offered catch-all, quick-fix solutions. Quick solutions inevitably involved the installation of incinerators and a tie into 25- to 30-year-long contracts. Waste problem solved! Despite this pressure, surprisingly, the National Waste Strategy actually leaned heavily in the direction of increasing the proportion of recycling, and the government made funding available to help local authorities build more of an infrastructure to do this. This was positive, but there was no real need to build any new infrastructure for recycling, nor to kick-start reuse: it was already being provided by community waste recyclers. Nor was there any reason for the government and SEPA to set up more government-led nationwide waste education initiatives. Despite this, Scottish Waste Aware Group was established to streamline waste education messages and provide education work for local councils, something that community waste groups were providing already.

A network of community and not-for-profit waste recyclers and reuse initiatives, Community Recycling Network for Scotland (CRNS), had been working for years behind the scenes. They survived by receiving environment and waste education grants, and some received donations or small fees for their services to the local communities. The beginning of an infrastructure was already in place in some areas on a local level: experts in segregating waste, transforming waste into compost, reusing furniture, providing education in their local areas and schools

– and lobbying and exposing inconsistencies in Scottish government policy. Campaigning by CRNS revealed that community recyclers and their contribution to the waste solution were being ignored in the whole National Waste Strategy process. This sector needed to be part of the solution, and not driven out of business by local authorities, which sparked off a campaign for funding and acknowledgement for community waste initiatives. The CRNS fight-back gained the sector £600,000 investment in 2003 to further support development and also the 'Increase Fund' to which community initiatives could apply to deliver crucial waste initiatives.

At the same time, waste campaigners were challenging the state to do better. Local authorities were making good progress with pushing more recycling, which was largely the outcome of the Best Practicable Environments Option process. However, rather than prioritising recycling, campaigners were pushing for much more focus higher up the waste hierarchy – on reducing waste, then reuse, with recycling as the last resort, in order to move more towards zero waste.

All of this largely left the commercial waste industry on the side lines in terms of addressing household waste, with its deeply unpopular option of incineration, although it did not entirely go away. While the Scottish Government took an interest in zero waste, it decisively undermined progress with the 2006 Renewable Obligation Scotland Order Act. Ostensibly designed to shift energy and heat sources away from non-renewable fossil fuels, the inclusion of waste as a 'renewable' fuel provided the incentive for the industry to develop incinerators. It gave the green light for so-called new burn technologies such as biomass and combined heat and power to qualify for Renewable Obligation Certificates and associated subsidies. These are technologies that run on renewable sources, biomass and 'residual waste', which is waste that local authorities and the waste industry insist you can do nothing else with and that you are left with after all recycling, reuse and reduce activities have been exhausted. But since they are still burn technologies, we will call them what they are traditionally known as, incineration. Under a zero waste philosophy, designing out would be the solution for residual waste and the most cost-effective, given the innovative materials and products that are constantly being developed.

Here lies the waste industry's assault on the zero waste process. In order to make waste industries' business viable, they needed to create a waste that nobody could deal with but them. Around this time the European Parliament was considering the Waste Framework Directive, which was to provide the legislative framework for the collection, transport, recovery and disposal of waste and to include a common waste hierarchy. Following a hard industry lobby led by pro-waste-industry UK Conservative Member of European Parliament Caroline Jackson, the Waste Framework Directive was agreed, in which the waste hierarchy was redefined to include recovery (of energy) inserted into the hierarchy. This opened the door for burn technologies to be included as a viable option within the waste hierarchy. The Waste Framework Directive of 2008 was the nail in the coffin for anything above recycling on the hierarchy, such as reuse and reduce, let alone designing out. In essence it guaranteed waste businesses all over Europe a supply of waste to burn.

Two years later the Scottish Parliament launched its Zero Waste Plan 2010, in which the definition of zero waste had changed to mean 'no waste to landfill'. This does not include removing waste from the outset – in other words, designing out substances that cannot be reduced, reused or recycled, a process that would do away with residual waste. While recycling continued, just, to keep its head above water in Scotland, in most places these events mark the end of striving for solutions that go beyond recycling and a hijacking of the term 'zero waste'.

Anti-incineration movement

The anti-incineration movement had been present in the UK before Scotland's National Waste Strategy. Scotland's only municipal incinerator at the time, in Dundee, has a chequered history and a legacy of resistance. It was located in the middle of public sector housing, including some of the poorest areas of Scotland. Concerns were raised regularly about health impacts from emissions and the original plant was closed in 1996 after failing to meet EU emissions standards. Despite campaigns by the community, trade unions and NGOs, the incinerator was replaced by a new Energy From Waste incinerator in 1999, a joint venture between a private consortium and Dundee City Council. The community, faced with further health risks, worked with Friends of the Earth Scotland to negotiate a Good Neighbour Agreement to force the company to be more accountable. There were initial concessions on emissions testing and vehicle movements, but the value of the Good Neighbour Agreement dwindled as the community lost its leverage and the incinerator was beset with a series of operational failures, explosions and emissions breaches (Scandrett, 2002).

At the same time, in North East England, the Newcastle Byker incinerator was condemned for dumping toxic ash from the facility on nearby allotments. These events and others fuelled a Greenpeace UK-led 'Incinerator Busters' campaign, which came just at the start of the National Waste Strategy process across the UK (Murray, 1999, 2002). Zero waste was put forward as the solution to the waste problem, not incinerators. The campaign resulted in the inevitable occupation of incinerators by Greenpeace UK in England. With the Greenpeace Incinerator Buster campaign ongoing, a small number of activists in Scotland were able to lobby the National Waste Strategy area groups to choose zero waste and not burn technologies, even under the requirements of Best Practicable Environmental Option. The aim of the activists was to educate local authorities on the dangers and negative effects of burning waste and to enthuse them about zero waste, despite what the waste industry would be telling them. The Best Practicable Environmental Option came out with largely recycling for tackling waste at that time. Although it would be nice to assume that the activists' lobbying had in part some influence on the decisions, it was more likely to do with the money the government offered to Local Authorities for increasing recycling facilities. There was no other activism in Scotland during this time on anti-incineration because Dundee was the only municipal household waste incineration facility in mainland Scotland. There was activism around landfill sites, the Landfill Directive and driving local authorities away from landfill as an option for waste. Community activists had largely won that battle, but another battle was brewing under the surface.

CRNS managed to have a high-profile zero waste conference in Scotland in 2005 with international delegates. This built on the back of its popular 'Towards Zero' newsletter, which aimed to educate on zero waste and give examples of zero waste in practice. The group coordinated a campaign for zero waste led by all the community reuse and recycling groups. Zero waste was at the core of the work of the community waste sector.

Internationally, incinerators and the so-called 'new burn technologies' of energy from waste, such as combined heat and power, gasification, pyrolysis and biomass, were gaining in popularity. Waste businesses were investing in a mass sales pitch, despite more information coming through on the dangers, health impacts, accidents and breaches in legislation in running the facilities (Murray, 1999, 2002). So much so that an international swell of activism erupted, mostly sparked by the Greenpeace UK Incinerator Buster campaign, which went global. A new international network of anti-incinerator campaigners, toxic specialists and waste experts gathered together to share information and help each other. However, this swell did not happen in Scotland.

The community waste sector past 2008 was up against the expectations that community waste groups would get funding only if they were reaching tough waste targets; further legislation on the way they dealt with their waste; and becoming 'social enterprises', which essentially meant forcing them into becoming businesses. Community composting and some of the most innovative reuse projects started to dwindle; waste education and nappy reuse projects suffered as well. Community waste groups started to become driven by targets and reporting, and doing less of the innovative work that made them valuable. Government funding moved away from facilitating the community sector for public and environmental benefit, and was now being used to control it and force groups into a not-for-profit business model or social enterprise.

After the EU threw the doors open for 'recovery' to be included as part of the waste hierarchy in the Waste Framework Directive and the Scottish Government redefined zero waste to include Energy From Waste, with a central aim of 'zero waste to landfill', it was pretty much a race against time for communities. Planning applications for Energy From Waste technologies came flooding in, and in 2008 Scotland was looking at no less than 12 applications for incinerators in a country of only 5.2 million people. For a country that had but one municipal household waste incinerator and a government offering money for large waste solutions, communities needed to organise themselves very quickly.

Like a reaction to shock, communities and individuals quickly started to form into groups around where planning applications were being proposed, with strong campaigns in the Highlands, in Aberdeenshire and several sites across the Central Belt from Irvine to Dunbar. A more considered and joined-up approach was also starting to happen by way of a Scotland-wide network of anti-incinerator campaigners at this time, with Green Alternatives to Incineration in Scotland (GAINS).

GAINS assumed no leadership and was made up of community activists, community development advisors, previous landfill campaigners reignited by the onslaught of incinerators and brand new campaigners. It also disappeared as quickly as it was set up. Why? Until a large amount of planning applications for mass burn technologies were being proposed, the movement had been driven by a very small, unsustainable number of people. This happened just after the 2006 Scottish Planning Act. The Planning Act was supposed to 'front load' the planning system to make it less adversarial, giving communities early opportunities to participate and developers an opportunity to incorporate community aspirations. In fact it served to incorporate communities into the interests of developers, although the latter remained unhappy with the 'burden' of community consultation. The aim of the Act was to make the planning process less complex and more 'accessible' to all. Clarification is needed here: 'accessible to all' actually means accessible to businesses, companies – the planning applicants.

Systems for opposing planning proposals are biased against communities from the outset. In order to have a system working equally for both sides of a planning proposal (for and against), they must be on an equal playing field, have the same rights and equally have the same amount of money to invest in arguing their case. There is evidence of adverse health impacts from incinerators, although it is complex and contested (Health Protection Scotland, 2009), but despite the clear importance of human health, community groups lack the resources to analyse, conduct new research and present the health argument. Similar problems arise for arguments about maintaining recycling rates and the contribution of incineration to climate-changing emissions. Community groups have access to this evidence but are constrained by not having the money to provide new research evidence and produce a flashy publication with a counter argument, or the resources to continuously lobby Parliament, or an office to work in a full-time job on the issue. Nor do they have a number of staff to help share the load and specialise in a particular area, or, more crucially, are they expert in planning law. There are far too many players that communities need to fight against. The Scottish Planning Act is not an exemplar of tackling inequality within the planning system.

Also, from a timing perspective communities are usually not involved in the planning process until the consultation point, which is determined (within certain legal requirements) by the developer, before which lots of decisions have already been made that question the validity of consultation processes. Consultations reveal the information only in the manner that the business wants it to be seen and are subjective, so communities are not exposed to all the information needed to make informed decisions.

During 2012–14 communities in Scotland found it very difficult to campaign against the large number of incinerator proposals. Because in very short time-scales, usually a brief window around the consultation announcement, they had to get themselves very organised. The waste industries, on the other hand, had a head start with their messages to politicians and other stakeholders. With no resources, and starting from little expertise in incineration technology or experience in responding to planning consultations, communities were digesting large amounts of unfamiliar information and hunting around for people and organisations that could help them. The undertaking of preventing such an attack on their local environment is not a small thing, and could be likened to shock treatment, although for a short time communities mobilised a strong opposition and deserve praise for their drive to take on the big companies.

GAINS was an attempt to bring anti-incinerator campaigners together as a coalition. They held a demonstration outside the Scottish Parliament, presented a petition and had a successful discussion hosted in the Parliament by Green Member of Scottish Parliament Robin Harper, where they shared information on technologies and the planning process. Subsequent attempts to bring the groups together to share skills and experiences and to create a bigger collective were unsuccessful. While the threat of incineration was the same for these groups, the feeling was that they were somehow very different. The geography of the groups was certainly different, some based in cities, some in rural areas and some on islands, so the demographics were different. The sizes of the technologies and how they work were different, although this is very deceiving because they all in effect ultimately do the same thing.

Another difference between the groups involved was motivation, whether be environmental, health or a large development issue versus local businesses, or community involvement. Typically, the groups of people who became involved in tacking proposals like these were middle class and possibly from more affluent areas, but some groups were not. Many of the working-class groups were highly experienced in challenging social and environmental injustices in areas that could be classed as 'sacrificial zones', where they are typically looking at any number of environmentally and socially destructive large-scale proposals from big companies and they know how things work. Some groups were already part of local interest groups such as a community council, but it may have been their first time looking at an environmental issue like incineration. These differences can make for complex relationships and can sometimes be taken as competition or some sort of level of distrust. They all start with confidence that what they are doing is right and with faith in the system – and because if they don't do something about it, nobody else will.

None of the national or local NGOs work on anti-incineration in Scotland, and this could be one way of explaining how exasperated communities can feel when they are left with little support to fight the proposals for these facilities. NGOs have been known to be a supportive force on most environmental and social issues in Scotland and beyond, but on tackling incineration this was not the case.

Regardless of this communities, can be good researchers and have reached out internationally for support, and some groups drew a level of success in their battles. One example was the Highlands' Invergordon Incinerator No to Waste group, which held a well-attended public meeting where it had managed to invite Dr Paul Connett, a well-known international campaigner against fluoride and toxic waste disposal from the US. This was something of a coup for the group. The business magnate Mohamed Al-Fayed had successful businesses in the area and he jumped on the campaign train in opposing the incinerator. The combination of these pressures led the Highland Council to reject the application for the incinerator. An appeal by the company meant that the case went to the Court of Session, at which it was again rejected. But a third appeal meant that the company in question, Highland Combined Heat and Power Ltd, was granted permission to proceed with the incinerator, as the previous decisions were overridden by the Scottish Government. The flawed Scottish planning system means that a company like Highland Combined Heat and Power can appeal as any times as it wants – and it usually has the resources to be able to afford to do so – but the community cannot appeal a decision even once, even if they has the necessary resources.

This behaviour is commonplace with large facilities, but no more so than with incinerators in Scotland. So, no matter the efforts of communities towards preventing incinerators, the decision will be challenged and challenged again by developers, with the government ultimately overriding rejections. This is what will determine the decision, and not the community. A lot of the incinerators proposed at this time were subjected to this process of appeal in the planning system, and 2018/19 is the time when construction of many of them will begin, if they are not being commissioned already (Edwards, 2017). On a more positive note, there are some groups in Perth and Aberdeen that have succeeded in preventing the development of incinerators. But without a doubt these groups would do well to link nationally, because groups who successfully prevent incinerators will be looking at a new application for a different site. The plans, technologies and companies stay the same and they don't go away. Had the GAINS network succeeded in bringing these activists all together, knowledge and education on the planning system would have been shared and would have played to the community sector's strength and might have provided some sustained attack against the waste industry, and sustained community resistance.

The Scottish planning system has turned out to be the biggest barrier for communities tackling developments in recent years, and has had a detrimental effect on community group dynamics. It has turned out that it is designed to bring lack of confidence, fracturing relationships, fuelling community burn-out and one of the unwritten outcomes of the planning review, which equates to a feeling of hopelessness and apathy. It does this by companies constantly raising the game: every time a group gets the support from its local authority and the decision is a 'no' to the developers, the company challenges that decision higher up the chain and communities are often failed by the politicians for whom they voted overriding the 'no' to a 'yes'. The continuation of this cycle is designed to drive out opposition.

Conclusion

I have the benefit of concluding from hindsight. My evidence is gathered from within on many sides in the waste sector and seeing the situations evolve. I worked for SEPA on the National Waste Strategy, and also in the community waste sector and as a waste campaign consultant and within community education and development. I also became an anti-incineration activist. Looking at the balance of power on this issue, my conclusion is to celebrate the communities' and activists' resolve and stamina against this system. The lack of an Equal Rights to Appeal in the new Planning Bill has left the community sector nothing to work with and no avenue for an equal footing of 'competition'; and with each wave of incinerator proposals there is a wave of activists asserting their rights in a democratic society, whether or not the system allows it. A worry is that with every wave there are fewer activists than before. The knowledge and education that need to be digested in order to take on the developers and the dirty games are no small undertaking.

The new wave of incinerator applications is currently well under way, still under the guise of 'zero waste', and is now part of Scotland's view of a Circular Economy Strategy, placed with the aim of 'making things last', and aims for no leakage within waste and that 'thermal treatments (including incineration) [be used when] we exhaust all options of retaining the value of those materials' (Scottish Government, 2016: 32). This is in direct contrast to the true meaning of zero waste, where the concept of designing out is the foremost starting point of a waste hierarchy. Waste incineration does not fit within a sustainable closed-loop circular economy model, as it merely replaces one waste stream with another by way of pollution and toxic waste. It also increases the demand for virgin materials, only to waste them at the other end.

With the Scottish Government holding these views, the current planning system working against activist groups and no improvement expected with the current revision of the Scottish Planning Bill, it is business as usual for communities. Lanarkshire community opposition had, for the second time, achieved a rejection of the proposal by the local authority, and the group warned that it will not be letting Scottish Ministers get away with overriding the decision. There are also three controversial applications for incinerators in Glasgow, which have now reached construction stage and which will create a toxic triangle for the local residents, who have been fighting for the last six years. The only thing left for communities is a judicial review, an expensive and time-consuming process that is not an option for most communities. However, a judicial review has previously helped to challenge the proposals for a coal power plant in North Ayrshire, Hunterston in 2012, when the company stopped submitting applications and appeals, after years of not taking 'no' for an answer. The Hunterston opposition is one example of lots of NGOs, local groups and individuals gaining support from Scottish Ministers and government bodies. It was an intensive investment to see off a powerful company, but many smaller organisations or groups don't have the resources to do this.

There is evidence that coalitions and networks that work across environmental and social justice campaigning, such as Scottish Climate Change Coalition and Scottish Environment Link, can achieve a fair amount of respect from the Scottish Government. If a larger alliance of anti-incinerator community activists across Scotland were to join together, as well as acting as their individual groups, it would create a much bigger resistance against developers, and would call out decision makers to account for their actions.

A new Planning Bill is under way and, at the time of writing, it looks as though there will be no improvement for communities. Hope lies in communities' resolve to organise themselves much more and build resistance together in larger numbers against a planning system that is designed for rushing through decisions on big developments. We have seen how forces have conspired against community development approaches to waste reduction, with the commercial waste industry taking advantage of quick-fix environmental solutions, exploiting legislative loopholes, defending the economic benefits for investors and acting against the interests of communities, health and the environment.

References

Edwards, R. (2017) 'Rash of new waste incinerators prompts fears for health and recycling', *The Ferret*, 23 October [online] https://theferret.scot/waste-incinerators-scotland-health-recycling/.

Health Protection Scotland (2009) 'Incineration of waste and reported human health effects' (with Scottish Environmental Protection Agency), Glasgow: Health Protection Scotland, [online] http://www.hps.scot.nhs.uk/resourcedocument.aspx?id=339.

Murray, R. (1999) *Creating wealth from waste*, London: Demos.

Murray, R. (2002) *Zero waste*, London: Greenpeace Environmental Trust.

Scandrett, E. (2002) 'Environmental justice', in L. Adams, M. Amos and J. Munro (eds) *Promoting health: Politics and practice*, London: Sage, pp 58–62.

Scottish Government (2016) *Making things last: A circular economy strategy for Scotland*, [online] http://www.gov.scot/Resource/0049/00494471.pdf.

SIX

An unfractured line: an academic tale of self-reflective social movement learning in the Nova Scotia anti-fracking movement

Jonathan Langdon

Introduction

> 'My friends, we are unfractured. And thereby hangs a tale. It's a tale in which we all are – each one of us is – a starring character and a co-author. We are the maker of this story that has been shaped by our unceasing, unrelenting efforts – all of which mattered and made a difference.' (Sandra Steingraber, New York State anti-fracking organiser, 22 January 2015)

'Frack Off, Gasholes!' screams a T-shirt in block letters. It is worn by an attendee at the third public consultation of the Nova Scotia Independent Review Panel on Hydraulic Fracturing, held in New Glasgow, Nova Scotia, Canada on 21 July 2014. The 11-member Nova Scotia Independent Review Panel on Hydraulic Fracturing was commissioned by the New Democratic (socialist) provincial government in Nova Scotia in August 2013 after it put in place a two-year moratorium on fracking in 2012. The review panel submitted its report in August 2014, and in November a legislated ban was brought in by the Liberal government that succeeded the New Democrats.

Several of us who drove up from Antigonish, where St Francis Xavier University is located, are wearing T-shirts that we have just purchased in the lobby downstairs. Our shirts are less direct, more tongue-in-cheek. Mine says, 'peas-full protest against fracking; protect local food from oil and gas drilling'. It has a drawing on it of peas on the march. With the exception of one vocal audience member, the room is full of anti-frackers – with T-shirts, buttons and signs opposing fracking on display. Still, even though we all oppose the process, people are in the room for different reasons. Some of these differences are clearly visible from the tone and approach of the T-shirts we wear, while others are less visible. For instance, there are several people in the room who would dispute that we are in Nova Scotia, instead insisting we are in Mi'kma'ki, the traditional territory of the Mi'kmaq First Nation – territory that was never ceded over the almost 300 years since the British and Mi'kmaq first signed a treaty. The Mi'kmaq are the main First Nation people in the Canadian Maritimes, with a traditional territory that encompasses all of Nova Scotia, Prince Edward Island, the majority of New Brunswick, the Gaspesie in Quebec and parts of Newfoundland, and in the US, the state of Maine. For me, having gone from being a member of the anti-fracking movement to being part of movement-organising and strategising over the past few years, I am in the process of learning about some of these tensions at first hand.

This public consultation comes at the height of our effort here in Nova Scotia/Mi'kma'ki to maintain an informal moratorium on fracking. At meeting after meeting, hundreds of people show up to voice deeply informed concerns about lifting the moratorium, and most call for formalising it. What strikes me is how diverse the crowds are, in their analysis, approach and where they come from; and yet we have common consensus on where we want to go. The emergence of this tacit consensus is what learning through social action is all about (Foley, 1999). In New York State their collective effort has also resulted recently in a ban on fracking, leaving the state as well as their movement 'unfractured' (Steingraber, 2015). This ability to maintain a common consensus throughout the struggle, despite fault-lines, is a major feat, and one that I believe we also achieved here in our struggle in Nova Scotia/Mi'kma'ki. This unity stands in sharp contrast to a long history of fractures in environmental and progressive organising in Canada, where environmental racism is often overlooked by largely white environmental movements. It is especially rare to see this unity across settler–First Nation lines, as the deep historic impact of divide and rule continues to pit communities against one another.

In the pages that follow, I share a personal narrative of what Foley (1999) has called social movement learning in struggle, and also my view of key reasons for why we remained unfractured. The story that follows explores my own learning and my experience of the anti-fracking movement here, where I was both directly involved in local organising in Antigonish's Responsible Energy Action (REA) and also REA's representative on the Nova Scotia Fracking Research and Advocacy Coalition (NOFRAC) steering committee. REA is a confluence of folks who came together initially to resist fracking in Nova Scotia but wanted to remain focused on positive alternatives, not just criticism. The membership is drawn from folks who live in the Antigonish area, a rural part of Nova Scotia/Mi'kma'ki. Its members include both settler and Mi'kmaq. Meanwhile, NOFRAC is composed of several organisations and individuals contesting fracking in the province. It was established in 2010 by the Ecology Action Center, an environmental justice NGO based in Halifax. Its steering committee is composed of long-time activists, as well as representatives from several local and provincial environmental and anti-fracking groups.

Central to this learning was my experience of the power and complex realities of building strong settler and Mi'kmaq First Nation alliances in the face of such an industry. An equally strong realisation was experiencing the power of pluralism in the movement, despite internal tensions, as it visibly prefigured how those of us living here can make informed collective decisions about our future together – a concrete moment of deliberative democracy in action. The story is told in three parts. Let me begin, though, by discussing learning in struggle.

Learning to struggle, struggling to learn

Since 2005 I have been studying social movement learning (SML), while also being involved in a number of social movements in different capacities. At times I have been a member of a demonstration or particular collective effort/campaign; at other times I have been directly involved in organising and strategising efforts. My scholarship on SML has largely involved documenting and sharing learning emerging from movements I have worked with and been part of; this is the first time I have turned the SML lens on myself.

Foley (1999) uses the term 'learning in struggle' to unpack the complex dynamics at play in SML. He describes non-formal, informal and incidental aspects, and is especially interested in how movement struggles lead to learning. However, he sees this learning as ambiguous, especially if it is not reflected upon – reflecting on learning in struggle allows movements to develop new strategies.

With reference to learning in the environmental movement in Australia, Foley identifies the tension between movement learning and individual member learning. A number of authors point to the usefulness of reflecting on activist and movement narratives (cf Butterwick and Elfert, 2012). hooks (1994), building on Freire's

(1970) notion of the pedagogy of the oppressed, notes the importance of learning through consistently challenging marginalisation and one's own assumptions. She argues for transforming power relations through engaged processes of acknowledging and challenging privilege. This echoes writing about environmental racism that highlights the blindness of much environmental organising to the impact of large-scale development on marginalised communities of colour, especially in the US and Canadian context. Grande (2004) challenges contemporary critical pedagogy for overlooking contrasting epistemologies of critique, such as those from First Nations contexts, and provides an important framework for thinking about how First Nations and settlers can build movements together without co-optation and assimilation of indigenous points of view – something Choudry (2007; 2013) has repeatedly pointed out as a danger. Leondar-Wright (2005) has described the challenges of building movements across similar divides and, like hooks, points to the reflective practice of those in dominant groups as a crucial part in this process.

My perspective on the Nova Scotia anti-fracking movement is arguably a limited one, but it is one through which I nonetheless have direct experience to share, and I can embed this experience in certain conversations, as well as compare it to experiences with other movements such as those I have worked with in Ghana. Colleagues from both Mi'kmaq and settler perspectives of this struggle have been kind enough to read my thoughts here and have deeply informed my framing of them. In a departure from much scholarly writing, where personal experience is dismissed to focus on the authority drawn from academic argumentation, I am purposefully putting myself on the line – the activist line – and drawing a line between my experiences and the wider movement learning. That said, I want to acknowledge that this article has gained tremendously from the feedback of Sue Adams, Janette Fecteau, Barbara Low and Molly Peters. (On reading this article, Barbara explained that she would not use the word activist to describe herself. To be an activist is to have a choice whether to act or not. As a Mi'kmaq defending the land, air and water, there is no choice.) Their suggestions, corrections and explanations have deepened my learning and improved this piece. These conversations have in and of themselves made writing the chapter highly rewarding. That said, any errors or omissions are of course my own.

An unfractured tale in three parts

Elsipogtog First Nation, New Brunswick

Without Elsipogtog, New Brunswick there would be no 'rest of the story.' The New Brunswick Conservative Provincial Government awarded Texas-based SWN Energy Co. a fracking exploration licence in 2010. This licence included large parts of the area around and near Elsipogtog First Nation and the nearby settler community of Rexton. Beginning in May 2013, First Nation and settlers established an anti-fracking camp to prevent SWN from conducting seismic testing by blocking SWN trucks from leaving their yard. On 17 October hundreds of heavily armed Royal Canadian Mounted Police (RCMP) officers descended on the non-violent camp, violently attacking and arresting camp residents (Howe, 2015). The movement remained resolute, and in December 2014 the new Liberal Provincial Government brought in a moratorium on fracking in the province.

But this part of the story is certainly not mine. I was not there, didn't make the trip to Elsipogtog, didn't get attacked by the RCMP in the early dawn, didn't get arrested. There were members of REA who *did* travel from Nova Scotia – although none was there when the attack took place. In response to the attack, large solidarity demonstrations were held throughout Mi'kma'ki, including here in Nova Scotia (something many of us in REA, including myself, participated in), in addition to countless protests across Canada and the US (CBC News, 2013). It was largely Nova Scotia Mi'kmaq groups who took the lead in organising the demonstrations here, with groups like REA offering support. Part of the proliferation of these protests can be attributed to the success of the Idle No More movement in laying the groundwork for a new conversation between First Nations and settlers in Canada and across this continent (Idle No More, 2013). It is crucial to recognise that people had been organising against fracking in Mi'kma'ki/New Brunswick and in Nova Scotia for years before this protest and subsequent attack in Elsipogtog (Smith, 2014). In doing so, they referenced the Peace and Friendship Treaties. In 1725, 1752 and 1761, Mi'kmaq leaders and representatives of the British Crown signed Peace and Friendship treaties that did not either cede the land or surrender the sovereignty of the Mi'kmaq. Canada's Supreme Court has acknowledged the strength of these treaties in several cases. The success of Elsipogtog stemmed from the fact that the front-line defence of the land, air and waters undertaken by members of Elsipogtog Mi'kmaq First Nation and the Mi'kmaq Warrior Society, along with the support of local Acadians (descendants of the first French settlers in Canada's Maritimes) and environmentalists from far and wide – settlers for the most part – survived the violence of the state and scared off a fracking company (Williams, 2013). For many months afterwards, four members of the Warrior Society remained in custody for defending their unceded land title and the Peace and Friendship treaties against SWN's incursions and the state's support (Williams, 2013). The legal battle for some of them ended only in 2015, when the company gave up its lawsuit against these activists.

My goal in highlighting Elsipogtog is to honour the efforts of those who truly stopped fracking in its tracks, here in Mi'kma'ki/Canada's Maritimes. The financial costs to SWN associated with the protest and work-stoppage it caused are claimed by the company to have been US$20 million (Smith, 2014). The costs for those attacked by the police are, by comparison, not so easily quantified, and neither is the well-being of generations to come who would have been sacrificed for corporate profit, had fracking gone ahead. As the four members of the Warrior Society facing charges attest, these costs were differently dispersed, depending on whether you are First Nation or not (cf Black, D'Arcy, Weis and Russell, 2014). This differentiation in who bears the cost for defending our collective future reveals the environmental racism at the heart of settler-colonialism (Walia, 2012). Since then, first Nova Scotia and then New Brunswick have both put in place stops on fracking (Nova Scotia now has a legislated ban, while New Brunswick has put in place a moratorium). Much work went into these stops, and much work still goes on to deal with the waste water produced from the fracking activity that had already occurred in New Brunswick, along with the limited number of test wells drilled in Nova Scotia. But hanging in the background in all of this work is the incredible effort of Elsipogtog. Without the potential of this protest being repeated again and again across Mi'kma'ki it is doubtful that so much could have been done to stop this process in other places.

The image of this protest that comes to my mind is the now iconic image of Amanda Polchies (Michelin, 2013) holding up an eagle feather, on her knees in front of a line of police. There is no doubt in my mind that this image of Polchies is a statement of the power of the Mi'kmaq to stop forms of development destructive to them and their communities. It also revealed the potential strength of the Peace and Friendship treaties between those who have come to settle on this land and the Mi'kmaq, which acknowledge that the Mi'kmaq never ceded this territory. The 2014 Supreme Court of Canada decision regarding First Nations land title has clarified that consent, and not consultation, is the test for proceeding with resource development projects, such as hydraulic fracturing (Hildebrand, 2014). This court decision echoes important free, prior and informed consent clauses in the United Nations Declaration on the Rights of Indigenous Peoples (UN, 2007). Where it is clear that the Mi'kmaq do not consent, fracking cannot move ahead. This teaching has been the backbone of my own feeling of hope – that, despite all the money the oil and gas industry has on its side, as a settler working to keep Nova Scotia unfractured, I am aligned with something stronger.

Lake Ainslie and the beginning of REA

In late 2010 Petroworth Resources applied to drill a conventional oil well near Lake Ainslie, Nova Scotia. Resistance to Petroworth's plans began in September 2010, when local residents near Lake Ainslie raised concerns about the company's planned exploration. Before this exploration could be started, the resistance had gained wider momentum, as nearby Mi'kmaq First Nations groups joined the protest. The movement was successful in putting this issue on local and provincial government agendas. Lake Ainslie resistance, along with the failure of earlier fracking test-wells, and clean-up costs in the Minas basin by another company, Triangle Petroleum, led to the initial province-wide moratorium on fracking in 2012. It also resulted in Inverness County, where Lake Ainslie is located, passing a by-law against fracking in 2013. Local resistance arose quickly from those who worried that this drilling would soon include hydraulic fracturing as well as those concerned with any drilling (Sue Adams, personal communication, 2015). Partially in response to the Lake Ainslie concerns, REA emerged in Antigonish over the next year. I got involved in some of this initial work, mostly through the efforts of some of my students at the time. REA members participated in several anti-fracking rallies between 2011 and 2013. During these early days I went when I could, and saw my role as supportive rather than taking an active organising role. At this time my energy was focused elsewhere, as I was very involved in work with a movement in Ada, Ghana, defending an artisanal salt-mining livelihood in the face of corporate and state efforts at expropriation (Langdon, 2011; Langdon and Larweh, 2015). This focused on documenting and being a part of the learning in struggle of this movement. My relationship with this movement has continued, even as my work with REA has deepened since 2010.

What struck me from the start with REA also resonates with my learning in Ghana. While REA emerged against fracking, it did so by learning about the practice – not by blindly opposing it. Similar to the Ada Songor Advocacy Forum, which collected knowledge about what governs their artisanal salt production practice and aired out long-standing differences of opinion about how best to address these structures, REA began by watching movies like *Gasland* and others about hydraulic fracturing, attending conferences, finding research and asking questions about its claims. It invited speakers who supported and opposed fracking to explain their positions, and it devoted time in its bi-weekly meetings for members to report on research they had done. An important early element of this informal and self-directed learning (Schugurensky, 2006) was about the Peace and Friendship treaties that frame how settler and Mi'kmaq communities should live together on this land. Janette Fecteau, a long-time REA member, recalls:

> [One] self-education session in REA [on 8 February 2012] was with Kerry Prosper from Paq'tnkek Fish and Wildlife Society, Band Councillor at Paq'tnkek First Nation, and REA member, talking about Aboriginal rights especially re the Treaties, land and resources. For me, it was a critical learning that informed my own work with REA all along. For the next several months we displayed copies of the Treaties in the meeting room as a way to frame all our discussions in the context of being on Mi'kmaq territory. (Not all settler members of REA were keen on emphasizing this, but most were.) (Personal communication, 2015)

REA also invited speakers who shared knowledge about fracking, such as how we could address our energy needs through job-generating efficiency processes, as well as investment in renewables. Looking back, it is clear that this long process of informing ourselves – learning before and during struggle – provided a perfect platform from which to engage with the fracking review. This type of internal, informal social movement learning is a very different story of activism than that which took place next door in New Brunswick, even as New Brunswick included extensive public education and movement-based learning (Sue Adams, personal communication, 2015).

Wheel in Wheeler

This part of the tale felt at first like a circus sideshow, but it became a sideshow that the anti-fracking movement here in Nova Scotia dominated and transformed into the main event. The review panel, chaired by Dr David Wheeler, began its work in 2013 with setting the terms of reference, establishing the panel of experts and then calling for public submissions, after which there were a series of public consultations where emerging conclusions from the review panel were shared. Finally, at the end of the summer of 2014, the panel submitted its report to the provincial Liberal government. In the lead-up to these public consultations, Sue Adams, REA's long-standing voice on NOFRAC, the Nova Scotia coalition of anti-fracking organisations, asked if someone else in REA would volunteer to be part of the steering committee of the coalition. I said I could do it.

It is clear that the Wheeler review panel was not prepared for the level of deeply informed public submissions that it received. More than a dozen of us from the Antigonish area had made submissions that dealt with concerns about the impacts of fracking on our health, on water tables and road networks, the level of methane (a far more dangerous greenhouse gas than carbon dioxide) produced or leaking from wells and the question of what to do with the waste water, replete with numerous harmful chemicals as well as potentially containing radiation, produced from fracking. My own submission focused on learning from Elsipogtog, and how passionate people are about defending their water, land and environment and the implications of going against this passion. Antigonish was only one of a number of places around the province with similar levels of submissions.

The Wheeler review panel highlighted 238 of the submissions it received from informed citizens, even as far more than this amount were actually submitted, as well as lengthy commentaries on the discussion papers published prior to the public consultations (Guy, 2014). Ian Mauro (2014), one of the panellists, noted that the submissions were incredibly well researched, and three-quarters called for a continuation of Nova Scotia's informal moratorium. And so, what Wheeler himself referred to as his 'roadshow' began, not so much as a desire for input, but rather as a strategy for disseminating the emerging conclusions of the panel. This did not go down well with the hundreds of Nova Scotians who came to hear these consultations.

I went to two such consultations – the one in New Glasgow, and one near the tail end of the process, in Whycocomagh – a community in Cape Breton with many nearby Mi'kmaq residents. The meeting in Whycocomagh was quite a tense one, as many of the speakers who came forward were highly critical of the panel, its members and its work so far. In fact, this tension and level of critique was entirely different from that displayed at the New Glasgow meeting – further reinforcing my sense of the plurality of this movement. At the same time, it was clear from my perspective that the countless questions and interventions made by well-informed audience members *had* had, over the course of the previous stops, a significant impact. We collectively forced what started as a slick, neutral 'pros and cons' presentation on the prospect of fracking to a much more definitive presentation that emphasised that Nova Scotians did not want fracking. For instance, as a result of the intervention of Barbara Low, a fellow member of REA who is a Mi'kmaq national, pointing out at Wheeler's first meeting that he ignored being on Mi'kmaq territory, as well as other interventions along similar lines, Wheeler became more conscious of honouring treaty relations, including acknowledging Mi'kmaq land title at the start of later meetings. The presentation in Whycocomagh also changed to reflect earlier critiques of the presentation itself. For example, in New Glasgow I had questioned the reliance by Wheeler on only one poll, by Corporate Research Associates, that showed that only 53% of the Nova Scotian population was against fracking, instead of also including the more recent and larger-size Abacus Data poll that put this figure at 69% (cf Colley, 2013). The Whycocomagh presentation included the more recent poll, albeit with a caveat that it had been 'commissioned'. However, as much as these changes may reflect learning on Wheeler's part, I would say that the changes, and the emphatic conclusion in the report that Nova Scotians did not want hydraulic fracturing in this province, came about as a result of the hundreds of people who came out to the public consultations, as well as the submissions to the panel. As Mauro (2014: 244–5) noted in his chapter in the report:

> [I]t is increasingly clear that citizens are highly capable of estimating hazard potential and the assumption that experts have superior risk judgment is now questioned (Wright et al, 2002). Dismissal of the public, assuming they are 'uneducated' and need to 'get the facts' regarding hydraulic fracturing, has been documented as a form of stakeholder silencing used by industry advocates to generate a pro-development discourse. (Hudgins and Poole, 2014)

This, to me, is an incredibly clear outcome of this movement. The power of a wide variety of people, writing to their particular concerns, deeply informed on the issue and with a common sense of what they want from their government, can have a profound impact on the kind of development that will happen. Literature on environmental racism suggests that it also matters who it is that makes this argument, as racialised communities often face huge obstacles, despite this type of preparation (cf Black et al, 2014). As alluded to earlier, one of the intentional early goals of REA was to educate ourselves and our communities through presentations, research, film viewings and discussions. It is clear that a similar mindset was informing folks in Mi'kmaq and settler groups across the province. Additionally, in submissions, in media stories, in public comments, what happened in Elsipogtog surfaced as something to be avoided here (Ross, 2014). For instance, Molly Peters, a member of the Mi'kmaq Paq'tnkek First Nation (near Antigonish) and supporter of the anti-fracking efforts said, "There's definitely going to be protests. I can guarantee. [...] Mi'kmaq consider water sacred, so that's why it's so important. It's the lifeblood of Mother Earth. It's the only thing that can sustain us" (Ross, 2014). The point drawn from the Elsipogtog example is the need for strong links between First Nation groups and settler activist communities on this issue so as to forestall the kind of state sponsored-violence of Elsipogtog by resisting this activity together before it comes – even while respect between the two groups has to be maintained regarding the different paths this activism takes. Yet, the leadership of First Nations actors in this context must be recognised if the type of liberal settler-colonialism that Coulthard (2007) and Walia (2012) document is to be avoided.

Learning through anti-fracking organising, concluding thoughts

Foley (1999) describes how individuals involved in social movements learn informally through social action, a process that he calls 'learning in struggle'. There is much that could be said through a participatory research lens, or many other qualitative research lenses, about learning in struggle in the anti-fracking movement in the Nova Scotia portion of Mi'kma'ki. This type of systematic and large-scale research has yet to be done in this context. What I share here is based on my own informal learning, my own learning in struggle. Even while I think the anti-fracking movement here in Nova Scotia has learned much from Elsipogtog, with so many folks from Nova Scotia visiting the protest camp and even getting arrested, Nova Scotia nonetheless has had its different path of learning in struggle. Besides the obvious difference of not having had state-sponsored oppression clamp down on our activities, there are less obvious differences that can be pointed to. For instance, the Anti-Fracking Alliance in New Brunswick is involved in litigation against the province, as are members of the Elsipogtog First Nation and the Mi'kmaq Warrior Society (MacIntosh, 2014). This is not something that we have had to strategise around here in Nova Scotia. In a very real way, then, our efforts here in Nova Scotia have been able to benefit from the sacrifices of Elsipogtog without paying nearly the same price. For this we should be exceedingly grateful – this gratitude being perhaps the greatest learning in struggle of our movement here.

Environmental justice literature suggests that we should consider who is asked to pay the price for environmental decisions (Hill, 2003). In New Brunswick and Nova Scotia this is First Nations and rural settler communities. In Nova Scotia, for example, much of the rural population relies on groundwater for its water supply (Mauro, 2014), a supply that is threatened by waste water. Indeed, Canada's history of resource extraction has long placed the burden of development on First Nations communities (Dhillon and Young, 2010; Black et al, 2014). It is a clear lesson from Nova Scotia and Elsipogtog that when settler and First Nation communities work together a strong alliance emerges for protecting what Molly Peters calls the 'sacred' water and the earth, as well as what Elder Albert Marshall describes as the 'the next seven generations' ability to sustain themselves' (Mi'kmaq Rights Initiative, 2014). And yet it is crucial to recognise and respect the differences between these communities, and not to try to subsume everyone under the tent of environmental defence. Instead, as Walia (2012) notes, settler activists need to find different paths to respect First Nation leadership and analysis in such struggles, without reducing this analysis to a singularity. This is what is invoked through the traditional symbol of the wampum belt, with its parallel lines of mutual respect and existence between the first people of this land and those who settled on it (cf Gehl, 2014). This is part of the learning I took away from the public consultation process. Many people came who were supportive of a legislated moratorium and against fracking, and yet their reasons for coming were very different. To assume that those defending local food had the same reason for being there as those who had a well on their property and as the urban activist who is committed to fighting climate change is highly problematic. Similarly, to assume that the various Mi'kmaq who attended the meetings came for the same reasons is actually missing the point of how unique this movement was. As Barbara Low described it in New Glasgow, the Mi'kmaq often disagree, which makes their agreement on this issue all the more powerful. The fact that many of the different Mi'kmaq governance bodies agreed on banning fracking was also telling of the strength of resistance that would likely emerge if this was pushed through. And yet the respective realities and processes of Mi'kmaq and settler communities necessitate different approaches that must be respected in order to avoid co-optation of indigenous organising (Choudry, 2007).

It is amazing to me that the potential fault-lines in both settler and Mi'kmaq organising, as well as between them, did not fracture the movement. Considering the colonial history of pitting communities against each other (Paul, 2006; Killen, 2016), this moment represents an important break from the past. A number of court rulings have found the Canadian state-led process of consultation with First Nations on resource-issues decision making to be deeply flawed. A 2014 Supreme Court ruling made it clear that Canada was not doing meaningful-enough consultation, and needed to move closer to consent. However, Mi'kmaq legal scholar Naomi Metallic (2016) argues that so long as consent is achieved with First Nations governance structures established through colonial imposition, this is simply the Canadian government talking to itself. There is also a long history of misuse of the language of consultation by various Canadian government and corporate entities. Hence, First Nation communities have become very careful about discussions that they get involved in officially, as these can be and often are used against them.

Elsipogtog showed us in Nova Scotia the dangers of what would happen if fracking began in earnest here, and the need to work across fault-lines in order to successfully stand up to the industry. The public consultation process showed many of us who took part the different and yet similar roles that we could play as First Nations and settlers in applying pressure for change. Voicing our various informed concerns from a number of contexts provoked enormous mutual learning. For my part, I now have a much better, nuanced understanding of why so many Mi'kmaq speakers were careful in what they said, lest this public consultation process be misused by various levels of settler government to imply that they had officially consulted with the Mi'kmaq on fracking. I understood this intellectually before, but witnessing it at first hand revealed so much of the everyday continuation of settler–colonial relations in this land.

This being acknowledged, the other major learning that struck me throughout this process was the plurality of activisms. Much as the settler-focused NOFRAC coordinated some activity here in Nova Scotia, it is also clear from the hundreds of submissions to the Wheeler review that people had informed themselves independently, and self-organised to effect this process. This is an important source of learning, as it undermines the idea that strong movements need to be under one tent, and rather suggests that there is real value in having diffuse sites of organising within movements, even when analysed through the lens of impact, and not just creating prefigurative dialogue and learning. Environmental justice writing often speaks of how environmental movements dominated by those of European descent silence the voices of indigenous communities and communities of colour (cf Hill, 2003). Leondar-Wright (2005) has described the pressure felt by working-class activists in cross-class alliances to table their issues in the interest of bigger strategic interests determined by middle-class activists. This kind of unity through silencing is not the diffuse yet aligned form of unfractured movement organising that the anti-fracking movement in Nova Scotia/Mi'kma'ki achieved.

In my experience with REA there is a different yet similar approach to ensuring that the movement remains open to self-organising, and rooted in a diversity of views. REA has been, and continues to be, a horizontal organisation where decisions are made collectively and our mutual learning is a key goal. Anyone can get more or less involved in REA. At the same time, a core group of REA members do a lot of the work, and feel a strong sense of investment in what the group stands for. REA's name and reputation has grown in the Antigonish area, so much so that it is now part of a discussion on how to transition the town off fossil fuels and onto renewable sources of energy. Many of us are also interested in municipal-level bans on fracking, and successfully pushed for the Antigonish Town and County municipal governments to pass an Environmental Rights declaration. This provides an important localised backstop to the legislated ban on fracking. In March 2018 this declaration was successfully used by REA and other allies to pressure the Antigonish Town and County to declare their public support for maintaining the fracking ban in the face of attempts by the oil and gas industry to get it overturned (CBC, 2018). The declaration is part of our own learning of focusing not just on the negative (what we don't want) but also on the positive (what we do want) in our community. It is through prefigurative actions like this that we live out the name of our group, taking responsibility for our energy future.

The pluralism of the movement is also prefigurative. Various different dimensions came together across various potential fault-lines in Mi'kma'ki in general, and in Nova Scotia in particular, to successfully overwhelm a well-resourced industry. This coming together happened in the spirit of a plurality of ideas and yet collaboration, to make a future that we can all live in. The effort here in Nova Scotia has shown that it is possible to work in peace and friendship and through this remain unfractured for today – and if we continue to remain open and learn from these lessons, we can perhaps hope to be unfractured for generations to come.

References

Black, T., D'Arcy, S., Weis, T. and Russell, J.K. (eds) (2014) *A line in the tar sands: Struggles for environmental justice*, Toronto, ON: PM Press.

Butterwick, S. and Elfert, M. (2012) 'The social movement learning of women social activists of Atlantic Canada: "What shall we do and how shall we live?"' Proceedings from the Canadian Association for the Study of Adult Education (CASAE) conference, Kitchener, Ontario, 28 May, pp 53–9, http://www.casae-aceea.ca/sites/casae/files/2012_CASAE_Proceedings.pdf.

CBC News (2013) 'Fracking protests thin across Nova Scotia', http://www.cbc.ca/news/canada/nova-scotia/fracking-protests-thin-across-nova-scotia-1.2125101.

CBC News (2018) 'Town of Antigonish rejects request to lift fracking ban', http://www.cbc.ca/news/canada/nova-scotia/town-of-antigonish-rejects-frack-ban-lift-request-1.4583414.

Choudry, A. (2007) 'Transnational activist coalition politics and the de/colonization of pedagogies of mobilization: Learning from the anti-neoliberal indigenous movement articulation', *International Education*, 37(1): 97–112.

Choudry, A. (2013) 'Saving biodiversity, for whom and for what? Conservation NGOs, complicity, colonialism and conquest in an era of capitalist globalization', in A. Choudry and D. Kapoor (eds) *NGOization: Complicity, contradictions and prospects*, London: Zed Books, pp 24–44.

Colley, S.B. (2013) 'Poll: N.S. wants fracking ban kept', *Chronicle Herald*, http://thechronicleherald.ca/novascotia/1162435-poll-ns-wants-fracking-ban-kept.

Coulthard, G.S. (2007) 'Subjects of empire: Indigenous peoples and the "politics of recognition" in Canada', *Contemporary Political Theory*, 6(4): 437–60.

Dhillon, C. and Young, M.G. (2010) 'Environmental racism and First Nations: A call for socially just policy development', *Canadian Journal of Humanities and Social Sciences*, 1(1): 15–30.

Foley, G. (1999) *Learning in social action*, London: Zed Books.

Freire, P. (1970) *Pedagogy of the oppressed*, New York, NY: Herder and Herder.

Gehl, L. (2014) *The truth that Wampum tells: Me Debwewin on the Algonquin land claims process*, Halifax, NS: Fernwood Publishing.

Grande, S. (2004) *Red pedagogy*, Lanham, MD: Rowman & Littlefield.

Guy, J. (2014) 'Most Nova Scotians don't appear to want fracking here', 30 July, http://www.capebretonpost.com/Opinion/Columnists/2014–07–30/article-3818612/Most-Nova-Scotians-don%26rsquo%3Bt-appear-to-want-fracking-here/1.

Hildebrand, A. (2014) 'Supreme Court's Tsilhqot'in First Nation ruling a game-changer for all: A case of "national importance" empowers First Nations, but may complicate big resource projects,, CBC, http://www.cbc.ca/news/aboriginal/supreme-court-s-tsilhqot-in-first-nation-ruling-a-game-changer-for-all-1.2689140.

Hill, R.J. (2003) 'Environmental justice: Environmental adult education at the confluence of oppressions', *New Directions for Adult and Continuing Education*, 2003: 27–38, doi: 10.1002/ace.107.

hooks, b. (1994) *Teaching to transgress*, London: Routledge

Howe, M. (2015) *Debriefing Elsipoqtoq: Anatomy of a struggle*, Black Point, NS: Fernwood.

Hudgins, A. and Poole, A. (2014) 'Framing fracking: Private property, common resources, and regimes of governance', *Journal of Political Ecology*, 21: 303–19.

Idle No More (2013) 'Idle No More urges support for Elsipogtog, Grassy Narrows and other actions', 1 November, http://www.idlenomore.ca/idle_no_more_urges_support_for_eslipogtog_grassy_narrows_and_other_actions.

Killen, S. (2016) 'Memories of an ex-Indian agent', in M. Battiste (ed) *Living treaties: Narrating Mi'kmaw treaty relations*, Sydney, NS: Cape Breton University Press, pp 83–94.

Langdon, J. (2011) 'Democracy re-examined: Ghanaian social movement learning and the re-articulation of learning in struggle', *Studies in the Education of Adults*, 43(2): 147–63.

Langdon, J. and Larweh, K. (2015) 'Moving with the movement: Collaboratively building a participatory action research (PAR) study of social movement learning in Ada, Ghana', *Action Research*, 13(3): 281–97, doi: 10.1177/1476750315572447.

Leondar-Wright, B. (2005) *Class matters: Cross-class alliance building for middle class activists*, Gabriola, BC: New Society Publishers.

MacIntosh, C. (2014) 'Chapter 10: Aboriginal, treaty, and statutory rights of the Mi'kmaq, in *Final Report of The Nova Scotia Independent Panel On Hydraulic Fracturing*, pp 281–304, http://energy.novascotia.ca/sites/default/files/Report%20of%20the%20Nova%20Scotia%20Independent%20Panel%20on%20Hydraulic%20Fracturing.pdf.

Mauro, I. (2014) Discussion paper: 'The environmental impacts of hydraulic fracturing in Nova Scotia: A public participatory risk assessment. Nova Scotia Hydraulic Fracturing review', http://www.cbu.ca/sites/cbu.ca/files/docs/hfstudy/Discussion%20Paper%20-%20Environment%20Impacts.pdf.

Metallic, N. (2017) Public talk on the implementation of UNDRIP. Delivered at St. Mary's University, Nova Scotia, 22 March.

Michelin, O. (2013) 'Amanda Polchies, woman in iconic photo says image represents wisps of hope', http://aptn.ca/news/2013/10/24/amanda-polchies-woman-iconic-photo-says-image-represents-wisp-hope/.

Mi'kmaq Rights Initiative (2014) 'Chiefs continue fight against fracking in NS', http://mikmaqrights.com/chiefs-continue-fight-against-fracking-in-ns/

Paul, D. (2006) *We were not the savages* (3rd edn), Halifax, NS: Fernwood Publishing.

Ross, S. (2014) 'Mi'Kmaq unanimously in opposition to fracking', *Chronicle Herald*, 12 August, http://thechronicleherald.ca/novascotia/1228780-mi-kmaq-unanimous-in-opposition-to-fracking.

Schugurensky, D. (2006) '"This is our school of citizenship": Informal learning in local democracy', in Z. Bekerman, N.C. Burbules and D.S. Keller (eds) *Learning in places: The informal education reader*, New York, NY: Peter Lang, pp 163–82.

Smith, H. (2014) 'Elsipogtog epic: How a tribe's fight against an energy company caught fire', http://grist.org/climate-energy/elsipogtog-epic-how-a-tribes-fight-against-an-energy-company-caught-fire/.

Steingraber, S. (2015) 'How we banned fracking in New York', Ecowatch, http://ecowatch.com/2015/01/22/banned-fracking-new-york/.

United Nations (UN) (2007) *Declaration of the Rights of Indigenous People* (New York: United Nations), http://www.un.org/esa/socdev/unpfii/documents/DRIPS_en.pdf.

Walia, H. (2012) 'Moving beyond a politics of solidarity toward a practice of decolonization', in A. Choudry, J. Hanley and E. Shragge (eds) *Organize! Building from the local for global justice*, Oakland, CA: PM Press, pp 240–53.

Williams, A. (2013) 'Elsipogtog anti-fracking struggle: where to go from here?' http://earthfirstjournal.org/newswire/2013/12/07/elsipogtog-anti-fracking-struggle-where-to-go-from-here/.

Wright, G., Bolger, F. and Rowe, G. (2002) 'An empirical test of the relative validity of expert and lay judgments of risk', *Risk Analysis*, 22: 1107–22.

SEVEN

'Mines come to bring poverty': extractive industry in the life of the people in KwaZulu-Natal, South Africa

Mark Butler

Introduction

Communities who happen to live where there's potential for big money to be made from mining the resources from under their feet face a daunting set of challenges. In the processes of working through those challenges, outsiders tend to instrumentalise local people in pursuit of agendas that are pretty much scripted and shaped prior to 'engaging'. This can be *as* true for outside actors in favour of extractive capital as it is for civil society 'white knights' opposed to it. Within local communities there is usually a range of questions, interests, prospects and views too. Many people are saying 'No' to mining capital, and many communities are divided on the issue. In this chapter we consider the thinking and praxis of militants from a number of areas in the province of KwaZulu-Natal (South Africa) who are thinking resistance to a wave of real and prospective new mining initiatives.

The chapter is based on the ongoing work of the Church Land Programme (CLP), a small, independent non-profit organisation based in KwaZulu-Natal province. CLP works to encourage, and learn from, the thinking and action of poor people who organise to resist injustice and to affirm humanity. (It initially focused on church-owned land while also challenging churches to engage in the national land question and transformation.) CLP relentlessly tries to break all-too-dominant patterns of civil society behaviour in favour of a disciplined praxis premised on the utterly simple idea that people think. We hope that we can continue our work on these issues and learn something about a new and democratic imagination of life and production, of culture and consumption, in the emancipatory spaces opened in popular militancy, thought and action.

Past

Extractive industry in the KwaZulu-Natal region of South Africa does not begin with the arrival of white people. At least since the Early Iron Age, during the first millennium CE, people have dug coal from the earth in KwaZulu-Natal to fire and fashion iron ore (Whitelaw, 1991; Maggs, 1992).

The patterns of pre-colonial society, including ferrous production, use and exchange, underwent dramatic shifts induced by western (especially British) colonial expansion, the arrival of which signalled a profound transformation through military conquest, racist political subjugation and capitalist economic predation, inaugurating the sequence to follow of colonialism, settler-colonialism and apartheid. KwaZulu-Natal's pre-colonial metal industry, specifically, was almost totally killed off by

> the flood of cheap though inferior industrial steel from Europe. Once Britain had established the colony of Natal, in 1842, the volume of imports began to rise…. First to feel the impacts would have been the smelting side of the industry. The labour intensive, traditional methods could not begin to compete with the mass production of the Industrial Revolution. (Maggs, 1992: 85)

Perhaps the key energy source of that industrial revolution was coal, and significant stores lay underground in KwaZulu-Natal.

The arrival of white, Dutch-originated Voortrekkers in the region in the 1830s inaugurated the small-scale use of local coal for the domestic needs of those early white farmers. But the establishment of the Dundee (Natal) Coal Company in 1889 signalled the shift to commercial, large-scale exploitation, and cemented Dundee's place at the centre of a geographic region with significant potential for commercial coal mining.

This scaled-up industry required the conscription of muscle power, but, from the beginning, the Natal coal industry found it hard to corral indigenous blacks in sufficient numbers because working conditions were so bad. As a result, 'indentured Indians' were vital to the colony's coal industry in the early years (Guest, 1998), and by 1902 they constituted 44.5% of the workforce. Bringing with them experience and skills gained in British coalfields, there were also a small but significant proportion of white workers during this early period. A deeply racialised hierarchy was sustained – and also entrenched in law (Stewart and Kumar Nite, 2017). Natal's coal industry evolved within its broader national economic context, and the provincial collieries had been fundamentally integrated with South Africa's larger coal scene by the early 1980s (Guest, 1998). Investments through this period were justified by increased domestic demand for coal during the 1950s and 1960s, and in the export trade in the 1970s. For the KwaZulu-Natal (KZN) coal fields in particular, the most important driver in that shift was selling to coal-fired electricity power stations established in the province.

Largely because of mining capital's colonial roots, it had not been integrated with emergent Afrikaner capital, but by the 1970s this historic bifurcation had been sufficiently overcome such that the conditions were ripe for the adoption of an over-arching sectoral strategy (Fine, 2008). The apartheid state tailored the overarching trade- and development-policy framework to encourage industrialisation on the basis of cheap energy inputs (Eberhard, 2011). The global oil crisis of 1973 also strengthened international demand for coal.

This post-Second World War period of rapid industrial expansion pivoted on the minerals–energy complex (Hallowes, 2011). It was Fine and Rustomjee's seminal 1996 political-economic analysis that identified this 'Minerals and Energy Complex' (MEC) as structurally central. In his later (2008) paper, Fine comments that the formulation of the MEC hypothesis became critical because

> it was inescapable that there was an integral partnership between state and private capital, and an equally integral connection between a core set of activities centered around mining and energy, straddling the public/private divide [and that it was important to understand how the economic and political interests] gave rise to a particular *system* of capital accumulation realised through the state and the market (as opposed to one versus the other). (Fine, 2008:1)

Subsequently, the country's coal sector grew strongly from the 1970s in response to expanded demand from public utility companies as well as export-led growth. Since then it has remained the foundation of the country's energy economy – and hence, also, its political economy (Burton, 2016). Crucially, production under the control of the corporations was vertically integrated, especially through the massive investments from the apartheid state into state enterprises supplying key industrial inputs like steel, power and fossil-derived chemicals (Hallowes, 2011). Not only did this underlying MEC structure concentrate economic power, it also

> led to one of the world's most energy- and carbon-intensive economies in the world ... Its carbon intensity and high emissions result from two fundamental and related reasons – its reliance on coal as its primary energy source and its policy of supplying cheap electricity to industry. (Hallowes, 2011: 8)

All instances of extractive industry must inevitably come to an end. That ending may well be directly consequent on exhausting the available resource at a particular site of extraction. But it's often a more complex mix of relative raw-material resource availability itself with other market and/or technological (and sometimes socio-political) considerations that determines whether extraction is considered to be viable or not.

National economic recession and reduced demand for steel in South Africa, coupled with worsening foreign market conditions, were bad news for the local coal industry in the mid-1980s. The KZN coal industry was severely battered when a number of smaller power stations that it supplied were closed down – and at the same time, exports were threatened by international sanctions against the apartheid regime (Binns and Nel, 2003). The number of coal mines in production fell from 44 to 21 by 1983, with massive job losses and devastating impacts on dependent local communities. This precipitous decline of the coal mining sector in KZN followed on the confluence of a number of factors that came together by the mid-1980s.

In the approximately 30-year period following the onset of the crisis, the KZN region lost nearly all of the approximately 30,000 jobs that the sector had provided (Nel et al, 2003). It's hardly an exaggeration when Binns describes the KZN coal mining sector of the late 1990s as having been reduced to a shadow of its former self, having shed more than 80% of coal mining jobs in the preceding two decades (Binns and Nel, 2003). And in terms of future prospects, holding just 4% of the remaining national coal reserve, the extant coal fields of KZN remain what Inggs describes as the 'poor relation' of the national coal industry (Inggs, 2007).

As the industry shrank and collapsed, its profound imprint in the region revealed itself. As Nel et al (2003) put it:

Whether as a result of the 'mineral cycle' based on the concept of inevitable resource depletion at some point in a mine's life-history or broader structural changes impacting on a mine's profitability, the end product is the same, namely the social and economic erosion of what are often mono-economies and the frequent absence of significant employment and development alternatives for those deprived of their former livelihood. (Nel et al, 2003: 369)

Present

Despite its relative collapse, the provincial coal scene remains important in the overall carbons and extractives picture. For one thing, the legacy issues of declining coal mining activity impact deeply on the people and their environments. For another, the decline of 'big coal' has not meant that there is no ongoing coal activity, even if there are notable changes in type and scale. And finally, there remain new 'opportunities' (some more apparent than real, it appears) for coal mining that are either actively being exploited or being scanned and scoped for potential exploitation.

A brief review of instances of the thinking and actions of people most directly affected by these developments points to key manifestations. During 2016, for instance, the Newcastle-based Kwazumkhono Environmental Justice Network staged protests against the Australian-owned Chelmsford coal mine, described by environmental justice NGO groundWork as 'a nightmare to the Normandien farm dwellers' (Mokgalaka, 2016). And early in 2017 hundreds of residents of the northern-KZN town of Utrecht were driven to take action against Uitkomst coal mine. They expressed deep frustration that the mine has failed to meet local people's expectations that it should contribute meaningfully to the development of the area since beginning operations in 2009 (Nkosi, 2017). Popular anger and resistance have become particularly pointed at Somkhele (KwaMbonambi), in the Fuleni district, where a large open-cast coal mine has been operated by Johannesburg-based Petmin since 2008. Residents of Somkhele village have become enraged at the devastation the mine has wrought on their lives, their houses, the land, the air and their water.

An 'opportunity' for further coal mining threatens adjacent regions of Fuleni, about 20km south-west of Somkhele – but with a couple of added twists. As the dust from existing mining at nearby Somkhele drifts across villages such as Mtubatuba, Nthuthunga and Ocilwane, people are all too aware of the downsides of extractive mining. And the proposed Ibutho coal mine here would be big and open-cast, with inevitably significant impacts. Not only will it impact directly on populated villages, but it would extend to within 40 metres of the boundary of the region's oldest-established protected wilderness area, the Hluhluwe-iMfolozi Game Reserve. A failure to consult with the people has added to their collective trauma, as do ongoing fears of what would happen next if the mining process were to proceed. Many of the people and villages in this area were victims of the notorious apartheid-era forced removals in the 1960s, so present threats are piled onto historic trauma.

With respect to the broader region of northern KZN, Schneider (2016) notes a number of other companies 'quietly nosing around' and pursuing mining proposals. Just across the provincial boundary is the site of an especially egregious instance within the Mabola Protected Environment and near the village of Wakkerstroom in Mpumalanga province. Here, Indian mining company Atha-Africa wants to mine for coal.

At the village of Makhaseneni, an Indian multinational mining company called Jindal has been prospecting for iron, apparently in cahoots with the local chief as well as people higher up the ladder of Zulu feudal power in the province. The local community were not consulted and the people and their *induna* (headman) have waged a careful but important battle with them, attempting to hold open a more democratic space within which people can think and contest these kinds of developments. The stakes are high, though, and local activists who question the mining and the deal making behind it are under threat of slander, violence and even assassination.

Across the region, then, the people face pressures relating to this widespread speculation about tapped and untapped coal and mineral reserves. One result is that a number of amakhosi [chiefs] are asserting a resurgent and aggressive authoritarian version of 'traditional authority' that claims proprietary rights to land and is also deeply intolerant of any forms of autonomous or popular organisation or power. Globally, this would fit a much wider pattern of resource extraction where big mining capital buys off local chiefs and their dependent local elite (for a relative pittance, compared to mining profits) in order to secure mineral rights and repress popular resistance. The political consequences for the people are clearly disastrous, as are their prospects for land access and use-rights. The environmental consequences of a resource-extraction boom in this region will certainly be disastrous as well. Furthermore, the continued and accelerated exploitation of coal for energy also reproduces the underlying political economy of South Africa's 'mineral energy complex'.

Notes from a meeting

The following section reproduces extracts from notes from a meeting of people active in at least seven mining-affected communities in northern KZN. The CLP was privileged to be present at the meeting but did not initiate it, and nor did it have anything to do with the agenda or content of the discussion. At the time of the meeting, grassroots resistance was under threat and a number of people present were effectively in hiding. Accordingly our notes did not (and do not) name the specific people, places and companies involved. In these notes a new paragraph constitutes a new speaker, but individual speakers or their villages have not been differentiated and the discussion has been presented as a collective argument.

Some terms used

Nkosi (pl. *amakhosi*): chief – hereditary or appointed leader of a 'traditional' or 'tribal' group of people or geographic area.

ubukhosi: the institution of, and governance by, chieftainship.

Induna (pl. *izinduna*): an overseer who is subordinate to an *inkosi*; part of the structure of *ubukhosi* – since colonial times, often rendered in English as a 'headman' (and indeed, almost invariably male).

abaNtwana: princes – usually male siblings of an *inkosi* (less usual. but can refer to princesses too).

abantwana: children (sing. *umntwana*: child).

ngaphansi kobukhosi: 'Tribal Authority area': chiefly power in a particular place – traditionally, the sphere within which the people gave their allegiance to a particular chief; from the colonial period onward, a defined geographic area ruled by a chief whose authority was given by colonial (then apartheid and now post-apartheid) government.

'A coal mining company works in our village. People were relocated and were promised to be compensated for their losses in properties, trees, arable fields, houses, schools and livelihoods – none of these were delivered fully. The company ganged up with the Tribal Authority/*ubukhosi* to change these agreements. They dug up our family graves without our consent. We were traumatised and never counselled to face the experience. We were never compensated. We told them that exhuming bodies was against our culture. We were against this because even the new burial sites were mass graves. There was no dignity in how our ancestors were treated. We want the mine to meet their promises – our demand is that our demands are met. Other villages next to us resisted more and fought hard for better treatment which led to them getting a better deal than we got.'

'When the mine is working, they deposit waste sludge in the streams where our cattle drink. The air is also being polluted and our kids are getting sick as well. The fields we had that were used to make a living are now destroyed and we are left to face poverty; we are left to dry. We were promised bursaries but these are set aside for certain select people.'

'Speaking about another village, many people in my place are convinced that the mine is going to be good because it will bring jobs and change livelihoods. People are being bribed to accept the propaganda of the mines. In fact, I no longer openly say that I am attending meetings for people who are against the mines. It is increasingly dangerous to openly resist. The Tribal Authority/*ubukhosi* has tightened its grip and they are defending the mines. I am now a target because I am against the mining.'

'In my area, which is a nearby village, no one wants the mine. We were told that we need to relocate to make way for mines. But we have had meetings in our area about the mining and we do not want to move from our place. We have livestock, fields, trees, large plots, water and recently built government housing with electricity and other infrastructure. What the mines will do is destroy all these things and bring us poverty. That is NOT development. No one can compensate for the things we have. We have heard that the village next door wants the mine badly.'

'Villages/*ngaphansi kobukhosi* are now divided and *izinduna* are in conflict because people were told there is lots of money ready to be paid to villages from the mining companies. What I know is that in my village, we don't want the mine. Sadly the people in the next village are weak and their local leaders are sell-outs. Clearly we can see that the Tribal Authorities, commercial farmers and mines are ganging up against the villagers.'

'In the village where a mine is already operating, the land is polluted, the air is polluted, the water is polluted and there is drought. All these things are caused or made worse by the mine. Now at the moment we want the mine to give us our compensation. The mine is playing delaying tactics to respond to our demands. But it is clear really that our demands will not be met. We no longer want the mine because it has caused so many problems. Is there a way to stop the mine?'

'At our place we were not told about the arrival of the mines. We heard about the troubles at that village where a mine is already established and we were concerned that this will happen in our place. We have seen how the Tribal Authority/*ubukhosi* sold out the people where there are mines now. We took the decision that we don't want the mine. We are not afraid of the Tribal Authorities because it is us who will suffer.

Our *inkosi* was called to a meeting by the people, and he confessed to signing an agreement with the mines. The *abaNtwana* have formed a committee for matters relating mines. They want the villages to agree to mines and be ready to relocate. They say all the land belongs to the *abaNtwana*.'

'The *abaNtwana* have become dictators and they do not want to listen to us villagers. Their strategy is to slander us and some individual leaders in the media that they control. We are concerned about how they are pushing us into agreeing to mining. What has happened has almost divided the villagers.'

'The people of our village had drafted a Memorandum of Agreement with the mine that was signed by both parties. However, mining work was stopped by the people, and all the mining machinery was removed from our village, because none of our demands were being met. Later that year rumours of an assassination of local leaders began to circulate. Then, the mining company, the *abaNtwana* and the party politicians wanted to meet with us, but in that meeting we opposed the return of the mining company. Then the slander and accusations against individuals began and rumours and warnings of hits against individuals have been circulating.'

'We know that the mines are making billions – therefore we need our share to change our lives. Instead, the money is going to the Tribal Authority/*ubukhosi* and not the people. We were fooled before but NOW we know this doesn't help. Whether they pay compensation or not, we don't want mines. Mines come to bring poverty. People must not be scared of the *abaNtwana* and *ubukhosi*. They take all our benefits and give us nothing. They don't scare us, they are nothing.'

'Well, in our village today we have youth that are vibrant, but the adults wanted the mine to continue because some of them work on the mine. The youth have often locked up the gates of the mine and stopped all activities. Adults saw this as unruly behaviour. Clearly the mine has divided people.'

'What we should do is to create platforms where we can speak freely about our reaction to the mines.'

'All villages must have a chance to speak and we need to connect them to speak to each other about their experience. For this to happen those activists in villages need to identify like-minded people and start organising. Of course this will be risky. Their immediate enemies are connected with the *abaNtwana* and their supporters. They will need to find careful ways of mobilising. It is going to be difficult.'

'As villagers from our place we speak in one voice on this: we don't want mines!'

'Having heard all what people have been saying, the question becomes how do we move forward?'

'Well, the issue of the *abaNtwana* and intimidation needs further discussion. We need to share the experience of dealing with the *abaNtwana* with all communities that are affected so that strategies can be developed and shared on how to stop them. From our case it is clear that the *abaNtwana* is basically functioning like a shield to protect mining interests. This behaviour is wrong – they should not be preventing villagers defending their rights.'

'We no longer trust the *abaNtwana*. We no longer listen to what they say. We are not scared of them. We should not be scared to say we don't want the mine.'

'The reason we get scared is that in my area I am the only one who is saying clearly 'I don't want the mine'. I am happy for you that you speak as a village but, where I am, I'm the only one. Other people do not want to speak out. They are not speaking with one voice. Even if they are in public meetings, they are scared to speak against the mines because they know it is protected by the *abaNtwana*. The mine has made promises to villagers of building houses when people are relocated. People are happy to have houses built for them as this also comes with promises of money for compensation.'

'The mine has been good at bribing people. Please people – don't believe anything that is promised by the mines! No one can build you a house. You have a house! Why should someone build you a house? We did not invite these mines.'

'It is intriguing that relocations are only threatened in our villages and not other built-up areas like white and middle-class suburbs.'

'We are tired of the mines. We need a big march that we go to the King.'

'People must not believe that they will all get jobs. They must not sign any agreements. In our place we took a resolution that, as a leader or a committee member you cannot be employed in the mines because there will be a conflict of interest. No matter how difficult it is to be unemployed, you do not take a job from your opponent.'

'It is clear from what's been said that there are many ways in which we have been made weak by the strategies of the mines and the *abaNtwana* but is it possible to look at the things that make us strong? The truth is that we all need each other in this struggle. We need to support each other to face the mines. But we can only support villages on what they want to do.'

'It has become so clear today that the mining companies, and the *abaNtwana*, and government cannot solve people's problems. They all look out for their own elite interests. Real change can only come through people organised into a strong fighting force. Fear exerted by the powerful groups cannot deter people from organising their own power. Promises made by others cannot solve our problems but the people, organised and democratic, can. So organising needs to take place in the places where the people live. That organising needs to hear, include and respect the voice of all who are there; it needs to build strength where the people can be strong on their own feet, in their own thinking and their own struggle and politics.'

'Yes, this is true. In our village, we can have meetings and we are ready to take the bull by the horns. We are free to talk and invite next door villages to our meetings as they cannot meet in their own places safely at the moment.'

'I am also grateful of this platform today. Fundamentally, we all agree – and we need this platform to encourage and support each other. We should continue and build this platform. *But* we do need to take this battle to our villages – that is the battlefield.'

'It seems we agree that this platform is important and that it is useful for us to draw strength from each other. Also that from here we will see in our villages how we can talk about our issues with all the people. Clearly, when we get back to our places we need to be strong and work towards building people's power.'

Praxis and politics

Civil society is important for state politics in allocating people to their place in the state system as 'beneficiaries', 'stakeholders' and 'interest groups'. (In many ways, civil society is to the neoliberal state what the missionary project was to colonialism.) Civil society sees itself (and is seen by many other elites) as an important bearer of knowledge, of skills, of resources, of the power to access and represent 'the community', or 'the poor', or 'the people' and so on.

Civil society tends to think for..., and to speak for.... It often assumes the it has the solutions, processes, strategies and theories – and that its role is to mediate these to 'beneficiaries'. It does so by workshopping, capacity building, facilitating, running 'teach-ins', info sharing. The real effect of this work is to relentlessly try to convince the people that they cannot think for themselves, that they cannot think their own politics and that they cannot take effective action in the world.

In civil society organisations the overwhelming tendency is to speak – and the unerring consequence is to reinforce the silencing of the people. In fact much civil society practice and thinking proceeds really on the assumption that speech is not a capacity of the people. The CLP has explored an alternative path. A central idea that emerged was that 'our voice is our praxis' – or indeed, 'our praxis is our voice' – and that the discipline of that principled praxis requires of the organisation much more listening than speaking. Thus, in CLP's understanding, since our voice is our praxis it then follows that it is who we *are* in the world, and what we actually *do*, that is the most the eloquent clarification of who we are. For CLP this praxis must frequently be a disciplined silence in order to listen. This is a break with the praxis of most NGOs in general. The majority praxis of NGOs reflects and re-inscribes power and control to speak for, to speak over and to mediate the representation of people's struggle and life. Finally, since our voice is our praxis, and our praxis is political, *it is always thought* – and therefore it always depends on thinking our principles in relation to a concrete situation, to what erupts and to what confronts us.

A key problematic that emerges through reflecting on grassroots discussions like those shared overleaf has been that people who want to think their resistance face the relentless instruction from political, economic and 'traditional authority' elites to 'stay in your place'. The instruction takes many forms, of course, from the subtle but overwhelming pressure of a hegemonic ideology of 'respect' and 'obedience', to personally targeted public slander and covertly issued death threats. And, together with the promises of jobs and development that the proponents of mining issue, it is not surprising that there is fear and division to different degrees in different locations in the region. But there is also a militant, popular, grassroots will to 'step out of order', and that is deeply significant. In the CLP's approach it signals the presence or possibility of politics proper, an emancipatory politics. A number of years ago, S'bu Zikode of the shack-dwellers' movement, Abahlali baseMjondolo, commented that 'A living politics is the movement out of the places where oppression has assigned those who do not count'. The decision to step out of order marks a rupture in the situation and inaugurates a liberatory sequence. It is invariably a moment of clarity and truth, thought and choice; an event that divides the situation-as-it-is from what could be.

The possibility of *this* emancipatory struggle is in response to a real clash provoked by the mining companies' actions and intentions. There was, of course, life being lived before the mining companies arrived – a way of living, of being, of struggle for life. The mining companies arrived in the midst of this life and not in a vacuum. So we start not with the mining companies but with the life of the people. We don't need to romanticise that life. We know perfectly well that it includes/d struggle for life itself under conditions shaped not only by that struggle but by histories of elite kingdom formation, of colonialism and apartheid, of capitalist domination, labour extraction and environmental degradation. Nonetheless, the most recent arrival of the mining companies has marked a new attack by capital on the life of the people here. Of course, those in favour of expanded mining have an extensive vocabulary to justify it – 'it'll bring development, there'll be jobs, it'll help fix the national energy crisis, we'll be able to help you people in so many ways through schools, bursaries, development trusts', and so on. But even if some of these promises were delivered, it's clear that they're there to facilitate capital's agenda – and that agenda is the thrust of the attack on the life of the people.

Even though it's for the interest of capital, it's presented as the general interest, the good of all. This is the classic function of a legitimating ideology. But when people choose to resist that attack, then the social synthesis is shattered by rupture from below. This is precisely what the instruction to 'know and/or keep your place' is meant to avoid at all costs! Its irruption into the situation is precious and vulnerable, powerful and fragile. It is the assertion of the human life of the people against the forces of death. In the 'No' of the people we discover anew and assert our humanity against the ravages of capital. As we've demonstrated, in meetings of grassroots militants the 'No' of the people has been clearly articulated.

And in this fundamental clash, the space is opened for a way forward. Provided that the struggle that unfolds remains in fidelity to the fundamental 'No' that originated it, then it stops simply reproducing or modestly reforming that world-as-it-is, but instead marks out an emancipatory future of what could be. Those clashes are all over – in the titanic struggles against transnational capital companies, and in the minutiae of daily refusals to become automatons of capital, in our neighbourhoods and households, in our formations, movements and organisations, within ourselves even.

References

Binns, T. and Nel, E. (2003) 'The village in a game park: Local response to the demise of coal mining in KwaZulu-Natal, South Africa', *Economic Geography*, 79(1): 41–66.

Burton, J. (2016) 'South Africa's coal sector: Energy security, ownership, and climate change', *Amandla*, 49/50 (December).

Eberhard, A. (2011) 'The future of South African coal: Market, investment and policy changes', Programme on Energy and Sustainable Development, Stamford University, Working Paper No 100.

Fine, B. (2008) 'The Minerals-Energy Complex is dead: Long live the MEC?'. Paper presented at the Amandla Colloquium: Continuity and Discontinuity of Capitalism on the post-apartheid South Africa, Cape Town, April.

Guest, B. (1998) 'Commercial coal-mining in Natal: A centennial appraisal', *Natalia*, 18: 41–58.

Hallowes, D. (2011) *Toxic futures: South Africa in the crises of energy, environment, and capital*, Pietermaritzburg: groundWork and UKZN Press.

Inggs, M. (2007) 'KwaZulu-Natal has viable resources, even in coal', www.miningweekly.com, 8 June.

Maggs, T. (1992) '"My father's hammer never ceased its song day and night": The Zulu ferrous metalworking industry', *Natal Museum Journal of Humanities*, 4: 65–87.

Mokgalaka, R. (2016) 'Uniting coal struggles', *groundWork Newsletter*, 18(3): 8–9.

Nel, E.L, Hill, T.R., Aitchison, K.C. and Buthelezi, S. (2003) 'The closure of coal mines and local development responses in Coal-Rim Cluster, northern KwaZulu-Natal, South Africa', *Development Southern Africa*, 20(3): 369–85.

Nkosi, X. (2017) 'Hire us or get out of here!', *Daily Sun*, 25 January 2017, http://www.dailysun.co.za/News/National/hire-us-or-get-out-of-here-20170124.

Schneider, K. (2016) 'SA locks onto coal despite water risks', http://www.fin24.com/Companies/Mining/sa-locks-onto-coal-despite-water-risks-20160422.

Stewart, P. and Kumar Nite, D. (2017) 'From fatalism to mass action to incorporation into neoliberal individualism: Worker safety on South African mines, c. 1955–2016', *Review of African Political Economy*, 44: 252–71.

Whitelaw, G. (1991) 'Precolonial iron production around Durban and in southern Natal', *Natal Museum Journal of Humanities*, 3: 29–39.

EIGHT

Ecological justice for Palestine

Simon I. Awad

Introduction

Palestine, throughout history, was the cradle of several civilisations, religions and cultures. It enjoys a privileged geographical location at the junction of three continents: Asia, Europe and Africa. Compared to other countries Palestine is a small area, yet its environment contains a wide range of temperatures, rainfall and topography. The Bible includes the earliest written descriptions of the diversity existing in historic Palestine. Its ecology and biodiversity make Palestine a natural museum.

The native people of Palestine, namely the Canaanites, also date back to early historical times, growing and changing with their natural environment. They have lived continuously in this land, developing a strong relationship and identity with the land, creating their own exclusive natural and cultural heritage. Unfortunately, the vibrancy of Palestine and its vital geographical location aroused the ambitions of invaders and rulers throughout history. It became a focal point for many colonial powers who realised its potential as a central hub for commercial routes. It also attracted religious groups because of its biblical significance. It endured intense wars to claim and reclaim prominent holy sites, as witnessed by the Crusades and the Zionist movement. The constant fight for land deprived the people of Palestine of the possibility of achieving political independence. However, their unbroken presence throughout the land gave it its identity and contributed to the evolving civilisations and provided a great gift to humanity in the Fertile Crescent, through the development of agricultural practices and domestication of animals.

The colonisation of Palestine

The most current foreign body to want Palestinian land is the Zionist movement, intent on the Jews 'coming home' to the land that was promised to them according to the Hebrew Bible. The Zionist movement was founded in 1897 by Theodor Herzl, who succeeded in promoting the idea of establishing a homeland for the world's Jews. Argentina and Uganda were among the proposed countries for this dream of establishing a homeland for the Jews, but Herzl encouraged Jews to migrate to Palestine. Organisations were then created to raise funds to buy land in Palestine and build colonies in order to create a fait accompli. Herzl mobilised support for the Zionist movement in other parts of the world.

After defeat of the Ottomans in the First World War, the fate of the Ottoman Empire and its controlled territories rested in the hands of the victorious Allied Powers. Mandates were distributed and assigned to the Allied Powers under the authority of Article 22 of the Covenant of the League of Nations, so that they could receive help in reaching full independence. In 1920 Great Britain was assigned the Mandate of Palestine, one of the Ottoman Empire's territories. The terms of the Mandate incorporated a letter known as the Balfour Declaration, written by the British foreign minister in 1917, to publicly state Britain's support for the establishment of a Jewish homeland in Palestine:

> His Majesty's Government view with favour the establishment in Palestine of a national home for the Jewish people, and will use their best endeavours to facilitate the achievement of this object, it being clearly understood that nothing shall be done which may prejudice the civil and religious rights of existing non-Jewish communities in Palestine, or the rights and political status enjoyed by Jews in any other country. (Balfour, 1917)

This letter was approved by the League of Nations and gave Britain controlling power in Palestine from 1922 until 1948. This promise was the turning point in the fight for land. Thus, while League of Nations mandates were designed to facilitate independence for indigenous peoples, this was not the case in Palestine, where Britain was mandated to facilitate the settler-colonial intentions of the Zionist movement.

At first the Palestinians welcomed the new wave of Jewish immigrants who came to Palestine before and during the Second World War and before the Second World War as victims of European persecution. However, when Palestinians realised the Zionist goals of expansion through displacement based on 'a land without a people for a people without a land' they started to struggle and to resist the Zionist movement. The land was a key element in Palestinian national revival (Figure 8.1).

Figure 8.1: Map showing Palestinian loss of land, 1917–2012

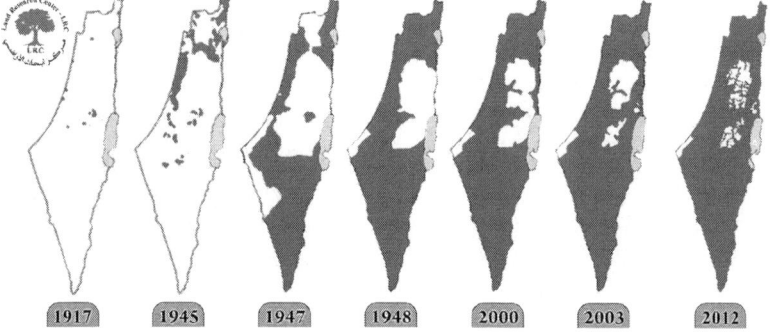

Source: Land Research Center

The Palestinian Nakba (catastrophe) and the environmental Nakba

Much of the environmental exploitation of Palestine has its roots in the work of the Jewish National Fund (JNF), which was established at the Fifth Zionist Congress in 1901 as a tool of the colonial movement to help raise funds for the purchase of Palestinian land for the development and expansion of Jewish settlements (Davis and Lehn, 1988). The JNF raised donations from world Jewry and other folk worldwide, especially Europeans, using various pretexts such as the conservation of natural resources and the cultivation of forests. Its purpose was to 'Judaise' the Palestinian environment, reconstructing the landscape to more closely resemble that of Central Europe, from where many of the Zionist settlers originated. This allowed for drying-up wetlands, reclaiming land, establishing plantation forests and developing infrastructure. Since the establishment of Israel, many projects have used similar justifications to continue the work of the British Mandate to make Palestine 'green' as envisioned by the western world. However, most of the preservation efforts were on the confiscated lands of Palestinian villages destroyed during the 1948 war, which destroyed the remaining fig and olive trees and grape vines that once surrounded Palestinian homes (Khalidi, 1992). Not only did the JNF have a hidden agenda to control more land, enabling the state of Israel to take away Palestinian property, but the introduction of non-native and exotic species to hide this agenda greatly damaged the flora and fauna that had flourished in this land for thousands of years. The greening of Palestine by foreign people using foreign species has led to the present-day efforts to reverse the negative effects on the ecology of Palestine. Because of these actions, most Palestinians regard Israeli environmental policies as anti-Palestinian policies. Palestinians have struggled to preserve the land, due to its ties with Zionist expansion.

Although organisations like JNF quietly grabbed land throughout the 1900s, the end of British control and the establishment of the state of Israel led to exponential land seizure in Palestine. The 1948 war, and its systematic displacement of the Palestinian population, was a major tragedy known to Palestinians as al Nakba (the Catastrophe). This ethnic cleansing operation drove 800,000 of the 1.4 million Palestinians from their villages and towns in what became the state of Israel. Most of them were displaced to a number of neighbouring Arab countries in addition to the West Bank (of the Jordan River) and Gaza Strip (then under Jordanian and Egyptian rule, respectively). Thousands of Palestinians who became under direct Israeli occupation rule were displaced internally. During the *Nakba* Zionist militias (terrorist gangs) carried out more than 70 massacres against the Palestinians, resulting in the deaths of more than 15,000 persons, and Israel seizing control of more than 78% of Palestinian land.

The change that took place in the natural environment of Palestine was just as rapid. The new state seized control of the many natural resources. It seized water resources, built thousands of kilometres of roads and new settlements. Large areas were seized for military purposes, damaging the natural environment, especially wetlands and forests. The new state also drained the ecologically significant Hula Lake (Hambright and Zohary, 1998) and diverted the water of the Jordan River to the Negev desert for agriculture (Zeitoun, 2012). These actions have greatly disrupted and damaged the delicate ecosystem in Palestine, as well as the people who previously depended on it (Isaac and Hilal, 2011).

Fifty years of occupation

In 1967 Israel occupied the remaining 22% of Palestinian land: the Gaza Strip and West Bank (including East Jerusalem). The continuous illegal occupation of Palestinian territory by Israel created many social and environmental difficulties for the Palestinians and their natural and cultural heritage. The protection of the environment was overlooked because of the 50 long years of occupation. Population growth, water shortages, increasing food prices, climate change and political instability have compounded the issues that Palestinians face every day.

Over the 50 years since 1948, Israel has demolished 48,000 homes, confiscated 586,000 acres of land in the West Bank and created 300,000 refugees. According to the Palestinian Central Bureau of Statistics (2017), 9% of the West Bank has been designated as a nature reserve, off limits to Palestinians and often converted to settlements. The occupation has increased the destruction of a unique biodiversity. Palestine represents about 3% of the world's total biodiversity, and many species are in danger due to the environmental problems. The planned strategies of dispossession, fear, violence and neglect that affect Palestinian livelihoods and daily life also result in the destruction of natural resources, wildlife habitats and migratory routes.

According to UN, the water resources needed in Gaza will increase by 60% by 2020, but much of the available water resources will be irreversibly damaged or unusable by that time (UNCTAD, 2015). Palestinians in the West Bank are able to use about 20% of the potential water resources in the area; the remaining 80% are appropriated by Israel. This puts the majority of Palestinians under the 100 litres of water per person a day recommended by the World Health Organization, while Israelis enjoy about 600 litres a day (Isaac and Hilal, 2011).

Land is central in the conflict between Palestinians and the Zionist movement/Israeli government. Israeli seizure and manipulation of the land has damaged the distinctive Palestinian environment and its people. Many Palestinians have forgotten the landscape of their homeland and can see no possibility of preserving it. However, the increased confiscation of land and natural resources and Israeli military control in the West Bank have led to the Palestinian struggle to preserve as much of their land and history as they can. Palestinians have come to acknowledge that without preserving the environment, and therefore identity, of Palestine they may never find lasting justice, freedom and self-determination. Much environmental destruction is irreversible, causing a new environmental Nakba.

In light of all of these issues, environmental concerns are often overlooked, despite the fact that they pose an increasingly perilous danger to Palestinians. Three cases show the direct impact on and destruction of the ecology of Palestine, caused by the Israeli settlements and the Apartheid Wall.

Illegal Israeli settlements

With the Israeli military occupation in 1967 and the imposition of full military control over the West Bank, Gaza Strip and East Jerusalem, Israeli governments began issuing military laws relating to the confiscation of land and natural resources: water, nature reserves, archaeological sites and forests. The main objective is to control the land for settlement purposes and to draw large numbers of settlers into these areas. At the same time, the Israeli occupation authorities prevent the Palestinians from building in these areas, strangling their communities and destroying geographical contiguity between them.

Although the construction of settlements is illegal under international humanitarian law, which prevents the occupying state from transferring its citizens to the territories it has occupied (Article 49 of the Fourth Geneva Convention), Israel has repudiated all applicable international norms and laws. By the end of 2017, the number of settlements established in the occupied territories had reached 144. About 524,000 Israeli settlers are living in West Bank settlements, including East Jerusalem.

Settlements in natural and forest areas pollute the Palestinian environment and devastate the landscape. They directly affect the biodiversity and cultural and natural heritage of the Palestinians. The Israeli settlements also violate the provisions of international humanitarian law, and resolutions of the Security Council and the General Assembly of the UN. The main source of pollution that the settlements create is the discharge of waste water from homes and factories into Palestinian wadis (valleys) and agricultural lands. The untreated waste water mixes with the clean water, with serious environmental impact. Similarly, solid waste from these settlements is discharged without any restrictions into Palestinian territories (al Butmeh et al, 2013).

The Israelis have used diverse methods to seize and confiscate the lands of Palestinian citizens to build settlements, infrastructure, highways and national parks, and to provide space for future expansion. Various types of settlements, such as residential, agricultural and industrial, have been identified as areas of national preference (or so-called development zones). Successive Israeli governments have provided land, water, subsidies, facilities, incentives and economic rewards to Israelis to get them to move to settlements in Palestinian territory. This has been done through the introduction of generous budgets from the state and through the Settlement Department of the

World Zionist Organization, while simultaneously violating the rights of Palestinians to property and self-determination.

The settlement of Jabal Abu Ghnaim

I began to follow this issue after the June 1991 statement of Yitzhak Mudai, Minister of Finance in the Israeli government, regarding the decision to confiscate more than 1,851 dunums (18.5 ha) of land on Jabal Abu Ghnaim, which were owned by families from Beit Sahour, Bethlehem and Um Tuba. I was working at the Palestinian Information Center for Human Rights in the Arab Studies Society in Jerusalem, which included documenting Israeli violations of human rights such as assassination, detaining, confiscation of land and demolition of houses.

The construction of the Har Homa settlement on Jabal (Mount) Abu Ghnaim is a strategic issue for Israel because it completes the settlement cordon around the Bethlehem area on all four sides and isolates the town from its historical extension with the city of Jerusalem. At the same time, it prevents any future expansion of the Bethlehem area and achieves the Israeli plan of a greater Jerusalem. The people of Bethlehem pursued the issue of the confiscation of their land through popular and legal struggle. The case remained in the Israeli courts from 1991 until 1996, when construction began. After interviewing the owners of the land in Jabal Abu Ghnaim I found that a small part of the land had been purchased in the years 1929–40, and a number of the owners confirmed that the sale was made to people known as 'Khojat' meaning British persons.

Jabal Abu Ghnaim is a forest that was planted by the Jordanian Ministry of Agriculture with 72,000 trees of several species of cypress and pine before the Israeli occupation in 1967. It is located north of Bethlehem and was considered the only natural haven for the Bethlehem area. After 1967 the occupation illegally decided to annex it to the municipal boundaries of Jerusalem. Afterwards, Abu Ghnaim was declared a protected green area because of its environmental importance and unique biodiversity, including Palestine oak, Palestinian pistachio, carob and hawthorn. This attracted dozens of species of animals and birds that made it their home.

The forest contains Christian archaeological ruins and was visited by pilgrims on their journey between the Church of the Holy Sepulchre in Jerusalem and the Nativity Church in Bethlehem. During my childhood I spent some time in Abu Ghnaim with my friends and enjoyed the diversity and beauty of the place. I remember the mountain on the back road linking Beit Sahour and Jerusalem, which I went to frequently, where I was constantly watching scores of gazelles, hundreds of chukar birds, foxes, migratory birds, wild flowers and other various kinds of wildlife.

Environmental impact

A forest of 60,000 trees that was considered to be a rich refuge in biodiversity and the only forest in the Bethlehem Governorate was removed, as well as other native trees. Deforestation and the construction of settlements was a disaster for biodiversity in the region. This led to habitat degradation and species decline, which in the future may lead to the extinction of certain species. It will also increase carbon dioxide emissions and thus contribute to climate change. Building the settlement of Har Homa led to the devastation of the natural landscape through the obliteration of the environment, destruction of aesthetic value, extinguishing important plant and animal diversity of biological and genetic value and destroying an important source of food.

The replacement of a forest with a settlement has significant negative impacts on the environment and will have undesirable consequences, especially the emission of gases and dust, building of roads, growing demand for water and the production of solid and liquid wastes.

Gusheri industrial settlements

Since 1967 the Israeli occupation has established more than 20 industrial settlements in the occupied West Bank. Because of the emission of airborne toxins, these settlements are built inside the Palestinian territory near Palestinian villages and towns so that, depending on the prevailing winds in the region, the pollution travels from Israeli areas towards the Palestinian communities. A number of these plants were located in areas close to Israeli communities, such as Kfar Saba and Netanya. However, they were transferred to the West Bank region of Tulkarm in the 1980s because of the decision of the Israeli courts to close the plants for environmental reasons. The transfer was due also to financial incentives and weak environmental legislation in the occupied West Bank. The Israeli industrial zones or so-called 'areas of death' are along the border with Israel, by decision of the Israeli military in the occupied territory. In 2006 all chemical factories inside the Israeli communities were moved to the industrial zones located on confiscated Palestinian lands in Tulkarm. These industrial settlements do not comply with Israeli or Palestinian environmental laws, and send their solid waste without treatment to the neighbouring

Palestinian towns and villages, regardless of any ethical, humanitarian, human rights or environmental standards. Israeli factories built in this zone pose a real danger to the population of the city and the surrounding areas because the toxic gases affect the health of humans, animals and the environment.

Death factories in the Geshuri area

The first factory built on confiscated land in Tulkarm was Geshuri, which produces pesticides and fertilisers and generates large quantities of hazardous waste. Geshuri employs hundreds of Palestinians manufacturing fertiliser, agrochemicals, building materials and animal-feed additives. Other industries are paper collection and processing; gas and compressed air tanks; heavy metal works; filters and water treatment for agricultural use.

According to Awad et al (2010), the chemical clouds of the Geshuri industrial settlement that spread over the city and its environs pollute all elements of the environment and living organisms. This lead to respiratory and skin diseases and have a long-term link to cancer. It has resulted in the destruction of the vegetation and animal diversity in Tulkarm and has a direct impact on human health, especially of children and the elderly, and on agricultural crops.

Hanoun (2014: np) indicated that 'the Israelis protested and succeeded in closing these factories in their areas, however, the popular and official Palestinian attempts to stop these factories have not succeeded'. Ironically, the factory west of Tulkarm faced a legal complaint from the Israeli kibbutz Oz (agricultural settlement). Following an examination by the Israeli Ministry of Environment, there was an outflow of dangerous gases and air pollution by opening the chimneys of the factory 24 hours:

> The defence's response to the court was that the winds in the area were to the east, and thus did not hurt the Kibbutz. The Israeli Ministry forced the plants of Geshuri to stop working if the direction of the winds is western and reach the Green Line and it can work if the wind is reversed. (Hanoun, 2014: np)

A recent unpublished study by the Environmental Quality Authority (EQA, 2016) 'proved the existence of a clear pollution in the soil and water, such as aluminium, cobalt, copper, cadmium, lead, zinc and nickel and acidic waste and asked for the closure of these factories, stressing the compatibility of the study with the United Nations Environment Program and the Arab League'. This provides international corroboration for the results of a Palestinian that study was financed by Belgian cooperation, and completed by a team of researchers from Palestinian universities in coordination with the United Nations Environment Program, despite Israeli obstacles. The study was presented to Prime Minister D. Rami al-Hamdallah, who authorised competent authorities to follow up the environmental, economic and social damage of the Geshuri factories.

The acute health impacts of this pollution have been described in an ethnographic study by Qato and Nagra (2013), who note disproportionate levels of asthma and cancer, and the significant impact on the local economy and livelihoods as a result of the polluting industrial zone at Gusheri.

Reporting for the human rights legal agency Al Haq, Pontin et al (2015) summarise:

> As well as health issues, this arguably engages the crime against humanity of indirect forcible transfer, which is an international crime under arts 7 and 8(2) (b) (vii) of the Rome statutes. To put Tulkarm case in perspective appropriate to the issue of universal crime, some further background is necessary: the factories had originally been located within the Israeli side of the green line. They were relocated into occupied territory once Israeli residents refused to tolerate their pollution and took legal action under the English common law of nuisance, which (to reiterate) is in force in Israel as a legacy of the British Mandate. By the terms of Israeli court injunction, the relocated enterprises were not allowed to operate at times when the wind blew in the Israeli direction of the green line. Here then is a case of the Israeli Occupying Forces (IOF), with the help (if unwitting) of the Israeli judiciary, actively contributing to local Palestinians suffering a toxic tort that Israelis found intolerable. (Pontin et al, 2015: 25)

Despite the damage, Israel continues to support the expansion of industrial settlements and allows the opening of new factories, in complete disregard of its responsibility for the safety of the environment and safety of the health of the civilian population as an occupying power.

The construction of the Apartheid Wall

While the idea of isolation and segregation walls existed previously within the Zionist movement, the Apartheid Wall emerged mainly after the outbreak of the Second Intifada (uprising) in September 2000, the 'Al-Aqsa Intifada'. The wall, according to Israel, aims at achieving security and protecting Israeli citizens from Palestinian terrorist attacks. However, Israel continues to support the construction of (illegal) Jewish settlements at an accelerated pace right next to Palestinian villages and towns inside the West Bank. There is a clear contradiction between these declared goals, which serves to conceal the implicit aim of taking over more Palestinian land.

In June 2002, Israel began construction of the wall. 'It is considered the largest construction project in the history of Israel, with a budget of 3.3 billion US dollars. 53 construction companies and more than 700 contractors, 5 barbed wire companies and 34 security equipment companies constructed the Apartheid Wall' (Stop the Wall, nd). The wall was expected to be about 708 kilometres long along the Green Line between Israel and the West Bank. However, Israel built more than 85% of the wall inside the West Bank. As a result, it has confiscated 9.4% of the West Bank, annexing it to Israel. The left-over land has isolated a number of Palestinian villages and towns, whose residents need special permits to access their homes and properties now on the other side of the wall.

In July 2004, the International Court of Justice (ICJ) stated that 'The construction of the wall by Israel, the occupying Power, in the occupied Palestinian territory, including in and around East Jerusalem, and its associated regime, are contrary to international law'. It found that

> Israel is under an obligation to terminate its breaches of international law; it is under an obligation to cease forthwith the works of construction of the wall being built in the Occupied Palestinian Territory, including in and around East Jerusalem, to dismantle forthwith the structure therein situated, and to repeal or render ineffective forthwith all legislative and regulatory acts relating thereto ... All States are under an obligation not to recognize the illegal situation resulting from the construction of the wall and not to render aid or assistance in maintaining the situation created by such construction. (ICJ, 2004: 15)

The map of the wall has been thoroughly studied and prepared by Israeli cartographers, in order to confiscate the most desirable Palestinian land, including the most abundant water sources and fertile agricultural lands. Taking water has destroyed the Palestinian agricultural sector while creating greater opportunities for Israelis. The continuation of such actions will render any future Palestinian state physically composed of nothing more than infertile, dry land, with little water, and that heavily polluted by untreated Israeli waste and sewage.

Israel's apartheid policies are clearly damaging the environment in the West Bank and Gaza Strip. There are numerous accounts showing Israeli actions against the environment. This includes the uprooting of trees, land annexation, building new settlements, restricting freedom of movement and garbage dumping. The wall not only limits the movement of Palestinians; it also restricts, and in some cases prevents, the movement of wildlife by cutting migration corridors and access to breeding areas. The 25-foot-tall barrier 'will lead to the destruction of natural habitat of great areas, fragmentation of ecosystems, removal and clearing of natural vegetation, disruption of the natural ecosystem balance, and endangerment of many species of plants and animals as a result from fragmentation, isolation and habitat loss' (State of Palestine, 2015). The natural balance will be shifted accordingly: more weeds, pests and pathogens will easily invade the disturbed areas. Animal populations will be fragmented and distribution patterns will be altered. The remaining small population would then be vulnerable to all of the problems associated with rarity, genetic deterioration from inbreeding, random drift in gene frequencies, and some species may even vanish completely. As for plants, thousands of trees have been uprooted, such as grapevine, olive, palm, almond, orange, fig and banana trees. Fruit-bearing trees are usually targeted in an effort to damage the agricultural productivity and economic prosperity of Palestinians living in the 1967 occupied territory as a collective punishment against the Palestinians. Furthermore, the wall has destroyed many archaeological sites located in villages surrounding East Jerusalem – Jenin, Nablus, Qalqiliya and many others.

The wall located on Bir Aouna in the town of Beit Jala was completed around 2017 and isolated thousands of dunums of land, which have been turned into national parks for the use of Israeli settlers. In the area in which the Environmental Education Center is located in the area of Sadr and Rass in Beit Jala, the wall was not completed, ostensibly due to objections from the municipality of Beit Jala and its residents. However, the real reason is the lack of alternative routes for settlers to reach Jerusalem in the event of disruption of the road in the tunnel area that links the southern West Bank with Jerusalem. As the situation worsens with increasing settlements, water shortages and climate change, education in proper environmental practices and activism becomes essential to preserve and protect endangered areas and to create avenues to build peace.

The sustainability of the environmental resources available to Palestinian society in the occupied territories is largely limited and marginal because of the actions of the Israeli occupation. As these actions are beyond the control of the Palestinian population, it is essential to educate and mobilise the people to implement the appropriate actions in order to preserve our natural heritage. However, this solution is dependent on continued effort to respect human rights and the support of the international community.

The Environmental Education Center

The Environmental Education Center (EEC) is a leading organisation for raising environmental awareness, protecting biodiversity, encouraging eco-tourism, promoting Palestinian identity and capacity building. It has implemented a wide array of programmes to work for eco-justice in Palestine. Through broad-based interactive educational programmes, the EEC reaches teachers, students, women, community members and officials, empowering Palestinians to work for positive, sustainable change in Palestinian society. It conducts scientific surveys and organises practical conservation activities.

Although there are inherent difficulties in promoting environmental sustainability in a land full of political and military struggle, EEC programmes are designed to take up some of the environmental challenges posed by the Israeli occupation in order to empower community members to take action for positive change and fostering positive public opinion. The EEC focuses on Palestinian youth and women to raise environmental awareness and acquire leadership skills necessary to educate others to achieve environmental justice in Palestine.

EEC has also launched a campaign of planting native trees each year and compensates farmers whose trees have been uprooted by the Israeli occupation. EEC's olive harvest festival is an opportunity for the farmers to sell their products.

The EEC has developed advocacy for environmental justice and sustainable resource management and economic development through an annual conference on eco-justice. It helps Palestinian citizens to realise their rights to sustainable livelihoods through capacity building, discussion groups and community activities. It also helps to cultivate community participation, tolerance for diversity and environmental responsibility. The EEC compiles lectures for the conference on topics such as biodiversity, water and energy conservation, climate change, food security, management of natural resources, sustainable development and the effects of the Israeli occupation on the environment. It works with community groups and local NGOs to prepare the conference, engage in dialogue and organise presenters. As part of the conference, a media campaign is undertaken, involving educational materials and other publications, in order to raise public awareness of environmental issues and create a platform to discuss critical environmental issues and justice in Palestine (for example, Awad, 2013).

In 2015 the Palestinian Council of Ministers adopted 5 March as the Palestinian Environment Day and the Palestine sunbird as our national bird as a result of an initiative launched through the EEC emphasising the importance of the environment in Palestinian society. These initiatives provide a platform for more environmental justice projects. During the month of the first Palestinian Environment Day more than 2,000 students and community members participated in various environmental service activities, including planting native trees and clean-up campaigns. These activities play a crucial role in developing future young leaders and environmental activists.

The EEC continues to work with a variety of organisations through coalition, networking, media and working groups. It has participated effectively in climate change conferences: COP22 Marrakesh and COP23 Bonn; the World Social Forums in Kenya and Brazil; and the International Union for Conservation of Nature World Conservation Congress Hawaii, in order to advocate for justice in Palestine, to connect with the rest of the world to seek justice together and to raise awareness globally of the impact of the Israeli occupation on the environment.

Hundreds of international visitors to the EEC each year are introduced to the impacts of the Israeli occupation on the Palestinian environment through the unique panoramic view at the site overlooking a landscape scarred by settlements, confiscated land and the Apartheid Wall.

The Palestinian and international churches have been an important avenue for promoting environmental justice for EEC. During the Christian season of Lent in 2016, in Jerusalem the EEC joined the Evangelical Lutheran Church in Jordan and the Holy Land and the

World Council of Churches (WCC) on a water justice campaign called Seven Weeks for Water, which focused on the inequality of water distribution between Palestine and Israel. This initiative engaged church leaders and Christians from local and international congregations and helped to draw out peace and justice issues surrounding the water issue – and was attacked by the Israeli government and Zionists from the US. During May 2016 the EEC hosted a meeting of the working group on climate change of the WCC in Bethlehem that focused on environmental protection and climate change mitigation and adaptation. Many of the WCC representatives were detained, interrogated and confined for several days by the Israeli government, some were deported and others were not allowed into Bethlehem. Many of the conceptual and theological ideas about how the EEC overcomes environmental challenges under the Palestinian context have been outlined in a chapter titled 'Advocacy for Eco-Justice in Palestine', written by EEC for a WCC book that discusses how religious leaders and organisations approach environmental issues (Awad, 2016).

The biogeography and socio-ecology of Palestine have provided the land with a unique environment that has been threatened by the Zionist settler-colonisation of Palestine, from the early days under Ottoman Empire, through the British Mandate and particularly since the establishment of the state of Israel and the military occupation of the West Bank and Gaza Strip. There has always been an environmental dimension to the injustices imposed on the Palestinian people and their relationship to their resources. While the current conditions of settler-colonialism make sustainable management of resources impossible, protection of the natural and cultural environment has become an important part of Palestinian resistance. The EEC is a unique organisation, overlooking the front-line of conflict along the Apartheid Wall and the expansion of settlements between Bethlehem and Jerusalem, providing an opportunity for education and action in support of the Palestinian environment.

References

al Butmeh, A., Peek, B. and Scandrett, E. (2013) *Environmental Nakba: Environmental injustice and violations of the Israeli occupation of Palestine.* Amsterdam: Friends of the Earth International.

Awad, H., Odeh, A. and Srouji, A. (2010) 'The reality of workers in the Israeli border factories west of Tulkarm Governorate'. Paper presented at the Israeli Industries in the Border Areas and Israeli Settlements: Bridges of Peace and Economic Development or Devastation of Humans and Environment? conference, Bethlehem.

Awad, S. (2013) *Eco-justice of Palestine*. The Environmental Education Center's Third Palestinian Environmental Awareness and Education Conference: Proceedings, December 2012.

Awad, S. (2016) 'Advocacy for eco-justice in Palestine', in G.J. Kim (ed) *Making peace with the Earth: Action and advocacy for climate justice*, Geneva: World Council of Churches.

Balfour, A.J. (1917) *The Balfour Declaration*, British Library, London.

Davis, U. and Lehn, W (1988) *The Jewish National Fund*, London: Routledge

EQA (2016) 'Environmental and health impact of the Geshuri Industrial Area in Tulkarm'. Summary of the final unpublished report (in Arabic), Ramallah: Environmental Quality Authority.

Hambright, K. and Zohary, T. (1998) 'Lakes Hula and Agmon: Destruction and creation of wetland ecosystems in northern Israel', *Wetlands Ecology and Management*, 6(2–3): 83–9.

Hanoun, S. (2014) 'Death factories in Israeli settlements and their consequences on the Palestinian environment: Geshuri as a model'. Paper delivered (in Arabic) to Eco-Justice between violation by the occupation and infringements by the community, The Environmental Education Center's fifth Palestinian Environmental Awareness and Education Conference, Bethlehem, December.

ICJ (International Court of Justice) (2004) *Legal consequences of the construction of a wall in the Occupied Palestinian Territory: Summary of the Advisory Opinion of 9 July 2004*, The Hague: International Court of Justice, http://www.icj-cij.org/files/case-related/131/1677.pdf.

Isaac, J. and Hilal, J. (2011) 'Palestinian landscape and the Israeli–Palestinian conflict', *International Journal of Environmental Studies*, 68 (4): 413–29.

Khalidi, W. (1992) *All that remains: The Palestinian villages occupied and depopulated by Israel in 1948*, Washington, DC: Institute for Palestine Studies.

Palestinian Central Bureau of Statistics (2017) *Press Release by Palestinian Central Bureau of Statistics (PCBS) and the Environment Quality Authority on World Environment Day (WED)*, Ramallah: Palestine.

Pontin, B., De Lucia, V. and Gamero Rus, J. (2015) *Environmental injustice in occupied Palestinian territory: Problems and prospects*, Ramallah: Al Haq.

Qato, D.M. and Nagra, R. (2013) 'Environmental and public health effects of polluting industries in Tulkarm, West Bank, occupied Palestinian territory: An ethnographic study', *The Lancet*, 382(Supplement 4): S29.

State of Palestine (2015) *Fifth National Report to the Convention on Biological Diversity*, Ramallah: Palestinian Environment Quality Authority.

Stop the Wall (nd) *Anti-Apartheid Wall campaign fact sheet, The Apartheid Wall, Palestinian Grassroots, Anti-Apartheid Wall Campaign*, https://stopthewall.org.

UNCTAD (United Nations Conference on Trade and Development) (2015) *Report on UNCTAD assistance to the Palestinian people: Developments in the economy of the occupied Palestinian territory*, http://unctad.org/meetings/en/SessionalDocuments/tdb62d3_en.pdf.

Zeitoun, M. (2012) *Power and water in the Middle East*, London: I.B. Tauris.

NINE

Learning and teaching: reflections on an environmental justice school for activists in South Africa

Bobby Peek and Jeanne Prinsloo

Introduction

'I live in a highly polluted community called Merebank [in south Durban] that is surrounded by industries. I want to learn more about how they are affecting the environment and how these effects are impacting on our health.'

'Growing up in a rural village I was surrounded by nature. When I went to primary school I used to cross two streams. On some days I could not go to school because the streams were overflowing and I ran the risk of being swept away. When I got to high school I still had to cross the two rivers. There was no longer the risk of being swept away, not because I was getting bigger, but because the water also became less and less. This bothered me. It's water. Water is important!'

'There is a notable reduction in space for action by Mozambican civil society, particularly for organisations that work with controversial issues (resettlement of communities, mining). Our organisation is regarded by government as anti-development.... The multinationals act as if they own this land, they grab, displace families and steal land, intimidate and use violence before the eyes of our unfazed governors.'

This chapter focuses on the Environmental Justice School (EJS) run by the environmental justice NGO, groundWork. Over four successive schools (of 20 people at a time, selected in pairs from the different organisations), participants have included black working-class men and women from both urban and rural spaces, mostly members of community-based organisations or activist groups. As the overleaf quotations, written by participants before their arrival at the school indicate, their contexts vary. Most live on the fencelines in urban areas and confront the consequences of industrial pollution and mineral extraction. Given the high rate of unemployment in South Africa, most are unemployed, apart from the self-employed waste pickers, who recycle waste for a livelihood. Those who live in rural spaces encounter environmental challenges of a different order and they increasingly have to defend their land against enclosure, notably by the mining industries. A few participants come from environmental NGOs. Over the years most have been South Africans, with a sprinkling from Namibia, Mozambique, Zimbabwe, Angola, Kenya and one from Sweden.

The choices made in designing the EJS are underpinned by an awareness of the spaces that the activists inhabit and the complex of power relations that produce the environmental injustices that affect their lives. Resistance to the ongoing environmental injustices fostered by a neoliberal economic order impels the nascent environmental justice movement that has emerged in South Africa since the 1980s (Khan, 2002), including groundWork and its EJS. To discuss the nature and form that the EJS has taken, we first provide an overview of the broad South African context before turning our attention to the specific circumstances that gave rise to the school, and the cyclical process that has informed the construction and reworking of the curriculum over several years. We then reflect on the EJS in terms of what it sets out to achieve, drawing on the evaluative responses of students as well as on interviews that we conducted with former activist participants.

The South African scenario

More than two decades after the election of Nelson Mandela as the first democratically elected South African president in 1994, disappointment and anger characterise many conversations about the current state of South Africa. Greater social equality was reasonably anticipated from a government that had promised to work towards 'peace and a better life for all' (ANC, 1994). The commitment to 'a better life for all' has been frequently repeated by the ruling party and its leaders, particularly during elections, and seeks to reassure that the 'development' of all South Africans is their serious concern.

Current President Cyril Ramaphosa has reiterated 'development' as government's priority; his interpretation of it is identifiable in the increased number of mining expansion licences granted within the first months of his presidency.

The state's notion of development is framed within a capitalist discourse that equates it with neoliberal economic growth. David Harvey (2010) has described 'accumulation by dispossession' as the process through which the rich get richer at the expense of the poor. While the mainstream Left of the 20th century directed their attention to the exploitation of labour, and in the process neglected other processes of dispossession, Harvey argues that neoliberal capitalism involves increasing forms of primary accumulation alongside labour exploitation.

Environmental injustices are effectively imposed on people through the exercise of three mechanisms of capitalism, subsequently referred to as the three Es:

> By polluting them, degrading their environments and coercing labour to work for less than it costs to live. This is called **externalisation** because corporations get a free ride by off-loading costs onto communities, workers, the public purse and the environment. (See Figure 9.1)

Figure 9.1: Externalisation

By dispossessing them and by privatising common or public goods. This is called **enclosure** because it eliminates or subordinates non-capitalist systems of production, so ensuring that all escape routes are closed and people cannot survive without capitalism. (See Figure 9.2)

Figure 9.2: Enclosure

ENCLOSURE

By **excluding** them from the political and economic decisions that lead to their being polluted or dispossessed. (Hallowes and Munnik, 2007: 13) (See Figure 9.3)

As in most southern countries, accumulation by dispossession in South Africa is a continuing process through, inter alia, the expansion of mineral extraction in rural spaces. The numbers of people affected by enclosures, and so made destitute, increase daily, resulting in South Africa being one of the most unequal countries in the world. Recent statistics indicate that more than half the population are poor, with poverty being correlated with race, class, gender and geographical location (Stats SA, 2017). Households headed by black women are most likely to be in the poorest 20%, women are poorer than men are and the poorest people are rural women living in the former apartheid-created Bantustans. The poor face higher effective inflation than the rich do, and many lack clean water, energy and food. The

Figure 9.3: Exclusion

EXCLUSION

unemployment rate, including those who have given up looking for work, stands at over 36%, and only 43% of working-age people are employed.

The country's neoliberal economy is dominated by the minerals–energy complex, in which a small number of large corporations hold wealth and power, aided and abetted by state policies, regulations and cheap energy. This concentration of power has resulted in South Africa having the dubious distinction of being among the most intensive carbon and energy economies in the world, a polluting economy that relies on coal as its primary energy source. The effects of the resultant pollution are felt most forcefully by millions of South Africans who live on the fencelines of dirty industries.

The policies approved by the African National Congress (ANC) are consistent with its neoliberal economic approach, including privatisation of water and the sale of electricity at below cost to multinational corporations. At the same time, a complex network of patronage characterised the presidency of Jacob Zuma with growing levels of corruption, nepotism and cronyism. State capture by an Indian family, the Guptas, through their relationship with Zuma, his family and his appointees, was established through investigations, including one by the Public Protector (Public Protector, South Africa, 2016). A robust investigative media and resistant set of opposition parties ensure that such abuse is articulated in the public domain. Regardless, the complex power relations ensure that certain loyalties persist in line with personal interests rather than for a better life for all.

The current organisation of power in South Africa and, indeed, the continent as a whole has its roots in colonialism (Mamdani, 1996). In the first instance, 'divide and rule' was the strategy of imperial capitalism that ensured the division of the population in African countries along the lines of race and ethnicity. Linked to this, and pertinent to this publication, is the usage of the terms development and community. Apartheid was euphemistically termed 'separate development'. The nature of the separation relied on constituting South Africans as racial subjects in the first instance and then creating a hierarchy in which the white colonisers were considered as citizens with the rights associated with the imperial country. The rule of indigenous people was indirect (Mamdani, 2001) and depended on 'containerized' indigenous people divided in terms of tribes located in rural areas, each with its own laws and economic obligations and answerable to the authority of the chief (Mamdani, 2001: 22), an authority granted by the state. Within customary spaces women were constituted as subordinate legal minors.

The expanded sense of democratisation since 1994 has not transformed this space of 'decentralized despotism' (Mamdani, 1996: 33): while power has been deracialised, rural areas have not been detribalised. Rather, the two-pronged division that is the legacy of colonialism – between town and country and between ethnicities (Mamdani 1996: 26) – continues. Customary power remains significant in terms of environmental justice in the current context. Secret deals made by some traditional leaders enable corporate enclosure of resources and are justified as development and job creation.

This organisation of power deploys the term community in ways that obscure heterogeneity and difference and fail to challenge the unequal power relations. People frequently use 'my community' to speak of cultural belonging along tribal lines. The idea of a white 'community' similarly erases the history of wars and struggles along language, religious and political lines. 'Community', in recent parlance, signifies black (African) people and, specifically, the economically marginalised.

It is increasingly evident that in post-apartheid South Africa corporates have gained more power and increasingly resist any form of mandatory regulation to enforce accountability (Butler and Hallowes, 2002). Clearly, then, resistance against environmental injustices must occur through active participation in official policy processes and on the fenceline.

Environmental justice as a resistant discourse

The environmental justice movement in South Africa has emerged within the context sketched earlier. In the country's earlier history, concern with the environment was articulated within a nature conservation discourse that foregrounded wildlife protection and landscape preservation (Khan, 2002). In contrast, South Africans marginalised by apartheid engaged with struggles framed as relating to social justice, including access to education, health and housing. While there is an overlap in struggles for social justice and environmental justice, for groundWork environmental justice rests on a critique of the relations of power that underlie the neoliberal economic system and its accompanying environmental destruction. It is mindful of the biophysical environment and acknowledges the consequences of the economic order on the ecology and the planet, and recognises the unequal distribution of economic advantage and negative environmental impacts.

The South African Constitution of 1996 was formulated as rights based and includes an environment-related right: 'Everyone has the right to an environment that is not harmful to their health or wellbeing and to have the environment protected through reasonable legislative measures' (Republic of South Africa, 1996: 9). The National Environmental Management Act 107 of 1998 states that 'environmental justice must be pursued so that adverse environmental impacts shall not be distributed in such a manner as to unfairly discriminate against any person, particularly vulnerable and disadvantaged persons'. While these policies can be counted as victories resulting from strategic and courageous engagement on the part of diverse social actors, environmental injustices continue and intensify.

The establishment of groundWork

In 1999 groundWork was founded as an environmental justice NGO. It understands environmental justice as being about 'empowered people in relations of solidarity and equity with each other and in non-degrading and positive relationships with their environments' (Butler and Hallowes, 2002: 6), and its purpose as supporting activist groups in communities affected by industrial pollution in the first instance, initially with people active on the fencelines of the major oil refineries, waste dumps and incinerators. groundWork's current campaigns include Climate and Energy Justice; Resistance to Coal; Environmental Health; and Waste Governance.

It views its role as enabling local resistance and the mobilisation of people acting on fencelines through supporting them in building organisations and providing technical and legal support. The community-based organisations, groundWork's essential partners, articulate their own concerns in relation to the powerful stakeholders of government and corporates. They inhabit marginalised spaces with complex sets of power relations and are aware that they are the objects of exploitation by capital. Their task is not only to resist, but also to develop awareness of these complicated power relations and their implications. In this context, the need for a strong, well-coordinated environmental justice lobby becomes increasingly clear.

groundWork's Environmental Justice School

From its inception, the EJS has been informed by an experiential cycle of seeing, judging and acting. Formulated by a Belgian priest engaging with Christian workers, the method became influential in the ecclesiastical resistance in apartheid South Africa (Nunes, 2000). The forms of seeing and judging that led to the formation of the school occurred on two levels. First, groundWork staff had been engaging intensely with people on the fencelines of polluting oil refineries, mines, steel mills, waste incinerators and toxic dumpsites in poor, working-class black neighbourhoods in urban and peri-urban industrialised spaces. The understandings gained led them to recognise the need for activists to be better equipped to organise and mobilise in relation to their specific struggles. Second, their awareness and critique of the global South African context and neoliberal economic order that produces poverty and dispossession led to the decision to create a school that would serve activists living on the fenceline.

The designing of the school constituted other moments of seeing, judging and acting, including scrutinising and consulting a range of progressive education initiatives and materials, both locally and internationally, and producing a draft curriculum. The first EJS design was produced in 2007; it was only in 2014 that the first residential school was run, over an intense two weeks. The school is conceptualised within the radical and critical approach of popular education and in keeping with the understanding of environmental justice outlined previously. Rather than focusing on reform that is superficial, its intention is to effect profound and systemic change in the long term and to shift power relations to effect greater democratic participation so that people might exercise more control over their immediate environment. Its aim is thus to build a cadre of informed environmental justice activists who will contribute towards the mobilisation, resistance and transformation to a just society.

The approach of the EJS has its intellectual roots in the understandings of hegemonic struggle of Antonio Gramsci (1999) and the critical education of Paulo Freire (1970). Gramsci's realisation that certain sets of ideas gained purchase and achieved hegemonic status led him to consider how consent is achieved within a society, or, in other words, how particular values and norms are accepted and become the 'common sense' of a society. He noted that intellectuals tend to act to legitimate or gain consent, albeit passive, to the status quo: 'traditional intellectuals' serve as 'the dominant groups' "deputies"' (Gramsci, 1999: 145). He proposed developing contesting intellectualism based on historico-political analysis. The new intellectual would engage 'in active participation in practical life, as constructor, organiser, permanent persuader' (Gramsci, 1999: 103) to confront, trouble and rethink 'common sense' in order to articulate different explanations and visions that contest the prevailing assumptions and norms. Consistent with these ideas, the EJS seeks to support the creation of organic environmental justice intellectuals through a curriculum design that interrogates the common sense of capital and all that attends it and develops critical awareness of this process to inform action.

Paulo Freire placed an emphasis on critical consciousness activated through the process of conscientisation (Freire, 1970) that leads to purposeful resistance and action. Consistent with Freire's position, the EJS acknowledges that emancipatory education needs to be experiential and so begin with people interrogating their situations. Arnold et al (1991) propose a five-stage experiential spiral including: the experience of the participants; looking for patterns in these experiences; adding new information and theory; practising skills, strategising and planning for action; and, finally, application in action. The spiral is re-entered with reflections on this action, and so on.

The EJS picks up on this spiral in its use of 'see, judge, act'. It begins with the group 'seeing' the concrete reality of their lives. To move to the next stage of judging their situation, participants need to be able to contextualise these circumstances and to understand how the political and socio-economic forces produce these circumstances. This necessary basis can then inform decisions about actions to resist, challenge and change their situation. In other words, an informed and critical understanding of hegemonic power relations is a prerequisite for any action. Freire linked notions of emancipatory pedagogy and 'praxis' (Freire, 1970). Praxis refers to informed action or, in other words, to the process of taking practical action while acting within a theoretical framework of thought. Consequently, this approach presumes that such education is critical in that it is concerned with unequal power relations and seeks to challenge them. It thus recognises that the struggle for hegemony is never finally and completely successful and so can be resisted and changed. Reflection is key and must occur at every point in the process.

EJS programme

In designing the curriculum process, at the outset we posed this question for ourselves: 'What do activists need to know in order to act and resist effectively?' Three aims were identified for the activists, namely:

- to acquire a strong knowledge base pertaining to contemporary environmental justice challenges – knowledge of the broad economic and social contexts, both local and global, that give rise to environmental injustices;
- to develop the skills appropriate for working within social groupings or communities for conceiving and managing campaigns and resistance strategies against environmental injustices; and
- to act creatively and strategically to foster social justice within a democratic framework.

Three major strands of learning constitute the curriculum design. The first provides a broad knowledge base of the neoliberal capitalist order of the economy and its critique, and the second addresses particular environmental injustices under the broad heading of the Gigantic Waste Creation Machine. These provide the opportunities for seeing and judging. The third strand focuses on Building Activism for Environmental Justice. The experiential dimension requires that participants link the ideas and knowledge to their own worlds.

As mentioned previously, the 'three Es' (externalisation, enclosure and exclusion) are employed to explain the workings of capital and are consistent with Harvey's notion of 'accumulation by dispossession' (2010). Introduced early in the process, the three Es are then revisited by the different facilitators in relation to different topics.

Strand one, our world, rehearses the aspects of seeing and judging, first at a personal level, then at a global level. 'This is my life!' calls for participants' personal histories and narratives to be presented and displayed on the walls, to be returned to during subsequent conversations. Over the course of the schools, we recognised the need to make this more central to the activist process, and this stage has expanded to include the creation of maps of their worlds, which participants add to at different stages and which later inform their presentations of and reflections on their activist projects.

To facilitate 'judging', the global ordering of the economy and societies is introduced through the prism of the three Es to pose the question 'Why is the world this way?' and to consider how power works in society. The history of capitalism, particularly imperialism and colonialism, and the attendant questions of what constitutes development, patriarchy and race are the broad focus here before the next question, 'How did South Africa get to this point?' turns attention to colonialism, capital expansion and the emergence of the mineral-energy complex (Fine and Rustomjee, 1996) in South Africa. The final element of this strand relates to rights and regulations relating to environmental degradation in South Africa.

Strand two moves to seeing and judging more specific moments of environmental degradation and injustices as the consequence of this economic ordering. Capitalism is viewed both as a 'gigantic accumulation machine' and 'a gigantic waste creation machine' (Hallowes and Munnik, 2008: 79). 'Waste' is the by-product of the neoliberal economic order that is dumped and contaminates the commons. This strand includes the topics of environment and people's health; waste in the air; waste in the water; waste of land and food; and solid waste: people and justice. Both strands introduce complex sets of ideas that are incrementally introduced and developed through games, case studies, film, toxic tours of industrial and urban degradation and various practical activities.

Strand three, the activist strand, draws on these ideas and is threaded throughout the course, and it is to this end that the EJS is designed. Prior to EJS, the participants consult with their organisation about possible activist projects to work on. Linking to Freire's notion of praxis, the strand stresses constant reflection using see, judge, act. The interactive sessions draw on certain advocacy models that require identifying the problem, clarifying the purpose, knowing the facts, understanding the system, timing, identifying target groups, anticipating obstacles, developing and delivering messages, building support, mobilising resources and monitoring and evaluation. Here, personal experiences are central to the process. Equally important is the introduction of a broad repertoire of potential activist strategies to introduce an expanded range of possibilities fit for different contexts and circumstances. The strand culminates in the specific projects worked on during the course of the school with the support of mentors appointed from groundWork staff.

The first iteration of the EJS in 2014 lasted for two weeks and, in response to participants' evaluations, the school was expanded to three weeks in 2015 and subsequently to three weeks with an additional return week three months later in 2016. During these three months the activists undertake their projects, or at least set them in motion. When they return for their final contact week, a structured cycle of seeing, judging and acting is used again to reflect on their projects and to plan ahead.

Reflections

At the end of each of the four schools, participants have undertaken evaluations of their EJS. They indicate that they value the EJS experience. They declare their determination to be informed activists and to engage with their projects on returning home. What is notable is the sense of empowerment that they describe: "equipped and informed", "highly empowered and encouraged by other comrades", "empowered, strong, capable and energised", "very excited", "more confident" and so on. Several identify their 'aha' moment in relation to learning about capitalism and the three Es; they consider this as valuable for their own seeing and judging.

While these evaluations speak to the responses at the close of the school, another important indicator of the value of the school lies in what activists do on their return home, first, in terms of their immediate project, and second, in the longer term. The projects undertaken vary enormously, and here we make brief reference to some of those initiated during the EJS that have been taken forward the spirit of the EJS, first those of fenceline activists and then those of NGO participants. In some cases participants have vanished back into their worlds without engaging with the organisations that identified them. Such attrition, while disappointing, is not surprising. However, many participants continue to actively take their struggles forward, much in the spirit of the intellectuals Gramsci envisaged. We now present two of the stories from participants whom we interviewed when working towards this chapter. Their accounts indicate how they are deeply engaged in complex struggles and they note the significant value they attribute to their EJS experience. In our reflections we deem these not only as success stories, but as stories that sensitise us continuously to the complexity of these struggles.

Mmathopelo Thobejane was born and lives in Sekukuneland in the Limpopo Province, a deep rural area dotted with mines in what was once an apartheid Bantustan. The land was originally "farming land", but "mining has wrecked the land". The streams are polluted and people are no longer interested in farming. She speaks of the enclosure of land by referring to the removal of people "and their graves as well" (the graves of ancestors hold deep cultural significance). Her analysis of the situation includes recognition of how people are being excluded from decision making. In effect, she is speaking of all three of the mechanisms that produce environmental injustice.

Following EJS, Mmathopelo returned to Sekukuneland to work on her project. In addition, she has been instrumental in the creation of the Sekukuneland Environmental Justice Network. This organisation decided to focus on a single pertinent issue, the pollution of its stream by the mines. Strategically, this focus incorporates the interests of livestock owners "because they are losing their livestock". Cattle hold a very important place in the cultural and economic life in this and other traditional spaces in Africa. Mmatophela acknowledges that livestock owners hold authority within this patriarchal space and "they are the ones to make people recognise the problem". In this way the livestock owners' interests become aligned with the struggle of the women who collect water and grow food.

The struggle has been taken to stakeholders at state and corporate levels and, significantly, the community decided against taking their issues to the Department of Mineral Resources charged with overseeing mining operations: "the mine did not want to engage with us". Instead they managed to get the attention of the water-quality manager of the district municipality and the Department of Water and Sanitation (DWAS), who took up their issue with the mining company. "That is when the mine started to respond – to the Department's emails and not ours ... We managed to sit with the government and the mine." At this stage a task team has been formed consisting of DWAS and "three representatives from the mine, three from the organisation and three from livestock owners". This is a remarkable story of tenaciousness, careful strategising and a determination to have community voices count. Mmathapelo also faces challenges as a woman in this patriarchal order: "community people do not want to take us seriously because you are a woman", yet she "keep[s] on pushing. I do not care what people say". This successful attempt to engage with the mines has, however, begun to shift attitudes: "because we are succeeding people are now interested. They are recognising us – they are asking how we get to sit with the mines."

Promise Mabilo, active in one of the organisations that make up Highveld Environmental Justice Network (HEJN), also speaks of the systemic challenges that the network confronts. The Highveld, with South Africa's central coal basin and rich agricultural lands, is exceedingly polluted. Living in the eMalahleni ('place of coal') township, she identifies the major environmental justice issues that people confront as emanating from the mining industry: "we are surrounded by those mines. They blast and we see the dust coming up [from the ground]. Our houses are cracking. People are suffering to get water. It's very scarce in the area and the air pollution is high. We are running out of water. The water streams are contaminated by the industries that are close to the streams that the community rely on."

Promise had heard about environmental justice in about 2006, but "did not take it seriously". However, when her son developed asthma and she had to resort to state health provision, she "started standing up to join the environmental group. I could understand the illness because of pollution."

While HEJN has communicated in writing to both mines and government about the impacts of mining, it is ignored and therefore has become sceptical about the will of government officials who merely deflect responsibility to the mines. Moreover, local government stands accused of failing to consult with people on other issues that impact on this environment, including the installation of a bulk sewage installation in a wetland. Despite being approached, government officials denied that they have to consult the community. Only after the threat of legal action did they provide information that the organisation had requested. What Promise's account reveals is the complexity of the activists' work and the necessity of knowledge about rights and procedures.

Participants from NGOs have developed projects of a different order, and two other 'schools' have come into being. A participant from Mozambique has developed an environmental justice school under the auspices of the environmental justice organisation Justiça Ambiental, based in the capital, Maputo, and designed to serve the activists it supports. It has run several smaller schools in Portuguese and in sites where people share particular forms of dispossession, notably as a consequence of mining ventures. Participants from the Centre for Environmental Rights in South Africa have designed a short school for activists so that they might better understand the legal rights and regulations relating to the environment and use them effectively to challenge environmental injustices and hold powerful actors accountable.

Finally, we turn to a few of the experiences and challenges that the school itself confronts. EJS operates in a space with a triad of players: the school, groundWork and the partner organisations that groundWork works with. Nurturing informed and confident activists potentially serves the interests of these organisations, and thus groundWork's work. However, both parties work intensely and often reactively in the environmental justice field; because of these work contexts, the EJS often becomes a casualty of this busy-ness. In spite of signed agreements, timelines and agreed processes, there is a tendency for groundWork staff and organisations to leave administration, decision making and participant selection to the last minute. At times they send forward candidates who are simply unsuitable. This is problematic on two levels. First, poor selection can result in undermining people, should they feel unable to participate meaningfully. Second, it impacts negatively on the school as a participatory learning space.

Another thorny issue in relation to selection pertains to language. The EJS is conducted in English, whereas participants speak various mother-tongue languages. Moreover, few of the presenters are fluent in a range of languages. While the EJS recognises the limitation of not working in people's first language, we do stipulate that participants must be able to speak and read English at approximately school-leaving level. When a fair number of participants who battle with English attend, the level of discussion and effective participation is negatively affected.

Then, the nature of the pedagogy chosen introduces a further challenge. It requires that the selection of people to run specialised sessions has to factor in whether they will be sympathetic to the pedagogical approach and prepared to design their sessions accordingly. In addition, groundWork staff are not educators in the first instance and their experience of education has been mostly of a more authoritarian, top-down approach. This has required an intervention in the form of a workshop on popular education, and which needs to be ongoing. In addition, the design of the curriculum presumes that groundWork staff mentor participants in planning their activist projects during the school and carrying them back to the field. Mentoring is a pedagogical process, and at the outset groundWork staff were not given sufficient guidance. We have become aware that the EJS requires interventions in the form of workshops and debriefings annually. After all, there are changes in staff; but more importantly, learning to teach is a constant and iterative process.

Reflections on the EJS and its needs frequently occurs outside the formal processes of evaluation. groundWork staff's experiences with activists far exceed their roles as EJS facilitators and mentors, for they constantly learn in the field too, and their reflections on these experiences impact on their engagement during EJS. The point to be made here is that not all reflections are formal, but rather the drip, drip, drip of gradual insights.

Conclusion

In concluding, we return to the interviewees. While their successes and drive are their own, they are explicit that the EJS has been an important and enabling experience. Mmathapelo spoke particularly about the importance of a network of activists. Since the EJS, she and her organisation have been active in environmental justice initiatives that incorporate other activists. She retains contact with her small EJS network – "a network to talk about issues with other people". This is consistent with the EJS's intention to develop a cadre or network of activists. Promise too describes the EJS as very significant in her life: "it made me a different person today. I did not know I had such power to engage in things happening in the area." She views herself as a "powerful understanding person"; she feels that she has the knowledge base she needs in her work "to tackle the impacts caused by industry". People who are reluctant to engage in public fora, "one by one they will knock on my door to ask me more about what I said in the mass meeting". She proposes that more people should attend the EJS, cautioning against those who want "just to chill". By mentioning this she is touching on one of the challenging aspects – the identification of appropriate people from the various organisations, people who will learn from what the school can offer and become engaged activists, or, as Promise puts it, "people who are responsible and helpful and will feedback". Promise is realistic and laments the lack of action: "we take a long walk for the struggle". Her impatience grows out of her activist zeal and desire to work for that elusive "better life".

The various processes of exclusion from decision making and the externalities that activists endure are deeply felt. Promise's account is an angry one and speaks to the cavalier manner in which local and national government and corporate representatives treat poorer communities in the Highveld. Certainly, for Mmatapelo's rural community the enclosure, or attempts at it, are more raw than for Promise, who lives in an urban space. There, enclosure is more elusive, as people live in townships originally built to serve industry; these circumstances are the consequence of the history of capitalist enclosure over centuries along the lines of race. She is born into this space of dispossession.

The account we have presented here is a partial one and we are mindful of the ongoing challenges that we face and how we have to engage in a constant cycle of reflection and action. Yet, our challenges pale into insignificance when considering the doggedness and courage that the participants display in their struggle against environmental injustices. The narratives we heard are produced by environmental activists who are able to *see* the issues, *judge* how best to address them and then *act* strategically from an informed base. They inhabit specific spaces and at particular moments in time, and the complex decisions they make come from a sensitivity to their lived worlds, a necessary characteristic of the organic intellectual.

References

ANC (African National Congress) (1994) *Manifesto 1994*, http://www.anc.org.za/content/1994-national-elections-manifesto.

Arnold, R., Burke, B., James, C., Martin, D. and Thomas, B. (eds) (1991) *Educating for a Change*, Toronto: Between the lines.

Butler, M. and Hallowes, D. (2002) 'Methodology for state of environmental justice'. Unpublished paper.

Fine, B. and Rustomjee, Z. (1996) *The political economy of South Africa: from minerals-energy complex to industrialisation*, Boulder, CO: Westview Press.

Freire, P. (1970) *Pedagogy of the oppressed*, New York NY: Continuum.

Gramsci, A. (1999) *Selections from the prison notebooks of Antonio Gramsci*, London: Elec Books.

Hallowes, D. and Munnik, V. (2007) *Peak poison: The elite energy crisis and environmental justice*, Pietermaritzburg: groundWork.

Hallowes, D. and Munnik, V. (2008) *Wasting the nation: Making trash of people and places*, Pietermaritzburg: groundWork.

Harvey, D. (2010) *The enigma of capital and the crisis of capitalism*, London: Profile Books.

Khan, F. (2002) 'The roots of environmental racism and the rise of environmental justice in the 1990s', in D. McDonald (ed) *Environmental justice in South Africa*, Athens: Ohio University Press and Cape Town: UCT Press, pp 15–48.

Mamdani, M. (1996) *Citizen and subject. Contemporary Africa and the legacy of late colonialism*, Cape Town: David Philip.

Mamdani, M. (2001) 'Beyond settler and native as political identities: Overcoming the political legacy of colonialism', *Comparative Studies in Society and History*, 43(4): 651–64.

Nunes, M. (2000) 'The young Christian workers and the struggle for a non-racial society', *Innovation*, 20: 38–40.

Public Protector, South Africa (2016) *State of capture*. Report 6 of 2016/17, 14 October, https://cdn.24.co.za/files/Cms/General/d/4666/3f63a8b78d2b495d88f10ed060997f76.pdf.

Republic of South Africa (1996) *The Constitution of the Republic of South Africa*, http://www.justice.gov.za/legislation/constitution/SAConstitution-web-eng.pdf.

Stats SA (2017) 'Poverty trends in South Africa: An examination of absolute poverty between 2006 and 2015', Report No. 03-10-06. http://www.statssa.gov.za/publications/Report-03-10-06/Report-03-10-062015.pdf.

TEN

The environment as a site of struggle against settler-colonisation in Palestine

Abeer al-Butmeh, Zayneb al-Shalalfeh and Mahmoud Zwahre with Eurig Scandrett

Introduction

The Zionist settler-colonisation of Palestine is primarily an ecological distribution conflict (Martínez-Alier, 2002) because it is focused entirely on dispossession of land, water and other environmental resources. The state of Israel since 1948, and its military occupation of the West Bank and Gaza Strip since 1967, as well as precursor Zionist colonisation under British mandatory and Ottoman empirical rule, have been predicated on dispossession of Palestinian resources. Unlike classical colonisation, which exploits indigenous labour for the purpose of capital accumulation in the colonising state, settler-colonialism has no long-term interest in indigenous labour. On the contrary, the settler colonial process actively expels or exterminates indigenous people in the process of resource dispossession (Veracini, 2010). Palestinian resistance to settler-colonisation should therefore be understood as a struggle for environmental justice.

In classical colonialism, value is extracted from the resources and labour of the colonised lands for the benefit of a colonising (usually European) country (Veracini, 2010). In such contexts, community development has often been used to integrate indigenous peoples into social, economic and political structures that serve the interests of the colonial power. By contrast, the purpose of settler-colonisation is access to land and resources by a settler population expelled from their origins, usually in Europe. The settler-colonist therefore seeks to remove and replace the indigenous population and has therefore largely not employed community development strategies. Britain, which had used community development strategies extensively elsewhere through its Colonial Office, did not do so during its Mandate of

Palestine, where the policy objective was explicitly to facilitate Zionist settler aspirations rather than Palestinian economic, political or labour integration.

Palestinian popular resistance to settler-colonialism has taken a range of forms, from scholarship and legal challenge, through non-cooperation and non-violent confrontation to armed struggle and the occasional targeting of civilians In the current context of an Israeli settler state, Israel's occupation of the West Bank, annexation of East Jerusalem and military blockade of the Gaza Strip, Palestinian community development has been employed in ways that both resist and collude with Zionist settler-colonisation. The distinction between collusion and resistance is a central tension, in response to environmental justice struggles against the settler-colonisation of Palestine.

Environmental justice and settler-colonialism

Dispossession of land and resources is at the heart of the settler-colonising process. By the beginning of the 20th century the early Zionist colonisers in Palestine had adopted a strategy of conquest of land by Jewish labour for their utopian experiments in social organisation and agricultural production, and established a range of institutions to facilitate this, including the JNF (1901) to obtain land exclusively for Jewish occupation (Davis and Lehn, 1988) and the Histadrut (1920) for exclusively Jewish labour (Piterberg, 2008). As Simon demonstrates in Chapter Eight, the JNF has been a means of ethnic cleansing and environmental injustice throughout its history, while portraying itself as an agent of environmental protection (see also Davis, 2010; Sahibzada, 2010; Benjamin et al, 2011; Sawalha et al, 2011). It contributed to the Nakba (Khalidi, 1992), and since 1948, as an arm of the Israeli state it has enforced apartheid discrimination within the Green Line, and facilitated the ethnic cleansing of Palestinian Bedouin in the Naqab/Negev desert. The Histadrut, meanwhile, has continued to pursue exclusionary and discriminatory labour practices while presenting itself internationally as a trade union.

Within the 1967 military occupation areas, Israeli policies in the West Bank pursue settler-colonial objectives, preventing farmers from reaching their land, justifying and legitimising barriers, evictions and confiscations. Access is blocked in the name of military orders, through selective confiscations, denial of permits, through classifying land as having natural or strategic value or through straightforward violent intimidation. Agricultural land is contaminated with raw sewage from settlements or the leachate of unregulated waste dumps. Untended land is regarded as abandoned and confiscated by the occupying state. Lack of regulation leads to pollution from Palestinian waste recycling (Applied Research Institute Jerusalem, 2012), construction (Gharib, 2013) and industrial development. Thus, through a range of mechanisms, Israel is progressively dispossessing Palestinians of their resources (al-Butmeh et al, 2013).

In Gaza, where 70% of the population are refugees, the occupation takes the form of a blockade and periodic military attack, with resultant environmental injustice. Exit from and entry to the Gaza Strip is tightly controlled by the Israeli military. Access to fresh water is close to zero (UNCTAD, 2015). The southern end of the coastal aquifer on which Gaza depends is depleted to the extent that it is saline with backfill from the sea and the over-pumped Israeli side, and close to collapse. Refill of the aquifer has been blocked by the damming and abstraction of water from Wadi Gaza in Israel (Koppelman and Alshalalfeh, 2012; al-Shalalfeh et al, 2018). Most of the agricultural land is located around the periphery of the Strip and farmers are regularly targeted by Israeli snipers (Safi, 2015). Israel imposes severe restrictions on the entry of agricultural materials, from fertilisers to wells. Internal movement to the West Bank and export of agricultural produce is significantly limited by time, quantity and arbitrary checks. Fishing, once a major industry in Gaza, is likewise decimated, as Israel's imposed coastal exclusion zone – and regular attacks on boats within it – restricts fishing, unsustainably, to young and reproducing fish that inhabit the (contaminated) area closest to the shore.

In the summer of 2014 Israeli bombardments from the air, land and sea resulted in over 2,000 dead, mostly civilian and around half of them children. Safi (2015) reports considerable additional damage to an already denuded environment in terms of food security, air quality, damage to water infrastructure, soil degradation, chemical contamination, coastal pollution and ecological destruction. Environmental health problems are considerable and expected to increase as a result of Israeli attacks, including the use of toxic chemicals in munitions (see also BMJ, 2009; Naim et al, 2012; Garrity, 2015).

Community development and anti-colonial struggle

The historical origins of community development in British colonial administration have been well documented. Mayo (1975), for example, describes the contradictory function of community development in British colonies, where it was promoted as a means to integrate colonised populations into a modern capitalist economy, democratic polity and labour discipline orientated around the interests of the colonial power in particular, and the western states in general. Based on an ideology of 'civilising' native populations, community development in British colonies was intended to improve the living standards of indigenous people – preferably at their own instigation, but failing which, with their participation (voluntary or otherwise) – while at the same time exploiting their labour and dispossessing their resources. Colonial community development policies were also designed to undermine threats from nationalist movements for independence, and later to shape movements for self-determination towards British interests post-independence, in particular to ensure that they were 'safe' from communism. Despite these manipulative intentions, community development programmes served to mobilise solidarity and collective action, and in some colonial contexts made considerable contributions to anti-colonial struggles (Mayo, 2008).

The colonial occupation of Palestine was unusual in several respects. The land has been successively colonised by British and Zionist occupiers since the Ottoman Empire, and it is Zionist settler-colonisation which has shaped social relations since the 19th century. The British Mandate of Palestine between 1920 and 1948, while falling under the remit of the Colonial Office, was orientated towards Zionist, not British, colonisation while protecting British interests. Mandates were established under the League of Nations and, although colonial, they were ostensibly designed to facilitate ultimate self-determination for the indigenous population. However, the Palestine Mandate embedded the policy of the Balfour Declaration of 1917, which committed the British government to 'the establishment in Palestine of a national home for the Jewish people'. Thus, rather than facilitating Palestinian self-determination, policies were generally orientated towards facilitating settler-colonisation by Zionist Jews, mostly from Europe (Kattan, 2009). The pressures on the Colonial Office and Mandate administration in Palestine were therefore somewhat different from other colonial contexts. Policies towards Palestinian Arabs were focused on repressing resistance to Zionist dispossession and there was little appetite for developing a Palestinian economy or encouraging Arab participation (Seikaly, 2015). European Jewish settlers imported their own models of community development such as the kibbutzim and labour Zionism, which were orientated towards the objectives of Jewish nationalism, utopian socialism, land appropriation, constructing a settlement economy and displacement of Arab labour. Although not operating along what would be regarded as community development principles, Palestinian welfare was somewhat dependent on the waqf (Muslim religious endowment) institutions well after this system had been abandoned in many other Islamic societies.

There was, however, a lively popular resistance movement against Zionist colonisation and British collusion, which grew in the 1920s and in particular following the 1929 riots and subsequent repression, and the 1936 general strike and Arab revolt, which was ultimately crushed in 1939 (Qumsiyeh, 2011; Cronin, 2017). As Qumsiyeh has shown, popular resistance has been a continuous part of Palestinian society throughout the Zionist occupation, at some times mobilising grassroots community development and at others involving more centralised structures on the basis of political expediency and possibility. This has periodically emerged into more active confrontation, such as the 1936–39 Arab revolt and the intifadas of 1987–93 and 2000–02. During the first intifada considerable numbers of Palestinians found themselves political prisoners in Israeli gaols, and this led to a structure of self-organised popular education in the prisons (Rosenfeld, 2011) that had a combined impact of strengthening the political organisation of the movement but ingraining a hierarchical structure somewhat divorced from community struggles. Some prisoners were released as part of the Oslo Accords, and elements of this structure transferred to the wider struggle, which potentially enabled a more focused, top-down organisation required for the armed uprising of the second intifada. After this was defeated in 2002, and the construction of the separation wall increased the confiscation of land, resistance became more grassroots and community led (Zwahre and Scandrett, 2014), mobilising the popular struggle committees.

In Palestine today there is another resurgence in popular resistance, employing principles of community development and non-violent confrontation as evidenced across the West Bank (the Bab al-Shams camp against the E1 extension of Jerusalem in 2013), Israel (Day of Rage against the Prawer Plan in 2013 (H, 2013)) and Gaza (March of Return in 2018 (Baroud, 2018)).

Community development as popular struggle

In Palestine, community development cannot be separated from popular resistance to the occupation that has been occurring since the early Zionist colonisation. As Qumsiyeh (2011) defines it, popular resistance involves six components:

Popular resistance in Palestine is a movement of direct action intended to accomplish what other similar movements have done before:
- pressuring opponents to understand the injustice that they engage in.
- weakening the grip of opponents on power.
- strengthening the community, including forms of empowerment and steadfastness (*sumud* in Arabic).
- bolstering the ability to withstand injustice and do something about it.
- building self-sufficiency and improving standards of living.
- achieving justice, including the right to return and self-determination. (Qumsiyeh, 2011: 30)

Just as community development under conditions of European colonisation was employed for the purposes of the colonisers and the colonised, so under Zionist settler-colonisation Palestinian community development can become part of the popular resistance or, alternatively, for normalising the occupation.

Al Ma'sara community centre

Al Ma'sara is a village in the Bethlehem Governorate with a population of under 1,000, with the main industry being agriculture (Applied Research Center Jerusalem, 2014). Land therefore constitutes a major source of employment, nearly all of which is in Area C and therefore under the control of the Israeli authorities. The village is surrounded by settlements that are continually encroaching on its land, and access to land is constrained by direct confiscation or indirectly through constant intimidation by settlers, their security guards and the Israeli military.

Use of A'-Shmoh Community Centre has changed over the last 20 years. In 2000–02, during the second intifada, when the Israeli army shut down most of the West Bank, schools were closed and movement was even more restricted than usual. In these extreme circumstances the community centre became a temporary school for the children, where they were taught by community volunteers.

When the intensity of violence subsided, schools reopened and the community centre focused on language lessons for the local community: English, French, Italian, Spanish, Hebrew: useful for the increasing numbers of European, North American and Israeli solidarity activists who were coming to the West Bank. In the following years land dispossession escalated: illegal settlement and infrastructure were constructed and the Apartheid Wall was erected. The A'-Shmoh community centre became a base for planning and training of non-violent resistance by villagers and international activists and a de facto headquarters of the Al Ma'sara Popular Struggle Coordinating Committee (Zwahre and Scandrett, 2014). In coordination with popular struggle committees in other villages, resistance took many forms: marches towards stolen land; blocking settlement roads; erecting 'counter' settlements; non-cooperation with the occupying authorities; varieties of unarmed and non-violent confrontation with the Israeli military with a view to forcing a crisis in the occupation and making the place ungovernable.

As settler and soldier violence increased and such direct confrontations became more dangerous, tactics changed and the popular resistance/community development diversified further: a kindergarten, financially supported by international supporters who are provided with information when family members are arrested; a women's cooperative producing traditional embroidery for international fair trade; alternative tourism for building international solidarity; community media training, arts projects, education in human rights: all take place in the context of anti-colonial resistance. Resource dispossession is being challenged through everyday Palestinian organic resistance. Living on and cultivating land right up to barriers with the illegal settlements, sometimes with international volunteers, helps to prevent confiscation. Farmers' cooperatives share the cultivation of the land of those farmers who are denied permits or imprisoned. Rights of access are insisted on, by group actions where necessary, and non-violent non-cooperation is practised with settlers and the military.

Youth and community in Aida refugee camp

The Aida Youth Center is among the few community centres in the Aida Camp in Bethlehem, of 5,500 inhabitants, all refugees from the 1948 Nakba and their descendants (UNRWA, 2015). The camp is now dominated by a 20-foot-high reinforced concrete wall punctuated by watch towers from which heavily armed Israeli soldiers monitor every activity. Although it is largely in Area A (and therefore 'security' is devolved to forces of the Palestinian Authority), incursions by Israeli soldiers into the camp are a regular occurrence and arbitrary arrests are frequent – including of children who are routinely held in administrative detention, without charge, trial, evidence or justification. Community centres such as the Aida Youth Center and nearby Lajee Center are regularly raided or fired at by soldiers. Peaceful protests are met with tear gas, rubber-coated bullets and, not infrequently, live ammunition (UNRWA, 2015). There have been instances of death threats announced by megaphone from armoured vehicles and of blackmail applied to Palestinian Authority police to repress their own children. In October 2015 an unarmed child was assassinated by an Israeli sniper (Levy, 2015).

Young people are presented with a narrow range of options between suicidal violence and traumatic collapse, but still regularly achieve imaginative yet fragile alternatives in the form of non-violent resistance. Community workers aim to facilitate this, and often demonstrate considerable creativity in combining arts, anger and defiance.

One project built a model 'train of return' for the purposes of carrying refugees back to the location of their family property now in Israel or on annexed land. The right of return of refugees is a legal entitlement according to international law, mandated by UN Security Council Resolution 194, yet persistently denied by Israel. The train was of course met with a violent response by Israeli soldiers. For the refugees of Aida, constructing and symbolically riding the train in the direction of the lands to which they are entitled (although many will never have seen) as far as the steel gates in the Israeli wall was a creative way to keep hope alive while confronting the Israeli forces with their rights. Such creativity in resistance – and community workers who promote it – is increasingly shunned by some international funders under pressure from Israel, either directly or via their own government, who prefer to fund projects that acquiesce in the occupation.

Food insecurity in Gaza

Food insecurity is an acute problem in the besieged and congested Gaza Strip, with a population of two million in a narrow strip of land 25 miles long (PCBS, 2017). Following the 2014 attack, the percentage of households requiring food assistance increased from 66% to 72% (Safi, 2015). The Union of Agricultural Works Committees (UAWC) operates at a level of grassroots organisation that seeks to challenge food insecurity through economic empowerment and technical support for farmers, and supporting cooperative work for improving quality and sharing of experiences. This work combines with political mobilisation in support of food sovereignty, which requires an end to occupation.

Community workers help to establish local committees of farmers and fisherfolk who organise collective responses to common concerns, most of which are dominated by the Israeli siege. The activities of UAWC include the repair and maintenance of wells and irrigation technology, largely dependent on the reuse and recycling of materials within Gaza: metals from bombed buildings are separated from rubble and smelted and recast in order to produce components for pumps. Where products can be imported, UAWC works with the committees to prioritise purchases of items of high capital value, such as boats, to optimise benefit for the community.

Export to Europe of high-value crops such as strawberries is an opportunity for income even though export licences controlled by Israel are unreliable. UAWC negotiates for international funds to invest in agricultural development for the committees for crop production, such as poly-tunnels and hydrological management systems to maximise crop production with limited access to water. Moreover, UAWC insists that food security is possible only with food sovereignty: for Palestinians to have control of their own resources. International funds that come with strings attached as concessions to the occupation are rejected as counter-productive.

The agricultural works committees with which UAWC collaborates become local sites of community mobilisation against the blockade that are independent of funding, NGOs and political parties, determining their own priorities, embedding inclusionary practices and linking social and economic development in the harshest of circumstances to political mobilisation challenging the blockade. In 2018, community organisations across the Gaza Strip mounted a sustained March of Return between Land Day (30 March) and Nakba Day (15 May), demanding their rights as refugees to return to the lands from which their families were evicted in 1948, and an end to the blockade imposed since 2007. Their unarmed protests were met with Israeli sniper fire, with 111 Palestinians killed and over 12,000 injured (Chughtai, 2018).

Women's resistance

In the Palestinian community, where women are still fighting for equal civil rights, the occupation policies and practices have different implications for women and men. The combination of the occupation policies and the conservatism of a large part of the Palestinian community hinders the status of women's rights. Also, it leads to a reproduction of violence against girls and women (see for example Clark et al, 2010; Haj-Yahia and Clark, 2013) that increases the exposure of women to risks from the occupation. Because women are believed to be less targeted by the occupation, their involvement in family affairs, which may involve movement inside the community, increases during tense political situations. Many women report taking over tasks from the men, such as buying bread and cultivating land, risking exposure to Israeli violence as well as harassment from Palestinian men (al-Shalalfeh, unpublished data). One activist woman explained that she was able to challenge the occupying soldiers by cultivating her land when her husband was in gaol to prevent it being confiscated (Zwahre, unpublished data).

Tense political situations not only give women more domestic tasks but also increase their political participation in acts of resistance. Some inside the Palestinian women's rights movement see that such situations give a woman a leadership role that she does not take in a normal situation but that she might be able to maintain at least partially. However, exposing women to more risk is just an extension to their traditional role, where they are expected to sacrifice for the greater interest of their families (al-Shalalfeh, unpublished data). The community is much less welcoming of women's representation in leadership roles, compared to delegating to them responsibilities that expose them to risks but do not increase their decision-making authority. In any case, the belief that women are less targeted than men is unfounded: sexual violence against Palestinian women has been explicitly advocated by Israeli police and Israeli political leaders (Aljazeera, 2017).

Women have been involved in the struggle for political and social independence since the 19th century, through charities at first and later politically. In 1893 women organised their first demonstration against the establishment of the first Jewish settlement in Palestine. In 1929, ten women were killed in the battle of Al Buraq. In 1929 women held their first national conference, which was followed by the formation of three women's unions. During the period from 1948 and 1967 women had active involvement in charitable work, which helped in relieving the bereaved families as well as equipping women professionally. In 1965 the General Union of the Palestinian Women was established as a popular feminist organisation. The establishment of the Palestinian Liberation Organization later in 1964 politicised the agenda of the women's movement as their role became one of representing the Palestinian political parties, providing social services and mobilising women for political action. This shift in the women movement's agenda was not reflected in their representation, constituting only 7.5% of the members in 1996. The work of the feminist movement was marked by the absence of a unified strategy until 1990, when the movement held a national conference in Jerusalem and drew a plan for the future. This conference coincided with the start of the peace negotiations. However, hopes for increased women's participation faded with the construction of the Palestinian National Authority. Women's organisations tried to gain independence from the political parties. In 1996 legislative elections, 49% of the voters but only 3.7% of the candidates were women. Five women were elected, which was a victory for the women's movement, although the Palestinian governments from 1997 to 2007 had only one or two women ministers. In the popular resistance, women have linked colonialism with sexism, both based on the under-estimation of women's power.

Community development as normalisation

Attempts at community development that do not embed resistance to the occupation collude with it. Any attempts to build community capacity, organise events, develop projects, identify collective learning needs, construct or renovate buildings or social enterprise activity inevitably encounter the Israeli military occupation. Community workers are faced with the choice of accommodating the occupation or confronting it. This causes particular dilemmas where funding is required. Almost all sources of funding for community development in Palestine are foreign, and many such international sources are reluctant to fund resistance to the occupation. In this context, funded community work can reify dehistoricised settler-colonial power relations and therefore promote Israeli objectives; development funding thus becomes 'political money' serving Israeli interests.

> International organizations – and many local Palestinian NGOs – project a view of development divorced from the power relations at play under Israeli settler colonialism ... As a result, the dominant development framework obfuscates, and thereby strengthens, the reality of Israeli settler colonialism in the oPt [occupied Palestinian territories]. (Hanieh, 2016: 33)

There are a number of community development initiatives in both Israel and the Occupied Palestinian Territory that serve to normalise the occupation and ensure that development is addressed only within terms set by Israel and the Zionist settler-colonial project – as well as a Zionist environmental movement eager to collaborate with Palestinians, strictly on Israel's terms (Tal, 2002). For example, the Israeli government has funded settlers of the illegal Efrata colony in the

West Bank to build ecological farms and agricultural schools on private Palestinian land from which Palestinians are excluded, and has called on international volunteers to work for this 'environmental' project.

In response to support in Britain for the Boycott, Divestment and Sanctions campaign, the Board of Deputies of British Jews (a body that claims to represent British Jewish interests but actually promotes pro-Zionist propaganda and attacks Palestinian solidarity in Britain) published *A better way than boycotts* (Moses, 2015), which lists initiatives that advocate 'peace' without decolonisation. Under the heading of 'Supporting peace by bringing people together', many of these appear to reflect community development values and practices to address collective problems while refusing to question the roots of the problem in the political context of settler-colonisation. The sub-text is that a solution to the 'conflict' can be achieved by Jews and Palestinians living peacefully together as coloniser and colonised, in which 'Israelis campaign for concessions to their government, and Palestinians doing the same with theirs' (Moses, 2015: 40). But Palestinian citizens of Israel are denied 'nationality rights', which limits on discriminatory grounds what concessions can legitimately be campaigned for. In the West Bank, Israelis in illegal settlements have full Israeli rights and access to the Israeli government, whereas Palestinians are subject to Israeli military governance. The complex of passes, permits and access rights across the occupied territories is part of the Matrix of Control imposed by Israel on Palestinians (Harper, 2000). Any concessions that question the settler-colonial foundation of the state are prohibited even in the Left's political ideology (Haaretz, 2017). At the time of writing, a precedent was established when the Israeli army evicted Palestinian communities on the basis of Military Order No. 757, which is meant to enable the evacuation of unauthorised settlement outposts: Israel has dealt with native Palestinian residents as illegal residents and has considered area C its own land (Hass, 2017).

One of these normalisation projects addresses environmental concerns in the region. EcoPeace Middle East (formerly Middle East Friends of the Earth – MEFoE) is an Israeli–Palestinian–Jordanian NGO that focuses on addressing environmental problems by bringing together activists of different ethnicities and nationalities, including through community development initiatives. The Board of Deputies its their work as:

> EcoPeace/MEFoE brings Palestinian, Israeli and Jordanian environmentalists to cooperate on environmental issues and to support sustainable development. Examples of successes

> include Israeli, Palestinian and Jordanian mayors agreeing to rehabilitate the Jordan River.
>
> The environment is a necessary area for mutual dependency, and this inter-dependence is highly significant. Since 1994, Jordan stores its water in Israel's Sea of Galilee in the winter, with Israel giving the water back to Jordan in the summer. EcoPeace Israel's Director, Gidon Bromberg, pointed to this project noting 'prior enemies can create positive interdependencies once they start trusting each other'. (Moses, 2015: 43)

EcoPeace's Jordan River project is an example of how normalisation operates to legitimise Israel's occupation. The Jordan River flows from the Syrian–Lebanese mountains, through the Sea of Galilee within the Israeli Green Line, to the Dead Sea along the border of the occupied West Bank and the Hashemite Kingdom of Jordan. Access to this water has been a source of conflict between Israel and the riparian Arab countries and populations of the region. There have been a number of internationally brokered attempts to provide an equitable sharing of access to this water between riparian countries on the basis of international law and conventions on transboundary watercourses. These have all been blocked by Israel, who instead constructed the National Water Carrier, a system of canals and pipelines that has diverted the Jordan water from the Sea of Galilee to central and southern Israel, forming a major source of water for domestic and agricultural use. The water flow in the Jordan River has since declined by more than 96%, with an accompanying ecological and social disaster (Isaac and Hilal, 2011).

EcoPeace's Jordan River Valley rehabilitation project involves a range of sustainable development and community development initiatives to manage and regenerate the valley, including increasing the amount of water being released from the Sea of Galilee. This has been possible only by collaborating with Israel (Abu Taleb, Alexander and Robillard, 2010), which has total control of the water, either directly or via the 'hydro-hegemony' through which Israel controls the Palestine Water Authority (Zeitoun, 2012). Access to the River Jordan is entirely determined by Israel, and is denied to Palestinians by military order. The EcoPeace approach to 'rehabilitation' of the Jordan Valley is dependent on, and therefore perpetuates, Israeli control through illegal annexation and military occupation (al-Shalalfeh, Napier and Scandrett, 2018). As a result of this and other normalisation projects,

EcoPeace was expelled from the Friends of the Earth International confederation.

Community development and international solidarity

Many authors have emphasised the centrality of solidarity to community development. For Bhattacharyya (2004), solidarity is the essence of community, whereas McCrea, Meade and Shaw (2017) argue that a practice of solidarity can be forged through the dialogue between community development practitioners and social movement activists. The struggle against settler-colonisation in Palestine has built international solidarity into its strategy, especially since 2005 with the Palestinian call for a campaign of Boycott, Divestment and Sanctions against Israel. The campaign focuses on three demands that represent the direct interests of three sectors of the Palestinian population: an end to the occupation of Arab lands (the populations of the Gaza Strip and West Bank, including East Jerusalem, as well as the Syrian Golan Heights); an end to discriminatory laws within Israel (Palestinian citizens of Israel); and the right of return of refugees (the refugee diaspora). This call has mobilised actions to promote boycotts of consumer products from Israel, of cultural events sponsored by Israel, of formal academic ties to Israeli universities; challenges to institutional links with Israel of trades unions; campaigns targeting companies that invest in or trade with Israel (especially arms manufacturers); and lobbying local authorities, churches, pension funds and so on to divest from Israeli companies. Such international solidarity efforts have facilitated considerable opportunities for community mobilisation and politicisation throughout the world, including in the global environmental justice movement.

The JNF has been subject to international mobilisations, in particular by Jewish groups opposed to Zionism. Fundraising efforts have been disrupted and legal and public campaigns have challenged the charitable and tax-exempt status of JNF branches throughout the world. Environmental organisations have joined with other civil society organisations publicly to distance themselves from the JNF's claim to be anything other than an agent of ethnic cleansing and colonisation.

Friends of the Earth Palestine, the Palestinian Boycott, Divestment and Sanctions National Committee and the Land Defence Coalition have coordinated a campaign to stop international cooperation agreements with Mekorot, Israel's state-owned water company responsible for implementing 'water apartheid': the pillage of natural resources in occupied territory, discrimination against the Palestinian people and vital support for the illegal settlement enterprise. Mekorot is a transnational corporation that commits the major part of its human rights violations in the location where it is based and uses international contracts to finance this. The Israeli water sector was developed to steal Palestinian water for Israeli colonisation. Mekorot has been responsible for water rights violations and discrimination since the 1950s, when it built Israel's national water carrier. At the same time it deprives the Palestinian communities of the possibility of access to water.

For environmental groups, the normalisation activities of EcoPeace have drawn attention to the nature of the Israeli occupation of Palestine. News of the exclusion of EcoPeace from Friends of the Earth International filtered down to many hundreds of community environmental groups.

Conclusion

Settler-colonisation, Wolfe insisted, is a process and not an event. The same is true of community development (Craig et al, 2011). These processes interact in Palestine, although the primary driver is settler-colonisation and resistance to it, both of which can employ the techniques of community development. Discerning the distinction is crucial for those engaged in community development in Palestine, and for the international community acting in solidarity. Community development that is based on Bhattacharyya's (2004) twin purpose of the promotion of solidarity and agency cannot be separated from resistance to the occupation, or from environmental justice, with access to land, to water, to resources. The Zionist project of settler-colonialism, since its origins, concerns basic dispossession of resources and removal of the Palestinian population. In that sense settler-colonialism is an ecological resource conflict, and Palestinian resistance, whether at community level, through wider movements or international solidarity, is a struggle for environmental justice.

References

Abu Taleb, Y., Alexander, M. and Robillard, C-E. (2010) *Why cooperate over water? Shared water of Palestine, Israel and Jordan: Cross-border crisis and a need for trans-national solution*, Amman, Bethlehem and Tel Aviv: I.B. Friends of the Earth Middle East.

Al Butmeh, A., Peek, B. and Scandrett, E. (2013) *Environmental Nakba: Environmental injustice and violations of the Israeli occupation of Palestine*, Amsterdam: Friends of the Earth International.

Aljazeera (2017) فلسطينية تروي قصة اغتصابها من جنود اسرائيليين, *Aljazeera*, 30 October, http://www.aljazeera.net/news/humanrights/2017/10/30/.

Al-Shalalfeh, Z., Napier, F. and Scandrett, E. (2018) 'Water Nakba in Palestine: Sustainable Development Goal 6 versus Israeli hydro-hegemony', *Local Environment*, 23(1): 117–24.

Applied Research Institute Jerusalem (2012) *The impacts of electronic waste disposal on the environment and public health in the Occupied Palestinian Territory: A case study from Idhna, Hebron Governorate*, Ramallah: Water and Environment Research Department in cooperation with Sunflower Association for Human and Environmental Protection.

Applied Research Institute Jerusalem (2014) *Al Ma'sara village profile*, http://vprofile.arij.org/bethlehem/pdfs/VP/Al_Ma'sara_vp_en.pdf.

Baroud, R. (2018) 'What Palestinians can teach us about popular resistance', *Al Jazeera*, https://www.aljazeera.com/indepth/opinion/palestinians-teach-popular-resistance-180410085806588.html.

Benjamin, J., Levy, M.B., Kershnar, S. and Sahibzada, M. (2011) *JNF – colonising Palestine since 1901 (eBook) Volume 4 Greenwashing apartheid: The Jewish National Fund's environmental cover up*, USA: International Jewish Anti-Zionist Network.

Bhattacharyya, J. (2004) 'Theorizing community development', *Journal of the Community Development Society*, 34(2): 5–34.

BMJ (2009) 'Norwegian doctors call for investigation into weapons used on Gaza', http://www.bmj.com/content/338/bmj.b170.full.

Chughtai, A. (2018) 'Palestinian' great march of return: The human cost', *Al Jazeera*, 16 May, https://www.aljazeera.com/indepth/interactive/2018/05/palestinians-great-march-return-human-cost-180516110538165.html.

Clark, C.J., Everson-Rose, S.A., Suglia, S.F., Btoush, R., Alonso, A. and Haj-Yahia, M.M. (2010) 'Association between exposure to political violence and intimate-partner violence in the occupied Palestinian territory: A cross-sectional study', *Lancet*, 375: 310–16.

Craig, G., Mayo, M., Popple, K., Shaw, M. and Taylor, M. (eds) (2011) *The community development reader*, Bristol: Policy Press.

Cronin, D. (2017) *Balfour's shadow: A century of British support for Zionism and Israel*, London: Pluto Press.

Davis, U. (2010) *JNF – Colonising Palestine since 1901 (eBook) Volume 2: Preparing for legal action. Focus: Canada Park*, London: Human Rights Legal Aid Fund.

Davis, U. and Lehn, W. (1988) *The Jewish National Fund*, London: Routledge.

Garrity, A. (2015) 'Rebuilding Gaza and the need to assess TRW risks', Toxics blog, 9 January, http://www.toxicremnantsofwar.info/rebuilding-gaza-to-assess-trw-risks/.

Gharib, A. (2013) 'Qatar's bad bet in the West Bank', *Daily Beast*, 3 July, http://www.thedailybeast.com/qatars-bad-bet-in-the-west-bank.

H, B. (2013) 'Thousands protest Prawer Plan in Global "Day of Rage"', *Palestine Monitor*, 4 December, http://www.palestinemonitor.org/details.php?id=qwhj0za5753ydbtz2pp89.

Haaretz (2017) אלף 80 לפנות אין ,הפלסטינים של בזכויות עוסק לא אני :גבאי יד כלאחר יהודים, *Haaretz*, 17 October, https://www.haaretz.co.il/news/politi/1.4516909.

Haj-Yahia, M.M. and Clark, C.J. (2013) 'Intimate partner violence in the Occupied Palestinian Territory: Prevalence and risk factors', *Journal of Family Violence*, 28: 797–809.

Hanieh, A. (2016) 'Development as struggle: Confronting the reality of power', *Journal of Palestine Studies*, 45(4): 32–47.

Harper, J. (2000) 'The 94 Percent Solution: A matrix of control', *Middle East Report*, 216, https://www.merip.org/mer/mer216/94-percent-solution.

Hass, A. (2017) 'Israeli army prepares to demolish hundreds of Palestinian homes in northern Jordan Valley', *Haaretz*, 13 November, https://www.haaretz.com/israel-news/1.822205.

Isaac, J. and Hilal, J. (2011) 'Palestinian landscape and the Israeli–Palestinian conflict', *International Journal of Environmental Studies*, 68(4): 413–29.

Kattan, V. (2009) *From coexistence to conquest: International law and the origins of the Arab–Israeli conflict, 1891–1949*, London: Pluto Press.

Khalidi, W. (1992) *All that remains: The Palestinian villages occupied and depopulated by Israel in 1948*, Washington, DC: Institute for Palestine Studies.

Koppelman, S. and Alshalalfeh, Z. (2012) *Our right to water: The human right to water in Palestine*, Ottawa: The Blue Planet Project.

Levy, G. (2015) 'An Israeli sniper shot me', *Haaretz*, https://www.haaretz.com/israel-news/.premium-an-israeli-sniper-shot-me-1.5409550.

Martínez-Alier, J. (2002) *Environmentalism of the poor: A study of ecological conflicts and valuation*, Cheltenham: Edward Elgar.

Mayo, M. (1975) 'Community development: A radical alternative?' in R. Bailey and M. Brake (eds) *Radical social work*, London: Edward Arnold, pp 129–43.

Mayo, M. (2008) 'Community development, contestations, continuities and change', in G. Craig, K. Popple and M. Shaw (eds) *Community development in theory and practice*, Nottingham: Spokesman, pp 13–27.

McCrea, N., Meade, R.R. and Shaw, M. (2017) 'Solidarity, organizing and tactics of resistance in the 21st century: Social movements and community development praxis in dialogue', *Community Development Journal*, 52(3): 385–404.

Moses, J. (2015) *A better way than boycotts*, London: Board of Deputies of British Jews.

Naim, A., Al Dalies, H., El Balawi, M., Salem, E., Al Meziny, K., Al Shawwa, R., Minutolo, R. and Manduca, P. (2012) 'Birth defects in Gaza: Prevalence, types, familiarity and correlation with environmental factors', *International Journal of Environmental Research and Public Health*, 9(5): 1732–47.

PCBS (2017) Indicators, http://www.pcbs.gov.ps/site/lang__en/881/default.aspx?lang=en.

Piterberg, G. (2008) *The returns of Zionism*, London: Verso.

Qumsiyeh, M.B. (2011) *Popular resistance in Palestine: A history of hope and empowerment*, London: Pluto Press.

Rosenfeld, M. (2011) 'The centrality of the Prisoners' Movement to the Palestinian struggle against the Israeli occupation: A historical perspective', in A. Baker and A. Matar (eds) *Threat: Palestinian political prisoners in Israel*, London: Pluto Press, pp 3–24.

Safi, A.S. (2015) *War on Gaza Strip: Participatory Environmental Impact Assessment*, Ramallah: Palestinian Environmental NGOs Network – FoE Palestine/Maan Development Center.

Sahibzada, M. (2010) *JNF – colonising Palestine since 1901 (eBook) Volume 1 (second edition) Introducing the Jewish National Fund*, Edinburgh: Scottish Palestine Solidarity Campaign.

Sawalha, F., Benjamin, J. and Sahibzada, M. (2011) *JNF – colonising Palestine since 1901 (eBook) Volume 3. Ongoing ethnic cleansing: Judaizing the Naqab*. 'Ar'ara, Israel: Al-Beit.

Seikaly, S. (2015) *Men of capital: Scarcity and economy in Mandate Palestine*, Stanford, CA: Stanford University Press.

Tal, A. (2002) *Pollution in a Promised Land: An environmental history of Israel*, Berkley, Los Angeles, London: University of California Press.

UNCTAD (United Nations Conference on Trade and Development) (2015) *Report on UNCTAD assistance to the Palestinian people: Developments in the economy of the occupied Palestinian territory*, http://unctad.org/meetings/en/SessionalDocuments/tdb62d3_en.pdf.

UNRWA (United Nations Relief and Works Agency for Palestine Refugees in the Near East) (2015) *Profile: Aida Camp*, https://www.unrwa.org/sites/default/files/aida_refugee_camp.pdf.

Veracini, L. (2010) *Settler colonialism: A theoretical overview*, Basingstoke: Palgrave Macmillan.

Zeitoun, M. (2012) *Power and water in the Middle East*, London: I.B. Tauris.

Zwahre, M. and Scandrett, E. (2014) 'Community development as resistance and resilience', *Concept*, 5(2): 1–9.

ELEVEN

Communities resisting environmental injustice in India: philanthrocapitalism and incorporation of people's movements

Eurig Scandrett, Dharmesh Shah and Shweta Narayan

A diverse, fragmented movement

In December 2014 hundreds of activists gathered in Bhopal for the 30th anniversary of the gas disaster at the Union Carbide insecticide factory in the city. At a gathering for solidarity activists from outside Bhopal and Mela (festival) of the Alternatives, diverse community groups, social movements and NGOs held stalls and exhibitions. There were activists fighting against nuclear power, uranium mining, coal mining, military testing, pesticides; advocating for the rights of Adivasis, Dalits, women, peasants, workers, displaced communities; and projects working in community development, alternative production, recycling initiatives, grassroots health promotion, social movement development and workers' mobilisation. A handful of those who had travelled to Bhopal for the anniversary had come from outside India: health activists from Japan, bringing solidarity from the victims of the Minamata mercury pollution disaster; a group of trade union occupational health activists from Scotland (including Eurig); a message of solidarity from Friends of the Earth International. But the vast majority of those present were from communities campaigning for environmental justice in different parts of India.

The anniversary event was organised by the International Campaign for Justice in Bhopal, an alliance of local community- and trade union-based survivors' groups and solidarity campaigns with international supporters, with a structure that ensures that the solidarity activists are accountable to the survivors. One group that was not present was the Bhopal Gas Peedit Mahila Udyog Sangathan (Organisation of Bhopal

Gas Affected Women Workers), a separate Bhopal survivors' group that organised commemorations with its own solidarity networks (Bhopal Survivors Movement Study, 2009). The event perhaps illustrates some core aspects of the Indian environmental justice movement more widely: the contradictory tensions of diversity, solidarity and division. The Bhopal survivors' movement, like the wider Indian environmental justice movement, has seen a few victories and many defeats in its struggle for justice.

Although the Indian environmental justice movement has seen some celebrated successes (such as the Dongria Kondh tribal community's iconic victory against British mining corporation Vedanta in 2014), there have been many high-profile defeats (including the completion of the Sardar Sarovar dam on the Narmada river in defiance of the long-running campaign led by the Narmada Bachao Andolan). Indeed, Whitehead (2003) has argued that the focus on celebrity environmental movements, or 'selective hegemony', has been part of the weakness of the movement, and we would add, an opportunity for exploitation that has not been missed by the interests of capital. Meanwhile, the number of fronts in the battle for environmental justice has multiplied. It is not that the vibrancy of the struggle has diminished, but rather that it is spread across India in fragmented diversity.

A major expansion of oil refining and extraction is extending along the coast and land adjacent to the Bay of Bengal and there is a proposal to develop a Petroleum, Chemicals and Petrochemicals Investment Region (PCPIR). This is expected to lead to large-scale petrochemical development through the entire coast of Tamil Nadu through a major extension to the polluting industries at State Industries Promotion Corporation of Tamil Nadu in Cuddalore (Narayan and Scandrett, 2014). Chennai is destined to be the coastal hub for export trade. This is part of the network of Special Economic Zones and interstate investment corridors that are expanding throughout India.

Communities around the Cauvery delta have been mobilising in opposition to oil extraction and the PCPIR. There have been some oil spillages, and local communities have organised protests. City-based environmental activists are supporting communities, filing Right To Information demands and collating information. A public hearing in connection with one of the proposed oil wells mobilised the community and environmental activists, who gathered information on environmental clearances that had been granted and thereby came to the hearing prepared. The community had already started organising before involving environmentalists; they were already aware that the oil developments were bad for their health and livelihoods. They organised protests that police have responded to with some arrests, so they had already experienced how the state responds to dissent, but decided to engage with legal process alongside protest. Communities made contact with environmental activists in Chennai (including Dharmesh), who have been able to respond with technical support, Right To Information requests, collating information and guidance on licences and environmental clearances and preparing for public hearings, and have been able to develop this material into a popular education format, but it was entirely dependent on the communities organising themselves in the first instance.

Historical context

The immediate post-independence period under Nehru has been categorised as 'passive revolution', in which a capitalist class, formerly held back by British colonial rule, lacked the strength to assume complete power in its own interests and was dependent on compromise with other classes – notably the urban political elite and bureaucracy and the rural landowning class. This period was dominated by scientific planning and state-led development ranging from major engineering projects such as large dams (Nehru's temples of development) to such technological interventions as the green revolution (the introduction of high-yielding varieties of crops, dependent on capital input in the form of agrochemicals and infrastructure). The emphasis on scale, coupled with the balance of class forces, led in both of these cases to highly uneven development, with economic (and, indirectly, political) power concentrated in the hands of narrow class interests – urban bourgeoisie and rural elites with large landholdings – at the expense of subaltern groups and the environment (Whitehead, 2003).

During this period, the Indian Ministry of Community Development embarked on an ambitious programme of rural development through the progressive empowerment and democratisation of village councils or Panchayat. Launched in 1952, by 1964 the programme covered the whole country. Workers were assigned to village Panchayats, there was a focus on agricultural production, economic development was promoted through cooperatives and there were initiatives to increase the participation of women and young people. Nonetheless, as Karunaratne (1976) points out, popular involvement in the project was negligible. Indeed, he suggests that the power structure of rural villages remained unchanged – or was reinforced. Decisions about rural development were made by the village elite and the workers under their patronage, while the majority of rural poor contributed only their unpaid labour – through deference and habitual obedience or coercion – to the construction of infrastructure, from which the elite castes and landowning classes primarily benefited. Additionally, at a regional level, a bureaucratic elite emerged with its own vested interests. Educational programmes largely focused on functional literacy, disconnected from the demands of rural communities. Community development became a top-down, target-orientated means of harnessing local labour for the interests of those with power.

As a result, community development became a discredited term for those engaged in local mobilisation and was replaced with the more politically infused 'community organising' in defence of excluded and disempowered communities, classes and castes. This was particularly important during the Indira Gandhi interregnum, from her first election in 1966 to her assassination in 1984. Rural interests achieved greater influence alongside a populist rhetoric of subaltern empowerment. Class conflicts intensified and state repression ratcheted up, particularly during the Emergency of 1975 to 1977 and into the 1980s. As Andharia argues:

> A generation of teachers and activists from 1980s onwards who began to associate themselves with mass-based struggles, discovered different strategies and new allies and questioned conventional moorings of western forms of institutionalized social work and its relevance to India. Grassroots empowerment took precedence over community development and saw greater involvement of community organizers and scholars in issues of exclusion, violation and assertion of rights, discrimination against dalits, tribals and other marginalized groups. (Andharia, 2009: 277)

Environmental justice conflicts played an important role in this development, including the iconic struggles of Bhopal and the Narmada river – examples of what Whitehead (2003) calls 'selective hegemony', the selection of struggles that resonate with western audiences through the attention of NGOs, funders and the mass media, distorting the influence of and generating division among different struggles.

In the 1990s, the introduction of the New Economic Programme (NEP) facilitated greater inward investment and privatisation and greater conflict between subaltern groups and ruling-class (and caste) factions (Corrbridge and Harriss, 2003). Dalit, Adivasi and Scheduled Caste groups increasingly resisted long-standing oppressions and humiliations, encouraged by state-level anti-caste pronouncements that were regularly betrayed by local state functionaries who were instrumental in violent backlash. As Corrbridge and Harriss contend, in some regions 'the price of labour ... is determined by the balance of forces between the armies of the upper castes (usually with police support) and the armies of the labouring poor' (Corrbridge and Harriss, 2003: 206). Further, such struggles have often been fought over the terrain of access to environmental resources as the Indian state sought to dispossess its poorest and most excluded communities, either directly or through facilitating dispossession by private interests. 'Because India lacks the colonial resource frontier that was available to the major European powers, it is forced to exploit its own resource base to meet the needs of its city-based or elite populations' (Corrbridge and Harriss, 2003: 207).

The Land Acquisition Act of 1854 governed the process of land acquisition in post-independence India and allowed for the dispossession of land for 'public purpose' by a government agency from individual landowners in return for government-determined compensation. Most developmental projects today owe their existence to this British-era legislation. It was not until 2013 that the Act was repealed, and then only after several mass movements over unfair land acquisition and misuse demanded a change. Most contentious was the 'public purpose' clause that features in most eminent domain legislations globally. This clause allowed the government to forcibly acquire land from farmers, often in return for poor compensation.

Farmers who found themselves with a piece of land earmarked for development were compelled to accept the compensation scheme, no matter how unfair. Until the 1990s, the Act was used to make way for projects of state-owned companies like Steel Authority of India, Indian Railways, Coal India Ltd., and so on. However, after liberalisation the Act continued to remain in use but the definition of 'public purpose' kept expanding in scope to include projects by private investors. These could range from luxury hotels to industrial corridors to car factories, and often land was devalued through bureaucratic connivance and owners were forced to sell at low prices. Many states, like Rajasthan, acquired land but failed to use it for the intended purposes, giving rise to a whole new politics of dispossession where the state usurped the role of the landlord.

Despite the widespread misuse of the legislation, successive Indian policy makers refused to repeal or amend the 1854 Land Acquisition Act. As the Indian economy continued to liberalise, the Act came to be seen as a piece of legislation aimed at reversing the achievements of the post-independence Land Gift Movement championed by Vinoba Bhave in 1951. Mass movements against land acquisition like the Narmada Bachao Andolan (against big dams) and the POSCO Pratirodh Sangram Samiti (against a steel plant, see Vijayalakshmi, 2015) raised the crucial question – was the state a landlord, a trustee or an owner? Moreover, was it above the law?

Such struggles, however, have not led to the progressive emancipation of subaltern groups or environmental controls. Indeed, various tactics have been employed to defend class interests and undermine such resistance, from the state violence of Operation Green Hunt against the Naxalite movement and Adivasi communities, to hegemonic control such as Hindutva and the civil society strength of the Sangh Parivar (in both cases involving complementary battles of cultural ideology and extreme violence). As Baviskar (2005) notes, the iconic (and often romanticised) Chipko movement in Himachal Pradesh found that association with Hindu nationalism rather than environmental justice increasingly served its interests.

Harvey (2005) argues that neoliberalism is distinguished by an increase in 'accumulation by dispossession', a form of return to primitive accumulation in which capital accumulation shifts more towards direct expropriation rather than exploitation of surplus labour value; and such accumulation is not accompanied by class formation but, rather, by pauperisation. As such, unlike the labour process, accumulation by dispossession leads to a fragmented and disempowered opposition, making anti-capitalist action difficult. Alliance-based movements such as the NAPM find it increasingly difficult to build wider political struggles from a progressively fragmented and defensive range of grassroots struggles. Victims of accumulation by dispossession include those subject to land grabs or through direct expropriation, neo-latifundisation or urban gentrification programmes, through foreclosure of assets, and climate refugees and so on. As Cox and Nilsen (2014) argue, social movement processes can go backwards during periods of intensive mobilisation by movements from above.

Violence has always been integral to enforcing Indian class discipline, since the British colonial era. Arguably, the current fusion of communal and state-sanctioned violence under Prime Minister Modi's Bharat Janata Party government, with the increasingly diverse mechanisms of dispossession, constitutes a war of manoeuvre in the implementation of neoliberalism (Gramsci, 1971). Such a war of manoeuvre may, however, be facilitating a war of position in which capital dispossession is occurring by hegemonic means through the incorporation of resistance through philanthrocapitalism.

Writing before the Modi government, Whitehead argued that neoliberal accumulation by dispossession in India has been accompanied by a 'reverse primitive accumulation' that has prevented the level of widespread destitution that might lead to revolutionary social unrest.

> High levels of capital intensity in industry, resource extraction on an unprecedented scale, and large-scale appropriation of smallholdings in agriculture through indebtedness, render the uptake of the majority of dispossessed small farmers and tribal populations in industrial work at presently high levels of capital intensity impossible. Nor would emigration, as occurred for the dispossessed of Europe in the nineteenth century, to 'empty', or rather emptied, settler colonies, be likely on a large scale either. Rather, India's contemporary capitalist development would be marked by large-scale accumulative dispossession accompanied by state attempts at reversals of primitive accumulation, so that the subsistence 'needs' of formally dispossessed agrarian and urban households would be continued in some form. (Whitehead, 2003: 287)

Resistance to this development, according to Whitehead, is failing. The traditional Left (principally the Communist Party of India and Communist Party of India (Marxist)) has engaged in electoral politics and often advocated the interests of subaltern groups, but their commitment to support for the postcolonial bourgeoisie, land reform, limited redistribution, industrialisation and neoliberalism (especially exposed through the violence of communist cadres in Nandigram in 2007) has exposed the limits of their value in transforming the prospects of the most marginalised, and contributed to their electoral collapse. The Maoist Naxalite movement is responding to Adivasi dispossession but has a tendency, Whitehead (2003) argues, towards the use of violence (for power and extortion) and the perpetration of superfluous, indiscriminate violence. Adivasi communities are frequently caught in the cross-fire and mutual violations between Naxalites and state forces and the latter's sponsored militia in the Salwa Judum.

Whitehead also criticises the social and people's movements that have emerged from environmental justice struggles. She argues that such movements, as typified by the NAPM, are constrained by romantic Gandhian ruralism and limited utopian ecosocialism. We would question that characterisation. While romanticism and utopianism are certainly present, and Gandhian ecologists have played an important role in the non-violent actions of the Narmada movement, the people's movements are more varied and complex than this.

The connection between affected communities and broader movements can be understood as social movement process (Cox and Nilsen, 2014). As Nilsen (2010) analyses in the Narmada Bachao Andolan, local rationalities of resilience can transform into militant particularism and social movement through a process of analysis of the limitation of struggle against 'movements from above', such as ruling-class realignment and power grab of neoliberalism. Activists from outside the communities can contribute to this process, not through 'leadership' but through a dialectical interaction between the local and the extra-local, or general, providing a stimulus for analysis (Freire, 1972).

Funding neoliberalism through philanthrocapitalism

Corporate social responsibility (CSR) is not new in India but escalated with the NEP to the point of being legislated for by Narendra Modi's government in 2014. Subsequently, funding has become highly politicised. The principal sources of funds for community organising are corporations' CSR budgets and international foundations (such as Ford, Rockefeller, Bill and Melinda Gates). CSR is primarily orientated towards humanitarian objectives and avoids any groups that are critical of corporations. Local CSR funding goes to projects that pose no challenge to the status quo, such as Modi's Swachh Bharat Abhiyan Cleanliness campaign, but no company will fund a fight against a company. The main alternative is foreign funding, but this is subject to different political pressures. The Modi government has taken a strong stand on international funding from a nationalist perspective, with vigorous implementation of the Funding Contribution (Regulation) Act of 2010 and high-profile NGOs like Greenpeace being targeted. While there have been narratives of suspicion concerning foreign funding since Indira Gandhi's allegations of the 'foreign hand', the anti-foreign funding rhetoric has become much more shrill and associated with Hindu nationalism. Meanwhile, the funding from international sources has become increasingly market orientated (Plank, 2017). The funding regime applies business models from capitalism, with superficial metrics, targets, monitoring and audit. There is a lack of honest critique as activists clamour for small pots of money, and marketing exercises compete as to who is more poor and deserving than whom. Philanthrocapitalism feeds on selective hegemony.

Through philanthrocapitalism, the narratives and priorities of the development sector have been increasingly dominated by the agendas of global capital. Smart Cities; climate resilience; air pollution; marine litter: these have become the core issues, due to philanthrocapitalist investment. This trend increasingly limits the space for questioning the capitalist structure that is causing waste, climate change, pollution or marine littering by plastics, or for a critique of the oil industry or the corporations. Through cultural hegemony (Plank, 2017) the agenda has become determined by the interests of corporate finance, dominated by a narrative of entrepreneurship, management, targets, technology and South Asian 'problems', rather than tackling the source of the problems: capitalism, consumption, western life-style, US-generated problems. In addition to this indirect influence, foundations also directly shape government agendas, through their offices in city administration buildings.

'Smart Cities' use information technology to increase operational efficiency and facilitate communication (or at least information) between government and the public. This looks radical and democratic, and gives the impression of addressing the problems, but in fact the terms of the problem are set by neoliberal capitalism, the problems of which are to be managed through more privatisation and corporate involvement. Civic polity and environmental management become dependent on corporate interests.

The discourse of climate resilience is also being distorted by philanthrocapitalism. The dominant narrative is about phasing out coal and generating electricity from renewable sources; however, the consumption of energy is not questioned, neither is the corporate ownership of renewable generation. India's massive growth in renewable energy has come at a cost in the form of land grabbing for corporate-owned wind and solar farms (Krishnaswamy, 2014; Ejatlas, 2017). The infrastructure of centralised energy generation is damaging and is subsidised by the central grid. This isn't challenging the politics of power. India's largest private energy company, Adani Power, is investing in solar parks and wind farms, which essentially constitutes a land grab. Rather than climate resilience, this is provoking dispossession.

Marine litter is the most recent western driver of funding by powerful NGOs, corporations and the world media. Even the term used, 'litter', serves to turn the narrative into a problem of management. It is focusing on managing plastics, not on getting rid of plastics, which would threaten the interests of the corporations. Campaigning groups like the Global Alliance for Incinerator Alternatives are arguing that plastic production must stop; never the less most funding goes towards waste management projects. Communities confronting landfill and incinerator plants don't get funded, nor does more radical waste work, including prevention, dematerialisation and organising rag pickers.

Zero Waste Cities – smart cities for waste – are redesigning how waste systems are structured to maximise efficiency. These are based on models of increasing waste, rather than efforts to decouple waste production from economic growth. Consumption, at the base of the waste pyramid, is not addressed. Assuming that the volume of waste produced will increase, technological solutions are sought. Hydrocarbon plastics are substituted by bioplastics manufactured from corn starch by the same corporate producers. Corn crops are thereby diverted from food production to meet consumption needs, risking food insecurity.

There is no transparency in the way that priorities are set by foundations and international NGOs. 'Stakeholders' are consulted but it is never clear who they are or how they are selected. Those groups best able to respond to these agendas are often the NGOs based in the main power centres and linked with grassroots campaigns, but not the locally based land, water, environmental justice groups themselves. Some communities are able to sustain a radical narrative, to call out the western agendas and expose the corporate links. However, civil society has become increasingly influenced by the funding from the major foundations, and co-opted. There is a real tension in groups committed to environmental justice work concerning where funding can be obtained.

Anecdotally, it is clear that some have become more accepting of foundations, more willing to compromise and less inclined to screen sources. Philanthrocapitalist funds can be laundered through intermediaries and 'whitewashed', and can drown out other sources. There is an increasing awareness that there is no clean money and that capitalist markets are funding work on social change. The lines are increasingly blurred, making it more difficult to determine the sources of funds and where the agendas come from. The increasing use of the Foreign Contributions (Regulation) Act (FCRA) is a factor that requires activists to consider how to maintain a radical agenda without a backlash against our work or the groups we support. The state is acting to force a binary between foreign versus corporate funding. Some of the grassroots groups choose to self-fund and are clear that they receive no outside funding. However, many city-based groups are increasingly required to negotiate the agendas set by philanthrocapitalist corporations. These foundations recognise that social change will happen, and want to ensure that it works in their interests, as a class.

It is too simplistic to say that all foreign funding distorts the environmental justice movement. Aruna Roy's Mazdoor Kisan Shakti Sangathan Right To Information movement receives international funding and is not distorted. It is very hard to discern what should and should not be funded, but the interests of the funders are always there. At the peak of the anti-Vedanta movement, Survival International was involved. The Indian government labelled it as 'foreign' and accused it of Maoist funding (Roshan, 2017). But the Dongria Adivasi movement's campaign to protect their land against Vedanta survived, and was funded by themselves. Survival International made the issue international, but the campaign would have succeeded without its intervention. Indeed, there was a degree of co-dependence. While the Dongrias resisted on the ground, Survival International hit Vedanta in its home country, where it was more vulnerable to public shaming. Grassroots groups don't need foreign funding. Many groups are able to find the resources they need locally. For example the Kudankulam anti-nuclear movement was funded by local fishermen. Similarly, the POSCO battle over the steel refinery.

The environmental justice movement in India largely remains without a clear direction, but small groups are trying to challenge environmental degradation. Environmental activists need to be able to respond to community demands, not go out with an attitude to 'save' them. In our experience, if communities see you as someone who will invest expertise and time in support of their interests, then they will come to you from a position of grassroots strength. If they come looking for funding, then their interests will be distorted by what they perceive as your interests. Environmental activists are few in number and remote from the communities on the front-line. There is an increasing awareness of the risk of attempting to organise or speak for the communities. In past decade or so more community voices have been coming up. There are still city-based groups who try to dominate and speak for everyone, but this is increasingly resisted by the communities themselves and we are hearing more diverse voices from the community. Previously a community member would be used as a prop for an NGO, but now there are increasing numbers of active spokespeople asserting the interests of the communities at global level.

Environmental justice activists are increasingly aware that we can work only with communities who are organising themselves; we can provide media, technical and scientific support. Communities take ownership, we only make small interventions. Often it is only small numbers of people in communities that take the initiative and contact the activists for support. They are not looking for money and we are clear that we are not able to provide financial resources. Communities organise their own resources: their reports are not fancy. There are other groups that emphasise communications and outreach, including interactive websites and toolkits, but it isn't clear whether this speaks to communities' demands. Only if it is a very big project of national significance, such as the PCPIR, then it is sometimes necessary for environmental activists to seek out the people who are mobilising in the community.

The environmental justice movement needs to be more self-critical. Capital accumulation is the key cause of the environmental injustices that we are fighting against, yet some of this capital is being directed at the movement itself. We need to understand how that issue of money can itself be challenged: how can movements renegotiate their work in the face of philanthrocapitalism? The movement is facing pressure to splinter, competing for the same pots of money. NGOs want to 'grow', to get more money. Grassroots communities don't need that money. The irony is that the movement risks becoming dependent on capital, which is causing the problems that it is resisting. This is a fundamental dialectic around which the movement is conflicted. It is dependent on consumer-capitalism to challenge consumer-capitalism. Some elements of the movement attempt to opt out, but then find that they can't be part of any change. The movement needs to be part of the problem in order to change it, but it needs to be conscious of this contradiction in order to force the change. Environmental activists need to reassess their strategies in order to support self-organised communities resisting the violators.

Conclusions

The environmental justice movement in India is faced with responding to the crisis of neoliberalism and dispossession. Grassroots resistance to capital expropriation of the environment – through resource dispossession, extraction, pollution, contamination and externalisation of environmental costs – is widespread, yet is fragmented. One of its key points of conflict is its own source of resources. There are many incidents of grassroots community mobilisation that draw entirely from their own resources to challenge corporations and the state, often making use of the expertise of environmental activists who themselves are limited in their access to resources. Such self-supported groups tend to be small, fragmented and limited in the extent to which they can coordinate with other such groups in order to build a movement to challenge the causes of the environmental despoliation in the accumulation of capital. They might win local concessions or even battles, but the main problem, the structure of accumulation, needs a broader movement. Where such groups are coordinated into a wider movement, they are often faced with the dilemma of funds.

The most available local funding source is CSR, which by definition cannot be used to challenge corporations. International sources of funding are distorted by several factors. The biggest sources of funds are global philanthrocapitalists, either foundations established by entrepreneurs, such as the Bill and Melinda Gates Foundation, or international NGOs. In both cases the means by which funding priorities are determined remain opaque, often apparently driven by media interest in the west, and the mechanisms of accountability for funding adopt a business model from capitalist enterprise, leading to superficial measures for monitoring and accounting. The impact of this on community organising is corrupting. Activists are torn between their accountability to funders and to the affected communities. Funding is disproportionately received by NGOs in the political centre with links to grassroots struggles. Communities compete in a 'beauty contest' to be the most needy, most iconic or most compliant with accounting procedures. Where campaigns are able to obtain more independent international funds that allow for community-determined challenges to the interests of capital in development (which corresponds with the interests of the neoliberal state), then these risk falling foul of FCRA regulations.

Thus, movements challenging the neoliberal causes of dispossession are often caught up in a contradiction of relying on funding sources that are themselves dependent on neoliberal dispossession. Refusing to do so can consign the struggle to, at best, local concessions and, at worst, irrelevance. Communities discern their own tactics on the basis of their local conditions. Environmental activists are able to provide limited support and accountability to communities, with a constant tension concerning sources of funds. Wider movements seeking to build alliances across multiple community struggles must try to hold together these disparate tactics and this is leading to a loss of direction. The movement needs to analyse this contradiction in order to challenge at source the neoliberal direction of increasing dispossession.

References

Andharia, J. (2009) 'Critical explorations of community organization in India', *Community Development Journal*, 44(3): 276–90.

Baviskar, A. (2005) 'Red in tooth and claw? Looking for class in struggles over nature', in R. Ray and M. Fainsod Katzenstein (eds) *Social Movements in India*, New Delhi: Oxford University Press, pp 161–178.

Bhopal Survivors' Movement Study (2009) *Bhopal survivors speak: Emergent voices from a People's Movement*, Edinburgh: Word Power Books.

Corrbridge, S. and Harriss, J. (2003) *Reinventing India*, New Delhi: Oxford University Press.

Cox, L. and Nilsen, A.G. (2014) *We make our own history: Marxism, social movements and the crisis of neoliberalism*, London: Pluto Press.

Ejatlas (2017) 'Wind farm CDM project in Kalpavalli Community Forest, India', EJOLT, https://ejatlas.org/conflict/wind-farm-cdm-project-in-kalpavalli-community.

Freire, P. (1972) *Pedagogy of the oppressed*, London: Penguin.

Gramsci, A (1971) *Selections from prison notebooks*. Edited and translated by Q. Hoare and G. Nowell Smith. London: Lawrence and Wishart.

Harvey, D. (2005) *A brief history of neoliberalism*, Oxford: Oxford University Press.

Karunaratne, G. (1976) 'The failure of the Community Development Programme in India', *Community Development Journal*, 2(2): 95–118.

Krishnaswamy, S. (2014) 'Solar good, but let us be careful', India Climate Dialogue, http://indiaclimatedialogue.net/2014/06/25/solar-good-let-us-careful/.

Narayan, S. and Scandrett, E. (2014) 'Science in community environmental struggles: Lessons from community environmental monitors, Cuddalore, Tamil Nadu', *Community Development Journal*, 49(4): 557–72.

Nilsen, A.G. (2010) *Dispossession and resistance in India: The river and the rage*, Abingdon: Routledge.

Plank, K. (2017) 'Philanthrocapitalism and the hidden power of big U.S. foundations', *Momentum Quarterly*, 6(3): 203–9.

Roshan, M. (2017) 'Adivasis in Odisha defeated Vedanta but are now caught between the state and the Maoists', Scroll.in, https://scroll.in/article/838121/the-dongria-kondh-defeated-vedanta-but-are-caught-between-the-state-and-the-maoists.

Vijayalakshmi, T.N. (2015) 'CAG blows lid off land grab in Odisha', *Down to Earth*, 30 March, http://www.downtoearth.org.in/news/cag-blows-lid-off-land-grab-in-odisha-37917.

Whitehead, J. (2003) 'Accumulation through dispossession and accumulation through growth: Intimations of massacres foretold?', in M. Ekers, G. Hart, S. Kipfer and A. Loftus (eds) *Gramsci: Space, nature, politics*, Oxford: John Wiley & Sons, pp 279–300.

TWELVE

Grassroots struggles to protect occupational and environmental health

Kathy Jenkins and Sara Marsden

Introduction

In this chapter we explore the interface between the community and the workplace in relation to environmental justice and, especially, in the forms of struggles for occupational and environmental health. We look at the connections, overlaps and parallels, both theoretical and practical, between workplace and worker organising, and community organising and development.

The chapter is based on three main sources of information. First is a series of interviews with activists from different parts of the UK and the US and less formal discussions with activists in the UK Hazards Campaign and the European Work Hazards Network. Second, we draw on information and experiences related both formally and informally during two conferences of the Asia Network for the Rights of Occupational and Environmental Victims (ANROEV) in Hanoi (2015) and Nepal (2017), on material in subsequent ANROEV email correspondence and the publication *Resistance on the continent of labour* (Panimbang, 2017b), which documents and analyses experience from ANROEV activists. Our third source is our own experience and learning as occupational and environmental activists over many years. Recurring themes have been identified. The chapter will use examples from sources to elucidate these themes.

In keeping with the activist nature of this project, as well as contributing to the book, a major aim in researching and writing the chapter was to contribute to the building of international networks and coalitions and the continued development of a global grassroots occupational and environmental health network.

Interviews

We interviewed the following activists:

Bryan Simpson, Unite the Union official and facilitator and activist with the campaign Better than Zero, supporting young precarious workers in Scotland to organise themselves; to identify major workplace issues including low wages, insecure or non-existent contracts and unsafe working conditions; and to take direct action to force employers to address these. Bryan also works with hospitality workers through the creation of Unite Hospitality branches.

Jawad Qasrawi, hazards activist and sub-editor of *Hazards Magazine*, a unique UK magazine combining top-level investigative journalism with reporting of and support for grassroots campaigns that challenge unsafe and criminal working conditions and act to protect workers' life and health.

Jessica Martinez, co-director of the National Council for Occupational Safety and Health (COSH), a US NGO and federation of local and state-wide COSH groups fighting for safe and healthy workplaces. National and local COSH groups involve grassroots alliances and collaboration among unorganised workers, workers' centres, trade unions, victims' organisations and occupational health and safety professionals.

Helen Lynn, coordinator of the UK-based Alliance for Cancer Prevention and a long-term activist with the Women's Environment Network. Her work emphasises the impact of chemical exposure in the workplace and the wider environment and she has been involved in organising and working with groups of women throughout the UK, particularly in relation to breast cancer. The Alliance has an explicit aim of bringing environmental and occupational activists together.

Hilda Palmer, Greater Manchester Hazards Centre, who has played a central role in the development of the Hazards Campaign, a UK-wide health and safety trade union activist network and movement. Hilda also provides the main coordination and support for Families Against Corporate Killers, a network of families bereaved through workplace death and active in campaigning for workers' right to come home each day alive and healthy.

Ted Smith, one of the founders of the California-based Silicon Valley Toxics Coalition and of the global GoodElectronics network. The network brings together trade unions, grassroots organisations, victims' groups, academics and occupational health and safety professionals who are taking action to protect workers and communities from human rights abuses and exposure to toxic chemicals used in the global electronics supply chain.

Sanjiv Pandita (via email), currently the Asia representative for Solidar Suisse, a Swiss organisation fighting for decent work, democratic participation and social justice worldwide, and former director of the Asia Monitor Resource Centre, which works to support a democratic and independent labour movement in Asia. Sanjiv is also a key activist in ANROEV.

The context of the global health and safety problem must be emphasised. The International Labour Organization (ILO) estimates that every day 7,400 people die as a result of occupational accidents or work-related diseases – more than 2.78 million deaths per year. Additionally, there are some 374 million non-fatal work-related injuries and illnesses every year. Sadly, this shows a large increase over the 2017 figure of 2.3 million deaths (ILO, nd).

Themes

Recurring themes include various aspects of the changing nature of the work environment, both in terms of the risks posed by work and in the way that work is organised. Our interviewees, in line with existing commentaries, spoke of the increasingly precarious nature of work – a global phenomenon; poverty and low wages; the impact of multiple layers of sub-contracting on workers' ability to demand and achieve reasonable working conditions; low levels of unionisation, discrimination against union members and fear of joining a union; higher-than-average risk levels for women, young and migrant workers; deregulation and lowering standards of enforcement of protective laws.

Activists pointed to the increasingly blurred boundaries between work and community, family and individual life and the broadening reality of what and where the 'workplace' is. The type and organisation of activism has responded to this changing world, both in terms of reaching individual workers and in recognition of the need to build coalitions and alliances: within the working world; between the working world and the wider community and environment; and among local, national and global activists and movements. Activists also reflected on the barriers they faced – with the increased need to fight for rights in what has become an increasingly hostile environment for social and environmental justice activism.

Context

Global political economy

It is possible to make sense of these themes and Occupational Health and Safety (OHS) activists' experience only in the context of structural shifts in the global political economy and, in particular, the developing complexity, depth and pervasiveness of the Global Production Network.

This is elaborated by Panimbang (2017a).

> The global political economy today is at a remarkable juncture with many multifaceted challenges. Two are specifically crucial. The first, we witness the competition between, on the one hand, the presently dominant power of corporations and financial institutions in local and global politics and, on the other, a multiplicity of counter-hegemonic labour and social movements fighting for social justice. The second is the threat to civilization posed by ever-expanding capital accumulation that leads to the risk of environmental catastrophe on a global scale (Barenberg, 2013). The increase in capital accumulation is reflected in the formation of cross-border production systems (also known as Global Production Network). (Panimbang, 2017a: 2)

Panimbang finds the absolute poverty of the past replaced in much of Asia by the poverty created by the use of cheap, vulnerable labour, now 76% of the workforce. Four major challenges are identified, which contribute to this: low wages, a growing proportion of temporary workers, unfavourable labour legislation and 'rampant' anti-union policies.

These challenges are echoed by all of our sources and backed up by the ILO (2015), which recently reported that only one quarter of global workers are in permanent, secure employment. The other 75% are employed on temporary or short-term contracts, working informally often without any contract, are self-employed or are in unpaid family jobs – almost all on low income; conditions which apply, in particular, to women (ILO, 2015). This ILO evidence is underlined by the International Trade Union Confederation's (ITUC, 2015) report, which reveals that only 6% of the workforce of 50 top multinationals are employed directly. This means that 94% are hidden in sub-contracting arrangements that enable the multinationals to escape responsibility. Sharan Burrow, ITUC secretary, states:

> Sixty per cent of global trade is now driven by big business which, without apology, uses a business model based on exploitation and abuse of human rights in supply chains. They must know their profits are too often driven by low wage levels that people cannot live on; that these profits risk safety with the result of indefensible workplace injuries and deaths; that these profits are increased by tax evasion or tragically linked to pollution of community land and water, even while their lobby teams are turning governments against the rule of law that would hold them to account. (Burrow, in ITUC, 2015: 4)

Organising for health and safety

Within this wider context of work and workplaces in a global economy, there are particular issues that face those organising specifically around health and safety. Sanjiv Pandita says: "Since the beginning of the Industrial Revolution and expansion of capitalism, control over workers' health and safety has been a contentious issue. Capital (industry) has always tried to use it as a tool to control labour by claiming it is a technical issue that needs expertise." Historically, most of the 'technical experts' have been under the control of industry. "Grassroots mobilisation has been a political movement to have democratic control of occupational safety and health by bringing it back to workers by demystifying it, including its technical jargons" (from interview with Sanjiv Pandita, 2018). It is this grassroots mobilisation that is described in this chapter.

Community development and organising

Throughout our interviews, and in drawing on other sources, we have looked at links between OHS organising and activism, and the principles and practice of community development. The history of now well-established OHS campaign groups lies in unofficial and community organising among workers, academics, students and scientists that challenged existing power structures in universities and industry. Examples include: the UK Hazards Campaign, which in part grew out of the British Society for Social Responsibility in Science and its early 'science shops' aimed at lay people; the Danish Activist Group of Workers and Academics, which involved the science shop at the Technical University of Denmark; the development of PPM in Austria, bridging the gap between academics and workers on OHS; science shops and alternative organising in the Netherlands and Germany, leading to the beginnings of the European Work Hazards Network (EWHN); COSH, which was formed to provide coordination of local community and worker advocacy groups across the US; ANROEV, whose roots are in community organising by and among victims of industrial disasters but that is now an alliance of victims (or survivors), workers, unions and academics across 14 different Asian countries.

A helpful summary of the principles linking OHS organising and community organising is given by Bunyan (2012):

> In the final analysis it was recognised that if community organizing is to play any significant role in galvanising local communities and their organisations to effect social change then the issue of power must remain central to the analysis and the action that is taken. To this end woolly notions of 'partnership' and 'empowerment', based upon pity and compassion for poor people will need to be jettisoned for, or at the very least, augmented by, a hard headed commitment to solidarity and to the building of alternative forms of collective power rooted in but transcending localities and capable of engaging with and unsettling the prevailing institutional order. (Bunyan, 2012: 14)

Bunyan emphasises the need to move from work at 'micro' level to 'meso' and eventually 'macro' levels. Most of our interviews reflect the attempt to work at 'meso' level, although work being undertaken to develop a Global Grassroots Occupational and Environmental Health Network is clearly 'macro'.

The relationship between occupational and environmental justice struggles

In our interviews we have also looked at links and divisions between OHS and environmental struggles. Here again, the history of now-established campaign groups is informative. Early gatherings that eventually fed into the establishment of the EWHN were linked to the German Green 'detoxification congress'. The 2010 change in the name of the Asian network from ANROAV (... Occupational Accident Victims) to ANROEV (... Occupational and Environmental Victims) reflected new processes to integrate the workers' occupational health and community environmental health movements. The concluding statements of biannual European Work Hazards conferences since 2010 have included a commitment to 'build links between workplace and environmental campaigns at local, national and international levels'. There have also been moves in this direction among individual trade unions and national and international union federations, although some impetus has been lost since the 2008 recession and the resulting attacks on basic working conditions. The cross-over among myriad areas of legislation also underlines the non-existence of any 'invisible' wall between workplace and environment (air, water and soil pollution, fire safety, waste management, chemicals).

A thematic presentation of findings

Work and community boundaries

All sources reported increasingly fragmented work organisation, with atomisation of individual workers and precariousness in employment. Employment rights are clearly less secure for many in these circumstances. Another important consequence is that the distinction between work and community, for an increasing proportion of workers, is becoming much more blurred. Internationally, the degree of casualisation, multiple layers of sub-contracting, bogus self-employment and migration for work all mean that people's work base is often their home, or their home is situated within or provided by their workplace. Both can result in poor and unsafe working and living conditions. 'The logic and model of working in the era of neoliberal capitalism has expanded into everyday life' (Panimbang, 2017b: 3).

These developments also highlight the urgent need for environmental and occupational campaigns to work together. It is well established that environmental degradation and hazards are found most often in working-class communities. This reality is reflected by Sanjiv:

> We realise that victims of occupational and environmental hazards are the same people exposed due to the same reasons. There might just be a wall separating them, but this wall is now becoming invisible due to home-based work. We have been trying to bring both these groups of people together to fight for justice. (ANROEV, 2015: 3)

In the UK and other parts of Europe and the US, migrant workers and low-skilled unemployed workers can find themselves working long distances from their family and community and housed in poor, dormitory accommodation. In the global South, internal and external migration results in the same phenomenon but multiplied many times. A high proportion of these workers are 'informal' – without contracts, which impacts not only on wages and working conditions but also on wider social protection. For example, in Pakistan more than 75% of the 68 million workforce are in the informal/unregistered sector. This denies them the right to social security and has implications for child labour and access to education (Khalid Mahmood, Labour Education Foundation, ANROEV email communication).

Although in much less drastic form, this lack of adequate contracts is impacting on workers in the global North as well. For example, Deliveroo workers in Scotland are among the bogus self-employed, denied guaranteed hours, paid on a piece-work basis, having to take responsibility for their own transport equipment and health and safety. Again, they have no 'workplace' and have had to search for ways to connect with their fellow workers. Social home-care workers in the UK are sometimes paid only for contact time in clients' homes, with no travel time between homes included.

The issue of (often low paid) piece-work pay is echoed in the experience and struggle of Samsung repair workers in Korea (Eun-Seok, 2017), who find this system used by the employer to reduce work, pay and security, particularly targeting union activists.

There are significant shifts in the gender make-up of the most precarious work. Semiconductor production in Vietnam draws young women from rural areas into huge industrial parks where they live, sometimes for years, in dormitories, with little prospect of an independent or family life. Women day labourers in the US are responding to an increase in private homeowners seeking day labour for (still) feminised jobs such as cleaning and cooking. Many of these women also have no contracts or are on zero hour/no guaranteed hours contracts. These workers also have no 'workplace' and have very limited (if any) chance to interact with fellow workers. Relationships between fellow workers and with the workplace have become much more intermittent, and perpetually temporary for many of those whose rights our interviewees fight for.

Another place where work and community blur is on the roads. Driving to and from, and for, work is a major hazard throughout the world. In the UK in 2012, the Department for Transport reported that 539 people were killed, 5,231 seriously injured and almost 45,000 slightly injured in collisions involving a driver or rider driving for work. The Bangladesh Occupational Safety, Health and Environment Foundation reports that 42% of the 1,242 reported work-related deaths in Bangladesh in 2017 are due to traffic accidents. In Turkey, ANROEV reports that transport is the leading cause of work-related death (ANROEV email correspondence).

Worker organisation response

Workplace organising is responding to these changes in the nature of work. Traditional approaches are still relevant to many workplaces but workers' organisations are also adapting to, engaging in and supporting new ways of organising outside of formal trade union structures, and sometimes outside the workplace altogether, in the community.

Two of our interviewees noted explicitly that the blurring of the distinction between community and workplace makes Jane MacAlevey's call to consider the person as a whole, not just a worker, highly relevant.

> The [2012] Chicago teachers' strike was an excellent example of transformational, whole-person organising ... By embracing the fight to defend Chicago's kids, parents and schools ... they provided yet another example of deep, relational, transformational, community-based approaches to union organizing. If more of the union movement understood their members as whole people, not simply as 'workers' – and if more civil society groups understood the urgent issues their members face at work and actively support them in efforts to unionize – we'd be well on our way to challenging the global dominance of corporations. There are no shortcuts to building the kind of power it takes to win meaningful change. Face-to-face organizing is

fundamentally about developing and unleashing the primary source of power available: ourselves. (MacAlevey, 2013: np)

Approaches to the organisation of workers have evolved in response to these new patterns of working and increasing worker atomisation. There has been a growth or, in some cases, regrowth in grassroots-inspired organisations (and organisation) both within and outside the structures of workplace/employers. This takes place within individual organisations and communities, within local industrial sectors and at national and international levels.

In different parts of the world, activists for OHS built alliances among different work sectors, between workplace activists, trade unions and radical OHS professionals, and sometimes also with environmental and community-based campaigns. Examples include the UK Hazards Campaign and the groups it coordinates. Hazards grew out of joint campaigning by radical scientists and advice workers with workplace safety representatives and shop stewards, and now includes several trade union, community and specific Hazards resource centres, occupational health projects, victim support groups, local trade union councils and specialist campaigns such as those around asbestos, pesticides and the construction and microelectronics industries. The EWHN brings together national Hazards groups that also include science shops and occupational physicians.

In the US, COSH grew out of state-level groups funded in the 1970s by federal grants to train workers in the new Occupational Safety and Health (OSH) Act. As COSH groups campaigned to protect, implement and extend OSH law they developed into an alliance with trade unions and workers' centres that in 2004 formed National COSH. In Asia, ANROEV is an alliance of grassroots campaigns, victim groups and national and sector-based networks. Maquiladora Health and Safety Support Network is an international network of 300 OHS professionals and scientists who volunteer to provide information and technical assistance regarding workplace hazards to worker and community organisations in the global South.

In addition, there are many single-issue and country-specific grassroots campaigns and professional and scientific research groups such as the Brazilian Ban Asbestos Campaign, Ban Asbestos Japan, Pesticides Action Network, the Industrial Health Research Group at the University of Cape Town, and local self-organised grassroots campaigns, sometimes with stimulation and or support from trade unions or organisations listed previously. Workers in the chicken-processing industry in the US are fighting for toilet breaks; CLEAN

(Community Labor Environmental Action Network) Campaign is organising car-wash workers in Los Angeles; Fair Hospitality is young people organising in the hospitality industry in Scotland.

Another kernel out of which organisation grows is victim activism. In South Korea, for example, people suffering ill health, injury and death through working for Samsung, and their families, have come together in the Supporters for the Health and Rights of People in the Semiconductors Industry (SHARPS) campaign. They have gained the support of Korean Confederation of Trade Unions and have been part of the development of the global Good Electronics Network. SHARPS work to reveal the truth about working conditions, to get proper compensation for victims and to gain fundamental worker rights. In recognition of the root causes of their struggle, they also state that their aim is to 'resist globalisation of neoliberalism'.

In the UK, Families Against Corporate Killers (FACK) has brought together people who have lost loved ones through workplace accidents. They campaign to stop others being killed in preventable incidents and help bereaved families to access emotional, legal and financial support.

Justice for Kentex Workers Alliance in the Philippines was set up by victims' families following a devastating factory fire in 2015 in which 72 workers burned to death. They have gained the support of trade unions through the Metal Workers Alliance of the Philippines and IndustriALL Global Union, as well as the Centre for Labor and Trade Union Rights and the Institute for Occupational Health and Safety Development.

Who is organising?

This last is an example of women increasingly taking a lead in organising. The Women's Environment Network in the UK has undertaken community research, development of community activist groups and campaigning from the 1980s until the present. Its work developed from an initial recognition of the health impact of chemical sensitivity to gathering detailed information about the environmental and occupational causes of breast cancer, undertaking a three-year Participatory Appraisal involving women in local areas throughout the UK. A total of 120 women's workshops mapped local sources of pollution against breast cancer clusters. The network created has continued to campaign in a range of ways about a variety of environmental and occupational hazards. It has been instrumental in forming the UK Alliance for Cancer Prevention. Challenge Breast Cancer Scotland is one of the few breast cancer charities that emphasise prevention. It is a network of women, most of whom have suffered from breast cancer, that is now reaching out to young women with breast cancer and lobbying the Scottish Parliament to strengthen the preventative element of its cancer planning.

In the US, the history of women organising goes back well beyond the tragic Triangle Fire in New York in 1911 and extends through the development of workers' centres from the 1970s to the present time among, for example, Southern black communities, Chinese immigrant communities and Hispanic migrant workers.

Another key group driving new ways of organising are young people. The UK Better Than Zero and Fair Hospitality campaigns are being driven by young people in precarious work environments. These campaigns involve some of the most marginalised workers in the UK. They work in pubs, cafes, restaurants and hotels, on minimum wage or lower, often have zero-hour contracts (no guaranteed working hours each week), work in unsafe and unhealthy conditions and have, historically, been poorly organised. With the support of some unions they have built a dynamic, creative and effective campaign to challenge the practices of their employers. Young people play a major role in some US Workers' Centres and campaigns, such as the CLEAN carwash campaign. Young workers are also playing prominent roles in parts of Asia, including in Indonesia's trade unions, the manufacturing sector in China and in South Korea within the struggle for unionisation of part of the Samsung Corporation (Panimbang, 2017a).

New ways of organising

There are increasing numbers of instances where much of the process of organising is located in the community and outside the workplace. The first moves to organise in response to a work-related injustice, and to make contact between those potentially affected, either self-organising or with active intervention by an external organisation, are increasingly found outside the structures of work and the workplace. Examples of how contact can first be made by external organisers include, for instance at Day Labor pick-up points (US) and at the point of entry and exit to workplaces. An example of the latter was in the early stages of the struggle to organise UK Sports Direct workers. To facilitate interactions various tactics are used, including offering information, advice or training. Worker centres are sometimes located close to Day Labour pick-up points, as well as within active community centres. Two examples were given of contact being made through language education, which was developed into a way of bringing workers together, providing education and advice on employment and health and safety rights, some measure of language justice and, eventually, organising the workers. These were Unite the Union working with Sports Direct workers in the UK and COSH and individual unions supporting precarious workers – often migrant workers – through workers' centres in the US.

Initial contact is also made in settings not directly related to the workplace. For instance, in the UK there are examples of workplace rights education delivered by Unite in communities in partnership with community groups (such as Castlemilk Against Austerity) as well as education in schools carried out by unions and congresses.

At a more formal level, there are organisations that provide information, education and training internationally. One example is Asia Monitor Resource Centre (AMRC), an NGO focusing on Asian labour concerns that works to 'support a democratic and independent labour movement in Asia'. In particular it promotes active worker participation in work-related issues and helps to organise occupational victims. AMRC provides major support to ANROEV as well as education, training, consultancy, advocacy, publications and network support. Hesperian Health Guides, a Californian non-profit organisation, supports local communities to realise their right to health through easily read material in over 80 languages and digital education tools. Interviewees also provided examples of first contact being made at or on transport to work. Contact was made with Sports Direct workers living in dormitories when they boarded the bus to take them to work, and on buses taking Mexican semiconductor workers to their workplace in Quadalarjara (Mexico's Silicon Valley).

Other community approaches include focusing on organising those who have been injured or made ill by work, or who are at risk of this. A number of UK primary care-based occupational health projects bring together experienced trade union and other OHS activists to work with primary care staff to make links between ill health and work. In addition to support and organising, valuable research is done into occupational causes of ill health. FACK is another example, as are groups organising around particular illnesses such as bladder cancer, breast cancer and others.

On a totally different scale is work done by ANROEV, which grew out of labour and victims' groups who organised following the industrial disasters of Kader and Zhil (1993 toy factory fires in Thailand and Shenzhen). Today it is a coalition of victims' groups, trade unions and other labour groups across Asia, all committed to the rights of victims and for overall improvement of health and safety at the workplace. It now has members from 14 Asian countries and territories, including Japan, Korea, China, India, Pakistan, Thailand, Indonesia, Vietnam, Bangladesh, Hong Kong SAR, Taiwan, Nepal, Vietnam and Cambodia.

Social media is increasingly being used to make initial contact with workers and to build networks and communities by promoting advice services and meetings as well as fostering online interaction. This can be aimed at a specific workplace or sector or be issue related, such as attracting interest and linking people in relation to low wages, unfair contracts, poor health and safety and so on. Better Than Zero, for instance, regularly initiates specific workplace and issue-based online groups. The use of WhatsApp in Asian social media, as well as acting as a first contact point, can be a key 'place' for many atomised workers to organise.

We heard of other novel uses of technology to organise, such as highly isolated Deliveroo riders in Scotland ordering pizza deliveries through a customer app in order to meet one another! *Hazards Magazine* is a printed and online source of up-to-date information and evidence on UK and international OHS hazards, regulation and enforcement, and on work-related injury and ill health. One of our interviewees told us that the magazine's job is to hold government and enforcers to account, to provide a high level of journalism and graphics in a form that provides on-the-ground workplace and environmental activists with knowledge and ammunition. The magazine has initiated a number of specific, largely digital, campaigns, including a recent (2018) impressive example: the Work Cancer Hazards website.

Specific tactics

Direct action: Activists gave powerful and creative examples of direct action taken in the workplace, in the community or on the streets. Examples can be drawn from Better than Zero, Sports Direct, the anti-Transatlantic Trade and Investment Partnership (TTIP) campaign throughout Europe, Samsung and other semiconductor workers in Asia, local, national and international asbestos campaigns. Tactics include demonstrations, street theatre (inside and outside the workplace), music, 'die-ins', occupations. A different kind of public expression is the internationally observed commemoration on 28 April of International Workers Memorial Day, whose slogan is 'Remember the Dead and Fight for the Living'.

Naming and shaming/brand shaming: Public naming of organisations that are exemplars of bad practice has also been used successfully. This can be aimed at the public as consumers, at politicians, at shareholders and other investors. It can take the form of active adverse publicity, such as awards for the worst employers. When at a nationwide or international level it can become brand shaming. Examples include Sports Direct, ending in the owner being called to give evidence before a parliamentary select committee; Better than Zero Cineworld campaign (response to cuts in late travel home allowances); and Samsung and Good Electronics Campaigns aimed at the Samsung brand. The use of campaign names, incorporating or echoing the target brand, can strengthen public recognition of such campaigns, for example Sports Direct Shame, Cineworld renamed Stingy World, Deliveroo renamed Slaveroo.

The power of testimony: The majority of our activists underlined the power of individual testimony. FACK supports people who have lost loved ones through workplace accidents. Sometimes, when a person is ready, FACK can help that person tell their story – to other workers, to employers, to politicians, to the community. This can help individuals and families but can also be a powerful tool to press for preventative action at workplace, sector and national levels. In the US, COSH harnesses the power of testimony, facilitating the public telling of personal stories of injury and ill health, with language support and interpretation being crucial in relation to many migrant workers. A moving and effective action taken by ANROEV is setting aside a part of each biennial conference to bring together and hear from victims campaigning across its 14 national constituents. In Kathmandu in 2017, the testimonies of ten victims from Indonesia, India, the Philippines, Korea and Pakistan were heard. Their stories were of tragedy brought about by factory fires, silica exposure, asbestos exposure, transport accidents, home humidifier poisoning, and of their subsequent and continuing commitment to work to prevent these tragedies happening to others.

Environmental links: Another tactic is making direct links between workplace and environmental or community campaigns that can both attract new activists and build stronger joint campaigns. In the early 1980s in Silicon Valley, California, chemical hazards had been identified in the semiconductor industry, but only early contacts existed with the non-unionised workers. However, when some of the chemicals leaked into the water system this became a community and environmental issue as well, and resulted in an effective and long-lasting Silicon Valley Toxics Coalition. The California CLEAN campaign brought workers and communities together over the hazardous chemicals being used in car washes. Environmental issues have been linked to workplace hazards in FACK campaigning, such as those involved in the waste and waste recycling sectors; the impact of silica dust on families at home as well as on workers. Two other examples, of UK-based campaigns, are a Hazards Campaign programme that provides training to workplace union representatives on air pollution and the Asbestos in Schools campaign, highlighting asbestos risk to teachers and other school staff and students. In the global South too, with its much greater levels of exposure, the issue of asbestos has brought workers and environmental campaigners together. In Chesterfield, England, joint work by a union and university highlighted the risk of bladder cancer from a Vinatex plastics factory. Links are made in the other direction too, an example being consumer pressure in the US for better treatment of chickens in the poultry industry, used to highlight the issue of toilet breaks for workers.

Building pressure on government at local and national levels: Many of the campaigns highlighted by activists used the tactics so far discussed to put pressure on elected politicians. In the UK the establishment of a review of health and safety in the construction industry followed a campaign highlighting the large number of deaths in the industry and their personal stories. Campaigns on zero-hour and other unfair contracts in the UK have also led to a government review, with some limited changes. In the US, COSH action in Massachusetts resulted in the enactment of the Temporary Workers Right to Know Act in 2012. In Europe, pressure from many unions and other groups has resulted in regulation to protect agency and temporary workers. In Scotland, the Fair Hospitality Campaign is lobbying local councils and the Scottish Parliament to support embedding its Fair Hospitality Charter into licence agreements. Trade unionists in Nepal have been fighting for improved occupational health and safety since 1995. In the 23 years prior to that they were part of the struggle for democracy. In 2017 the government finally passed national labour and social security laws: union activists said that the challenge now is to make these reality on the ground. 'For 23 years we fought for democracy. Now we are fighting within democracy for OSH' (ANROEV conference, Nepal, 2017).

Working together/alliance and solidarity building

A major theme that emerged from all sources was the centrality of developing alliances and coalitions and the importance of solidarity, support and action. Alliances include those among unions, those between self-organised workers and unions, those between self-organised workers and other organisations (NGOs and single campaign groups, or coordinating bodies such as UK Hazards, US COSH, Asian ANROEV), those between victims/survivors and unions and/or other organisations, those involving professional or expert advice and support to workers and victims/survivors, those between workers and community groups, and between those addressing occupational and environmental issues. Alliances are local, sectoral, across geographical areas, nationwide and international.

There is rich evidence of alliance building and solidarity support relating to more specific campaigns. The Save Spodden Valley Campaign in the UK was a campaign against a housing development being built on land contaminated by asbestos from the Turner & Newall asbestos textile factory. Residents and the community together with the Greater Manchester Association of Trade Union Councils and Hazard Centre campaigned to oppose the development.

The Justice for Kentex Workers Alliance brings together the Kentex Fire Accident Victims Network and Metal Workers Alliance of the Philippines with input from the Institute for Occupational Health and Safety Development. The alliance has also involved and been supported by ANROEV. As well as campaigning for Kentex worker justice, the Alliance has offered support to others, for example the Justice for HTI Workers campaign (HTI was the company that owned the Kentex factory).

Informal workers in the gem-polishing industry in India and the contracted workers in factory units in China face a major health hazard through exposure to silica. In India, as many workers are home based, families are exposed as well. Both groups of workers have been supported by local organisations: in India, the People's Research Training Institute and in China Labour Action China. Both of these organisations are active members of ANROEV. Through this link they were brought together and have since shared information, experience, best practice and training (Pandita, 2017). Another example from ANROEV is the sharing of experience and learning within Asia on occupational lung disease – the struggle to get recognition, diagnosis and, finally ,compensation. Victims from China have led this struggle and their victories have motivated others. There has also been alliance with the Human Rights network in Asia to claim compensation for informal workers where employment status cannot be proved.

In Scotland the Better Than Zero Campaign has built many alliances and, through them, done wide-ranging work. It is supported by Unite the Union and together they work with the Bakers' Union. It has also built strong links with the communities from which its precarious-work members come. Through local meetings and work in schools, it provides education and advice, and through links with a trade union employment rights organisation it is connecting with migrant workers. It has run workshops with community rights workers on hatred of injustice, know your rights, build confidence to fight back – with the overall aim of raising people's political and moral consciousness. It has linked occupation and environment through issues such as cleaning chemicals and the impact of towel washing in hotels.

One of the main roles of national COSH in the US is building and maintaining alliances. COSH involves individual workers and groups of workers, workers' centres, trade unions, health and safety professionals. It helps to coordinate the work of and to learn from its local COSH groups and workers' centres throughout the US. It also works closely with other organisations, for example the National Day Labour Organising Network and the online network Protecting Workers Alliance.

This alliance-building and coordinating role is mirrored by the Hazards Campaign in the UK. An important example is the marking of International Workers' Memorial Day (IWMD) in the UK. This day is marked throughout the world. UK Hazards and *Hazards Magazine* play a major role in stimulating unions, trade union councils and others to put on local events and in providing and identifying speakers, including members of FACK. They also provide crucial support in the form of information and briefings, graphics for publicity/posters/public displays, IWMD ribbons, car stickers.

The Good Electronics Network is an example of an alliance that has brought together individuals and organisations from across the world to improve human rights in the global electronics supply chain. This includes individual professionals, unions, victims' groups, environmental groups, NGOs, consumer groups.

Barriers and possible solutions

The last major theme that we have drawn from activists is the difficulties and barriers faced in organising, and suggestions for things that could be improved. We should start by referring back to our introduction and underlining the major structural barriers created by the now global neoliberal economic model, the putting of profit and economic growth before the health and well-being of workers and communities. This global system drives the changes in the nature of work that we have outlined, in both developing and developed countries. However, here we focus on identifying more specific barriers and difficulties that might be changed in the short to medium term.

Perceptions of conflicts of interest among working people: Among low-paid and precarious workers, tensions between local and migrant workers have been stoked in employers' interests. Migrants are portrayed as a threat to the jobs of local workers and adding to pressure on community resources such as housing and healthcare. This can be and, in some places (such as Scandinavia), is being tackled by strong union organisation and sector collective bargaining that insists that all workers are paid the same rate for doing the same job – improving the situation of both migrant and local workers.

Perceptions of conflicts of interest between environmental protection and jobs: In the UK this includes open-cast coal mining, fracking, nuclear power and nuclear submarines, air pollution and car industry workers. In other countries it can include the tobacco industry and other cash crops for export that threaten both communities and the land. These conflicts divide unions, communities and environmentalists, with all being weakened. They can also lead to counterproductive competition between unions for members, reducing the possibility of collective, strong union pressure for change. There is recognition that part of what is needed is debate and action on Just Transition away from industries that endanger the environment and public health and into those that protect and enhance quality of life. Just Transition is a framework developed by the trade union movement that encompasses social interventions needed to secure workers' jobs and livelihoods when economies restructure to more sustainable production. This includes moves to avoid climate change, protect biodiversity and end war. We have to find a way for jobs and livelihoods relying on industries such as coal, oil, military weapons, mining that destroys land and communities to be replaced by new jobs. The ITUC developed a Just Transition Centre in 2016.

Falling union membership/weak unions and pressure against unionisation: Activists identified weak trade unions as being a major barrier to effective organising and campaigning. Weakened unions are in part a result of the changing nature of work and partly due to anti-trade union policies of governments and employers. The situation is made worse by communication problems among workers due to language differences and low literacy. In some countries trade unions' independence is compromised or non-existent.

In Asia, rampant anti-union policies are a major issue. A striking example of this is the Samsung company, where there are well-documented anti-union and union-busting activities alongside clear and now accepted work-related risks to workers' health. Interviewees in the UK and US have also identified fear of forming or joining a union as a major barrier to organising marginal workers. This fear is sometimes created by the businesses themselves, for example Deliveroo and Sports Direct, and sometimes, for migrant workers, by immigration authorities.

The impact of trade deals: International trade deals or proposals, for example the North American Free Trade Agreement and TTIP, have major implications for workplace and environmental standards. The struggle in Europe that stopped TTIP going ahead was an example of transnational collaboration by unions, environmentalists, food safety groups, scientists.

Global and local supply chains: The impact of sub-contracting on workers throughout the world is huge. Responsibility for working conditions becomes very difficult to disentangle. In Denmark a campaign by construction unions has succeeded in getting regulation that ensures that the employer at the head of the supply chain is held responsible for what happens in all companies involved in the chain. In the UK work is being done to address this through the development of ethical procurement policies within the public sector.

Political impact on funding: Funding is a major issue for most of the organising and campaigning organisations we have discussed. An additional problem is that funding often depends on the current political climate. National COSH has been hit by major funding cuts since the election of President Trump. In the UK, falling funding for local authorities as a result of the government's austerity agenda has impacted on a number of local campaign groups that relied on local authority funding. Many campaign groups in Asia depend on NGO support that is also impacted on by political climates and changing donor priorities. One of the necessary actions discussed by our interviewees was to diversify funding streams so as to reduce this vulnerability.

Social media: Social media is seen as an important organising tool, but also a complicated one. It is crucial that it not be seen as taking the place of on-the-ground, face-to-face organising, but as an additional tool.

Conclusion

This chapter has used snapshots of current activity that identify themes reflective of the realities facing grassroots activists throughout a world enmeshed in neoliberal capitalism. Researching and writing it has already stimulated discussion, and at least in some cases an expansion in the scope and tactics of organising. It is also contributing to discussions aimed at developing a global grassroots occupational and environmental health network.

Sanjiv Pandita has said that "the exchange with grassroots movements in the US and Europe have been of great help and support in building the movement in Asia" (personal e-mail communication, 2018). Exchanges among activists have been very important, including, for example, those involved in the struggle for justice in Bhopal following the 1984 gas disaster; the work of the Workers' Health International Newsletter (WHIN), which played a crucial role in international communication prior to the internet; the work of European and US workers' centres. Sanjiv continues:

> technical sharing by experts often does not help but sharing on the level of movements is very important since people in other places (like the North) may have been through the same struggle and it helps communities or workers who are being exposed now. Examples of this are struggles against exposure to asbestos and chemicals in electronics. Both the International Ban Asbestos Secretariat (IBAS) and the [International] Campaign for Responsible Technology (ICRT) have played an important role in this. (Personal e-mail communication, 2018)

There is a fallacy of 'technology transfer' – that support between North and South, university and trade union, NGO and survivors' group is based on technical expertise in the former. The examples here demonstrate that, wherever the technological expertise lies, alliances are effective only when built on the basis of solidarity and agency. Indeed, all the examples support a conclusion that power relations are central to effecting social and political change. Just as Bunyan (2012: 14) concludes in relation to community organising, this requires 'a hard-headed commitment to solidarity and the building of alternative forms of collective power rooted in but transcending localities and capable of engaging with and unsettling the prevailing institutional order'.

References

ANROEV (2015) 'Prevention of occupational diseases and improving workplace safety', in *Proceedings of the ANROEV Conference 2015, 4–5 September. Hanoi, Vietnam*, New Delhi: ANROEV.

Bunyan, P. (2012) 'Partnership, the Big Society and community organizing: Between romanticizing, problematizing and politicizing community', *Community Development Journal*, 48(1): 119–33.

Eun-Seok, C. (2017) 'Organizing warranty service engineers at Samsung Electronics Service Sector in South Korea', in F. Panimbang (ed) *Resistance on the continent of labour: Strategies and initiatives of labour organisation in Asia*, Hong Kong: AMRC, pp 55–72.

ILO (nd) 'Safety and health at work', International Labour Organization, http://www.ilo.org/global/topics/safety-and-health-at-work/lang--en/index.htm.

ILO (2015) 'World employment and social outlook 2015: The changing nature of jobs', International Labour Organization, http://embargo.ilo.org/global/research/global-reports/weso/2015-changing-nature-of-jobs/WCMS_368626/lang--en/index.htm.

ITUC (2015) *Scandal: Inside the global supply chains of 50 top companies*, ITUC Frontlines Report, https://www.ituc-csi.org/IMG/pdf/pdffrontlines_scandal_en-2.pdf.

MacAlevey, J. (2013) *Transformation*, https://www.opendemocracy.net/transformation/jane-mcalevey/organizing-as-whole-people.

Pandita, S. (2017) 'The bottom-up international labour solidarity: Victims' organising in the Asian Network for the Rights of Occupational and Environmental Victims', in F. Panimbang (ed) *Resistance on the continent of labour: Strategies and initiatives of labour organisation in Asia*, Hong Kong: AMRC, pp 303–20.

Panimbang, F. (2017a) 'Labour struggles in Asia', in F. Panimbang (ed) *Resistance on the continent of labour: Strategies and initiatives of labour organisation in Asia*, Hong Kong: AMRC, pp 1–10.

Panimbang, F. (2017b) *Resistance on the continent of labour: Strategies and initiatives of labour organisation in Asia*, Hong Kong: AMRC.

Conclusion

Anne Harley and Eurig Scandrett

We asked contributors to this book to reflect both practically and theoretically on their engagement with struggles for environmental justice and how these connect to community development and popular struggle. As academics or activists, all provide rich reflections on these processes. The process of producing the book has been a joy, although not without its difficulties. The contributors are all engaged in some way with struggles against the exploitations of neoliberalism. Activists constantly operate to time-scales determined by the situation in which we and our comrades find ourselves. Academics in all parts of the world also face the sustained imposition of neoliberal practices on our working conditions. It is important to protect the space in which university employees engage with committed scholarship in solidarity with communities of struggle, as well as engaging with struggles in which our own labour is expropriated; and this book has facilitated this. It has been a privilege to work with such a range of committed activists and scholars.

Many of the chapters have been co-produced, a process that has been a generator of new insights. Co-production has been informally shaped by a discipline of Freirean dialogue. Eurig, working as an activist-academic with a range of friends and comrades from India, Palestine and Scotland, found that the production process — the dialectical integrity of content and narrative, experience and theory, urgency and reflection — has taken a different form with each. In the cases of Scottish-based activists Jennifer, Kathy and Sara, as a co-activist Eurig was able to participate in discussing the chapters prior to editing, but their chapters are essentially their work. Kathy and Sara's Chapter Twelve is in itself a significant contribution to the struggle, involving detailed discussions with a wide range of community-based, trade union, anti-toxics and environmentalist groups engaged in the contradictions of class struggle over environmental health in the workplace and community. The production of the chapter has thus made a contribution to developing the grassroots network on occupational and environmental health struggles that was proposed at a conference between the Asian and the European movements a few years ago.

Many of the chapters began as dialogues between two or more of those involved in a struggle or acting in solidarity. Dharmesh and Shweta's (Chapter Eleven) significant experience and current dilemmas with the Indian environmental justice movement were captured through a series of Skype interviews with Eurig, documented and then subjected to a process of dialogical counter-critique. Chapter Ten was initially written by Eurig from material provided by Abeer, Zayneb and Mahmoud in many different ways – through written input and interview, but mostly through Eurig's direct experience of participation in solidarity activities in Palestine, hosted by the other contributors – and then collectively revised. Similar processes were used by others: reflections from experience were debated, written up and then shared for further discussion (Patrick with Berenice (Chapter Three)); Jeanne and Bobby (Chapter Nine); Mark with others at CLP (Chapter Seven); and/or activist-scholars interviewed those involved in various struggles, capturing different voices (Richard and Daniel, Chapter Four); or, in the case of Jonathan's self-reflection of his experiences and the wider movement learning (Chapter Six), shared with others involved in the struggle for suggestions, corrections and explanations to deepen his learning.

As a body of work, the chapters have explored issues familiar to environmental justice activists, including coal mining (Mark, Chapter Seven), oil and gas (Hilary and Laurence, Chapter Two), fracking (Jonathan, Chapter Six), waste (Jennifer, Chapter Five), pollution (Richard and Daniel, Chapter Four) or a combination of these (Dharmesh and Shweta in Chapter Eleven; Jeanne and Bobby in Chapter Nine), but also the ways in which environmental justice issues may be hidden as part of broader processes: for example, how colonial appropriation of environmental resources is part of the Zionist settler colonisation of Palestine (Simon in Chapter Eight; Abeer, Zayneb and Mahmoud in Chapter Ten). Patrick and Berenice's account in Chapter Three of the remarkable popular uprising in Buenaventura is rooted in both a human ecology of some of the most excluded populations of Colombia and the violation of the port-city population through the accelerated export of extracted resources. In Chapter Twelve Kathy and Sara illustrate the ways in which environmental injustices interact with new forms of labour exploitation – and of trade union organising – throughout the world.

During our editing process we found that we had started to edit out some of the most interesting and insightful material in order to accommodate the core arguments and diverse contexts in which these struggles are occurring. Much material that we risked losing occurred in sections in which contributors allowed themselves the opportunity to step out from their campaigns and struggles and the requirements of academic scholarship, and to reflect, critically and honestly, on their activities. These insights, stimulated by the process of writing, are so often the content that academic writing excludes in the current competitive climate of league tables and productivity ratings. They relate to some of the more difficult and challenging reflections that activists and academics face in their praxis. We have, wherever possible, included these insights in the chapters themselves but want to highlight the 'generative themes' (in Freirean terms) that the book has collectively generated. We believe that these have the potential– through a dialectical process of testing against concrete reality – to produce understanding in praxis at a deeper, richer and 'thicker' level.

We have been struck by the extent to which, in reflecting on these themes, we are continually drawn back to Bhattacharyya's understanding of the core purposes of community development as *solidarity* and *agency*. Solidarity is an essential characteristic of community, while agency, he argues, is what development should be about:

> The ultimate goal of development should be human autonomy and agency – the capacity of people to order their world, the capacity to create, reproduce, change, and live according to their own meaning systems, to have the powers to define themselves as opposed to being defined by others. (Bhattacharyya, 2004: 12)

Practices that go by the name of development, in contrast, do the opposite. As our contributors show, 'development' means coal mines in KwaZulu-Natal, a power station in Slovakia, a gas pipeline in Ireland, land grabs for oil extraction or solar farms in India, incinerators in Scotland, fracking in Nova Scotia, unregulated chemical industries in occupied Palestine, expansion of a private port in Colombia and casualised employment in multiple sectors and locations across the globe. In all these cases, development is an attempt to exclude, silence, fragment, segregate and disempower; it is precisely solidarity and agency that are under threat (Bhattacharyya, 2004). Both have been undermined at micro and macro levels through industrial capitalism, the rise of the nation-state and ideologies such as instrumental reason. Through this process, commodification and radical individualism have come to permeate every aspect of life, while identity and subjectivity have been threatened by cultural domination. 'Cultures that do not obey the market logic of capital are labelled as irrational' (Bhattacharyya, 2004: 20). None of these eroding forces is likely to go away anytime soon; and thus community development, operating in this context, needs to address macro factors while working in microenvironments.

The chapters have reflected the problematics of how solidarity and agency are to be practised with integrity in the microenvironments of particular struggles and concrete contexts while addressing the macro factors that are often the origins of these eroding forces. The accounts of micro-level struggles, and those taking place on a more macro level, identify tensions around how particular struggles relate to each other or the ways in which activists from outside the communities directly affected by environmental injustice (as is the case for many environmental activists and activist-academics) engage with those within. While the practices of activists seek to prefigure emancipatory ecological humanism, the contributors demonstrate that the embedded subjectivities of colonialism, settler-colonialism and class, racial and gendered oppression (as well as the functional incorporation of civil society) cannot easily be left outside the door when we enter the location in which the terrain of struggle is most acute. 'Communities are not uncomplicated homogeneous entities. They are multidimensional and fragmented by different inequalities and competing interests, and at times they are fractured by overt conflict' (Kenny, 2016: 24).

A number of the chapters thus speak to potential or actual faultlines or fractures in struggles at micro or macro level: such as gender, in one of the interviews in Jeanne and Bobby's Chapter Nine on South Africa; class and ethnicity in Richard and Daniel's Chapter Four on Slovakia; settlers and indigenous populations in Canada and Palestine (Chapters Six, Eight and Ten). However, accounts show the various ways in which solidarity can be built (in the case of the Nova Scotia fracking struggle (Chapter Six), or Patrick and Berenice's account of the Buenaventura strike (Chapter Three)); or indeed faultlines recreated or newly created (as in the Slovakian case (Chapter Four), where environmental justice struggles, manipulated by class interests, served to reproduce and exacerbate conflicts along ethnic lines; or in Dharmesh and Shweta's account (Chapter Eleven) of how philanthrocapitalism in India fragments and divides struggles). By contrast, Hilary and Laurence (Chapter Three) show how a community can hold a struggle together despite disunity. As Simon in Chapter Eight, and Abeer, Zayneb and Mahmoud, in Chapter Ten, point out, a call for unity can be distorted by colonial interests as Zionists seek to use environmental protection as a cover for normalising and legitimising the expropriation of Palestinian land and resources.

As Shaw and Mayo (2016) argue in *Class, inequality and community development*, a class analysis needs to be central in any discussion of community development; and environmental struggles help us to see this. Class is dynamic, driven by economic and social pressures and mediated through the environment: extractive and manufacturing 'development' produces new working classes and bourgeoisie; racist discourses of pollution consign unwanted populations to an ethnically defined 'underclass' through settler-colonisation, expulsion and ghettoisation; accumulation by dispossession of resources fragments class fractions; post-industrial workers are casualised into precarious transience, including through the proletarianisation of academic work.

Current environmental struggles take place at the micro, community level; and play themselves out on a global stage. They are fraught with issues of power. Understanding the macro–micro connections, relations of power and the possibility of agency is possible through this environmental justice lens. We return to Bhattacharyya's (2004) insistence that there is a need to separate out the purpose of community development from its premises and its methods, the purposes of agency and solidarity.

What is clear from these stories is that solidarity involves work, and especially by those of us who have been privileged – in however compromised and conflictual ways – by the eroding forces of capital accumulation and hegemonic patriarchy. The account of the struggle against fracking in Nova Scotia/Mi'kma'ki (Chapter Six) makes this particularly clear. Similarly, in Chapter Seven Mark includes a snapshot of 'the good stuff' (see Butler et al, 2010: 4) of radically democratic and militant humanism that the CLP has come to recognise through reflective critique on its engagement with communities engaged in struggle in KwaZulu-Natal.

Authentic solidarity requires an assumption of agency, and aspects of the agency of communities have been identified by our contributors through practices of what is variously called prefigurative politics, popular struggle, or non-violence – the ways in which the means by which we conduct the struggle reflect /are consistent with/are infused with the purposes for which we struggle (and the expectation of emancipation): civic organisation and the grassroots puntos in Buenaventura (Chapter Three); decolonising alliances between settlers and First Nation peoples in Nova Scotia/Mi'kma'ki (Chapter Six); the intellectual work of those threatened by mining in KwaZulu-Natal (Chapter Seven); economic self-reliance of Adivasi struggles in India

(Chapter Eleven); popular resistance in Palestine (Chapters Eight and Ten); new forms of community-based labour organising in Scotland (Chapter Five).

The stories captured in the book are reflections on a 'war of position' in Gramscian terms between the interests of capital and that of popular community agency and solidarity. In the reflections of some activists, movements from below are experiencing set-backs and retreats in the face of aggressive mobilising by the capitalist class: India's philanthrocapitalism has contributed to a retreat by the environmental justice movement (Chapter Eleven); European business influence on policy has defeated community waste and anti-incineration movements in Scotland (Chapter Five); and Slovakian Romani agency is so thoroughly excluded that environmental justice campaigns have become little more than struggles between sections of the bourgeoisie (Chapter Four). As Cox and Nilsen (2014) point out, social movement processes can go backwards as well as forwards. In other contexts, movements from below are thriving, developing new forms of engagement, and in some cases (Buenaventura (Chapter Three), Nova Scotia/Mi'kma'ki (Chapter Six)) making some advancement against the interests of capital mobilising from above.

Some of the pivotal issues concern the connection between the micro and the macro, the extent to which multiple communities engaged in particular struggles are able to link together to challenge the interests of structural power, such as capital, colonisation or patriarchy. For those engaged in community development – as local activists, environmentalists, community workers or academics – this is a crucial question. Through a dialectic of agency and solidarity, communities are able, with or without the involvement of community workers from outside, to respond to environmental injustices through mobilisation, informal education, collective action and engaging in forms of militant particularism. Moreover, such militant particularism can be understood as a component, alongside other forms of popular struggle, in a 'social movement process' (Cox and Nilsen, 2014) that also includes building connections among communities with common struggle: 'joining hands to join the dots'; collective conscientisation as people generalise from their particular struggle and learn from their abstractions; single-issue and multiple-issue campaigns and wider movements that at times make claims within, and at other times seek to transform hegemonic social relations.

The capacity for communities to transcend their concrete struggles and challenge the 'eroding forces' of capital can be constrained by the ferocity of the battle against them, but also facilitated by their connections with other communities or, at times, with outsiders willing to listen. Solidarity requires outsiders to engage in serious dialogue that starts from a genuine presumption of the thinking and agency of people. The struggle for environmental justice requires sustained engagement with these processes, for the environment to be valued through human agency, not, as is currently hegemonic, as economic investment (Martínez-Alier, 2002). Community development, as agency and solidarity, is part of this.

References

Bhattacharyya, J. (2004) 'Theorizing community development', *Journal of the Community Development Society*, 34(2): 5–34.

Butler, M. with Dennis, C., Ndlazi, T., Ntseng, D., Philpott, G., Sithole, Z. and Sokhela, N. (2010) *Finding our voice in the world*, Pietermaritzburg, SA: Church Land Programme, http://www.churchland.org.za/wp-content/uploads/2013/02/Finding-our-voice-in-the-world.pdf.

Cox, L. and Nilsen, A.G. (2014) *We make our own history: Marxism, social movements and the crisis of neoliberalism*, London: Pluto Press.

Kenny, S. (2016) 'Community development today: Engaging challenges through cosmopolitanism?', *Community Development Journal*, 51(1): 23–41.

Martínez-Alier, J. (2002) *Environmentalism of the poor*, Cheltenham: Edward Elgar.

Shaw, M. and Mayo, M. (eds) (2016) *Class, inequality and community development*, Bristol: Policy Press.

Index

Page numbers in *italics* indicate figures.

A

Abu Taleb, Y. 165
accumulation by dispossession 137–138, 178–179
African National Congress (ANC) 136, 139
Afro-Colombian communities 32, 34
agency 8, 10, 26, 213, 214, 215–216
Agenda 21 (UNCED) 3, 4–5
agriculture 154–155
  Union of Agricultural Works Committees (UAWC) 160–161
Ahern, Bertie 15, 16
Aida Youth Centre 159–160
air pollution 53
al Butmeh, A. 122, 155
Al Ma'sara community centre 158–159
Alexander, M. 165
Al-Fayed, Mohamed 78
Aljazeera 162
Allen, R. 21
alliances 80, 204–206
Alshalalfeh, Z. 155
al-Shalalfeh, Z. 155, 162
Andharia, J. 176
anti-fracking movement 83–85
  Elsipogtog First Nation 87–89, 94, 95
  Lake Ainslie 89
  learning in struggle 93–97
  Responsible Energy Action (REA) 84–85, 89–90, 96
  Wheeler review panel 91–93
anti-incineration movement 72–79, 80
apartheid 140, 141
Apartheid Wall 127–129
Arnold, R. 143
Asia
  poverty 192
  trade unions 207–208
Asia Monitor Resource Centre (AMRC) 191, 201
Asian Network for the Rights of Occupational and Environmental Victims (ANROEV) 194, 198, 201–202
  alliances between members 205
  name change 195
  pressure on government 204
  testimony 203
  work and community boundaries 196, 197
Awad, H. 125, 131
axiom of equality 8

B

Balfour Declaration 118, 156
Bangladesh 197
Baroud, R. 157
Barrington, B. 18
Bethlehem 123
Better than Zero 190, 200, 202, 205–206
better way than boycotts, A (Moses) 164
Bhattacharyya, J. 10, 166, 167, 213–214, 215
Bhopal 173–174
Binns, T. 104
Black Communities Process 34
Board of Deputies of British Jews 164
boundaries 195–197
Bourdieu, Pierre 54
boycotts 166
brand shaming 202–203
Brennan, M.A. 10
Broadhaven Bay 15
Buenaventura
  civic strike 29–52
    historic march 21 May 2017 *43*
    learning in struggle 46–50
    legacy 50–52
    negotiations 44–46
    origins 30–32
    police response 40–44, *41*
    preparations 34–37
    roadblocks (*puntos de encuentro*) 37–38
    women's march 3 June 2017 *48*
  location *31*
Bunyan, P. 194
Burke, Ray 16
Burrow, Sharan 193
Burton, J. 103
Butler, M. 140, 141

219

C

Cabral, A. 8
campaigning knowledge 22
Canaanites 117
Canada
   anti-fracking movement 83–85
   Elsipogtog First Nation 87–89, 94, 95
   Lake Ainslie 89
   learning in struggle 93–97
   Responsible Energy Action (REA) 84–85, 89–90, 96
   Wheeler review panel 91–93
capital 1, 3, 70
   mining capital 101, 103, 106, 114–115
capital accumulation 2, 3, 4, 8, 192
capitalism 1
   Buenaventura 51–52
   Environmental Justice School (EJS) 145
   mechanisms of 137–139
   and sustainable development 3–5
   see also philanthrocapitalism
capitalism 1, 137, 145
   and sustainable development 3–5
   see also philanthrocapitalism
Carter, E.D. 6
Catholic church 34–35
Centro Nacional de Memoria Historica 32, 33
Challenge Breast Cancer Scotland 199–200
Chicago teachers' strike 197–198
China 205
Choudry, A. 50, 86, 95
Christian churches 130–131
   see also Catholic church
Chughtai, A. 161
Church Land Programme (CLP) 101, 113, 114
Circular Economy Strategy, Scotland 79
Civic Strike to Live with Dignity in Buenaventura 29–52
   historic march 21 May 2017 *43*
   learning experiences 46–50
   legacy 50–52
   location of Buenaventura *31*
   negotiations 44–46
   origins 30–32
   police response 40–44, *41*
   preparations 34–37
   roadblocks (Puntos de encuentos) 37–38
   women's march 3 June 2017 *48*
civil society 113
class 59–61, 77, 96, 215
CLEAN campaign 203
climate change 130, 131
climate resilience 181
coal industry 101
   community resistance 105, 106, 107–113, 113–115, 147–148
   history 102–105
   licensing 137
   present day 105–107
coal-burning power plant 53–54
   development 54–56
   map *55*
   public resistance to 57–58
   and social class 59–61
coalition building 204–206
cohesion 20–21
collective consciousness 46
Collins, C. 5
Colombia
   civic strike 29–52
   historic march 21 May 2017 *43*
   learning experiences 46–50
   legacy 50–52
   negotiations 44–46
   origins 30–32
   police response 40–44, *41*
   preparations 34–37
   roadblocks (*puntos de encuentro*) 37–38
   women's march 3 June 2017 *48*
   map *31*
colonialism 1–2, 153
   South Africa 102–103, 140
colonisation, Palestine 117–119, 153–154
   and community development 156–157
   and international solidarity 166–167
   as normalisation 163–166
   as popular struggle 157–163
   and environmental justice 154–155
community 6, 7
community (self-) education *see* self-education
community and work boundaries 195–197
community composting 69, 75
community development 2, 4–5, 9–10
   British colonies 155–156
   consensual 25
   and neoliberalism 6–7
   oppositional 25
   Palestine 156–167
   and international solidarity 166–167
   as normalisation 163–166

as popular struggle 157–163
community organising 176, 180, 193–194
Community Recycling Network for Scotland (CRNS) 71, 74
composting 69, 75
conflicts of interest 207
Connett, Dr Paul 78
consensual community development 25
consensus 84
corporate social responsibility (CSR) 180, 185
Corrbridge, S. 176–177
Corrib gas field 15, 18
COSH *see* National Council for Occupational Safety and Health (COSH)
counter-expertise 22
County Mayo 15, 16
Cox, L. 5, 19, 178, 180, 216
Cronin, D. 157
Crowley, Gerry 17
cultural hegemony 181
Curtin, C. 25
Czechoslovak Energy Company 55, 56

D

Davis, U. 119, 154
Deliveroo 196, 202, 208
Denmark 208
development 1, 6, 137, 213
direct action 202
discrimination 53
  see also racism
displacement 120
dispossession through participation 5
division of labour 2
Dundee (Natal) Coal Company, South Africa 102
Dundee, Scotland 73, 74

E

Earth Summit 3, 4, 5
Earthlife Africa (ELA) 5
Eberhard, A. 103
Ecology Action Centre 85
EcoPeace Middle East 164–166, 167
education *see* Environmental Education Center (EEC), Palestine; Environmental Justice School (EJS), South Africa; self-education
Ejatlas 181
El Espectador newspaper 51
El Tiempo newspaper 33
Elsipogtog First Nation 87–89, 94, 95
emancipatory education 143
emancipatory politics 114
embodied social structures 54
employment 192–193, 195
enclosure 138
energy 56, 72, 102, 139, 181
  see also extractive industry; Responsible Energy Action (REA)
Energy from Waste 69–70
  anti-incineration movement 73–79, 80
Enterprise Oil 18
environment 1
  political economy of 1–2
environmental degradation 34
Environmental Education Center (EEC), Palestine 129–131
environmental health *see* occupational and environmental health
Environmental Impact Assessment (EIA) 56–58
environmental justice 9–10
environmental justice conflict 59
environmental justice movements 2, 5–7, 10
  India 173–174, 182–185
  historical context 175–180
  South Africa 141
  unofficial 21
Environmental Justice School (EJS), South Africa 135–136, 142–146
  challenges 149–150
  participants' evaluations 146, 150
  participants' struggles 146–148
environmental justice struggles, map *11*
environmental links 203–204
Environmental Quality Authority (EQA) 125–126
environmental racism 84, 86, 88, 93
environmental rights 141
environmentalism 3
environmentalism of the poor 6
equality, axiom of 8
Erris
  resistance to gas pipeline 15–18
    campaign goals 21–22, 24
    cohesion among activists 20–21
    counter-expertise 22
    impact on radical politics 19–20
    knowledge transfer 24
    police violence 17, 18, 23–24
    professional activists 25–26
    radical self-education 23
Escobar, A. 32, 34
ethnic cleansing 120
Eun-Seok, C. 196
European Commission 69
European Parliament 72–73
exclusion 138, *139*
expertise *see* counter-expertise

externalisation 137
extractive industry 101
　community resistance 105, 106, 107–113, 113–115, 147–148
　history 102–105
　licensing 137
　present day 105–107
Eyerman, R. 22

F

Faber, D.R. 5
Fair Hospitality 200, 204
Families Against Corporate Killers (FACK) 199, 203, 204
Fecteau, Janette 90
Filčák, R. 62
Fine, B. 103, 145
First Nation people *see* Mi'kmaq
Foley, G. 84, 85, 93
food insecurity 160–161
fracking 19, 24
　anti-fracking movement 83–85
　　Elsipogtog First Nation 87–89, 94, 95
　　Lake Ainslie 89
　　learning in struggle 93–97
　　Responsible Energy Action (REA) 84–85, 89–90, 96
　　Wheeler review panel 91–93
free trade agreements 32, 33, 208
Freire, Paulo 143, 180
Friends of the Earth 4, 73, 166
funding 208

G

gas pipeline
　resistance to 15–18
　　campaign goals 21–22, 24
　　cohesion among activists 20–21
　　counter-expertise 22
　　impact on radical politics 19–20
　　knowledge transfer 24
　　police violence 17, 18, 23–24
　　professional activists 25–26
　　radical self-education 23
Gaza Strip 121, 155, 160–161
gender 2, 161–163, 196–197
Geoghegan, M. 9
Geshuri industrial settlements 124–126
Gharib, A. 155
ghettos 54, 62
Glasgow 80
global political economy 192–193
Global Production Network 192
global supply chains 208
Good Electronics Network 191, 206
Gramsci, Antonio 8, 143, 178
Grande, S. 86

Great Britain 118
Green Alternatives to Incineration in Scotland (GAINS) 75, 77, 78
Green Party, Ireland 17
Greenpeace 57, 74
groundWork 105, 141–142
　Environmental Justice School (EJS) 135–136, 142–146
　　challenges 149–150
　　participants' evaluations 146, 150
　　participants' struggles 146–148
Guest, B. 102, 103
Guha, R. 3, 6
Guy, J. 91
Guy, W. 61

H

Hallowes, D. 103, 104, 140, 141, 145
Hambright, K. 120
Hanieh, A. 163
Hanoun, S. 125
Har Homa settlement 123, 124
Harper, Robin 77
Harris, J. 176–177
Harvey, D. 7, 137, 178
Hazards Campaign 190, 198, 204, 206
Hazards Magazine 190, 202
hegemony 3–5, 50–51, 144
　hydro-hegemony 165
　selective 174, 176, 181
health and safety 193
Health Impact Assessment (HIA) 58
health impacts, industrial settlements 125, 126
health issues *see* occupational and environmental health
Health Protection Scotland 76
hegemonic struggle 143
Herzl, Theodor 118
Hesperian Health Guides 201
Higgins, Michael D. 17
Highland Combined Heat and Power Ltd 78
Highveld Environmental Justice Network (HEJN) 148
Hilal, J. 120, 121, 165
Hildebrand, A. 89
Hill, R.J. 94
Histadrut 154
home-care workers 196
hooks, b. 86
Howe, M. 87
human rights violations 44
Human Rights Watch 33
Hungary 57–58
Hunterston 80

Index

I

Idle No More movement 87
incineration 69–70, 71, 72, 79–80
  anti-incineration movement 73–79, 80
India
  environmental justice movement 173–175, 182–185
    historical context 175–180
  home-based workers 205
  Land Acquisition Act 1854 177–178
  New Economic Programme (NEP) 176
  Petroleum, Chemicals and Petrochemicals Investment Region (PCPIR) 174
  philanthrocapitalism 180–184, 185
indigenous communities
  Colombia 31–32, 34
  Nova Scotia 84, 85, 86, 94–95
    Elsipogtog First Nation, New Brunswick 87–89, 94, 95
    Lake Ainslie 89
    Wheeler review panel 92, 93
  South Africa 140
industrial settlements 124–126
Inggs, M. 104
institutional racism 60–61, 63
International Campaign for Justice in Bhopal 173
International Court of Justice (ICJ) 127
International Labour Organization (ILO) 192–193
international solidarity 166–167
international trade deals *see* free trade agreements
International Trade Union Confederation (ITUC) 193
Invergordon Incinerator No to Waste group 78
Ireland
  oil and gas regime 15–16
  Shell to Sea 15–18
    campaign goals 21–22, 24
    cohesion among activists 20–21
    counter-expertise 22
    impact on radical politics 19–20
    knowledge transfer 24
    police violence 17, 18, 23–24
    professional activists 25–26
    radical self-education 23
Isaac, J. 120, 121, 165
Israel 119–120
  Apartheid Wall 127–129
  community development 163–166
  illegal Israeli settlements 122–126
  occupation of Palestinian territory 120–121, 154–155

J

Jabal Abu Ghnaim 123–124
Jackson, Caroline 73
Jamison, A. 22
Jewish National Fund (JNF) 119–120, 154, 166
Jones, T. 21
Jordan River 165
Just Transition 207
Justiça Ambiental 148
Justice for Kentex Workers Alliance 199, 205

K

Kader and Zhil 201
Karunaratne, G. 175
Kathmandu 203
Kattan, V. 156
Kenny, S. 9–10, 214
Khalidi, W. 119, 154
Khan, F. 136, 141
Killen, S. 95
knowledge transfer 24
Koppelman, S. 155
Krishnaswamy, S. 181
Kumar Nite, D. 103
KwaZulu-Natal (KZN)
  Church Land Programme (CLP) 101, 113, 114
  coal industry
    community resistance 105, 106, 107–113, 113–115
    history 102–105
    present day 105–107
Kwazumkhono Environmental Justice Network 105

L

Laborov
  coal-burning power plant 53–54
  development 54–56
  map 55
  public resistance to 57–58
  and social class 59–61
  Roma population 53, 54, 57, 59–60, 60–61, 61–62, 63, 65–67
  sugar factory 54–55
  waste management 53, 61, 63–66, 64, 66
Laborov First 57, 58, 59–61, 63
labour, division of 2
Labour Party, Ireland 17
Lake Ainslie, Nova Scotia 89
Lanarkshire 80

Land Acquisition Act 1854, India 177–178
land 16
see also Church Land Programme (CLP)
land grabs
India 187, 181
Palestine 119–120, 121, 122, 123, 128
land rights
Colombia 34
Nova Scotia 87, 88–89, 90, 92
Palestine 117–119, 154–155
South Africa 106, 109
landfill 70–71, 74
Langdon, J. 89
Larweh, K. 89
leadership 48–50
learning in struggle 84, 85–86, 93–97
Lehn, W. 119, 154
Leonard-Wright, B. 86, 96
looting 40–41
Low, Barbara 92, 95
Lynn, Helen 190

M

Mabilo, Promise 148, 150
MacAlvey, Jane 197–198
Machado, Temistocles 51
MacIntosh, C. 94
Maggs, T. 102
Mahmood, Khalid 196
Mamdani, M. 140
Mandela, Nelson 136
Maquiladora Health and Safety Support Network 198
marine litter 181–182
Martinez, Jessica 190
Martínez-Alier, J. 3, 6, 153, 217
massacres 120
Matarrita-Cascante, D. 10
materialist environmentalism 6
Mathers, A. 30
Mauro, Ian 91, 92, 94
Mayo, M. 155–156, 215
Mayo, P. 24
McCarthy, D. 5
McCrea, N. 166
Meade, R.R. 166
Mekorot 166–167
Metallic, Naomi 95
Michelin, O. 88
Middle East Friends of the Earth see EcoPeace Middle East
Mi'kmaq 84, 85, 86, 94–95
Elsipogtog First Nation, New Brunswick 87–89, 94, 95
Lake Ainslie 89

Wheeler review panel 92, 93
Mi'kmaq Rights Initiative 94
Minerals and Energy Complex (MEC) 103–104
mining 101
community resistance 105, 106, 107–113, 113–115, 147–148
history 102–105
licensing 137
present day 105–107
mobilisation 47–48
Modi, Narenda 12, 178, 180
Mokgalaka, R. 105
Moses, J. 164–165
movements from above 2, 7, 11, 178, 180
Mozambique 148
Munnik, V. 145
Munster 16, 24
Murray, R. 74

N

Nagra, R. 126
naming and shaming 202–203
Narayan, S. 174
National Council for Occupational Safety and Health (COSH) 190, 198, 203, 204, 206
National Environmental Management Act, South Africa 141
Nel, E. 104–105
neoliberalism 4, 5, 32
accumulation by dispossession 137–138, 178–179
and community development 6–7, 9
and environmental justice movements 6
impact on Roma population 61
and philanthrocapitalism 180–184, 185
South Africa 139
waste industry 70
networking 24, 80, 150
see also alliances
New Brunswick, Nova Scotia 87–89, 94
New Economic Programme (NEP) 176
New York State 84
Newcastle Byker incinerator 73–74
NGOs (non-governmental organisations)
alliances with 6
Czechosolovak Energy Company 56
Ecology Action Center 85
EcoPeace Middle East 164–166, 167
funding 184, 185
incineration 77–78

Index

transparency 182
vanguardism 8, 113
see also groundWorks; Laborov First
Nilsen, A.G. 5, 178, 180, 216
Nkosi, X. 105
'no arrest' strategy 17
No Consent project 24, 25–26
North Ayrshire 80
Nova Scotia
 anti-fracking movement 83–85
  Elsipogtog First Nation 87–89, 94, 95
  Lake Ainslie 89
  learning in struggle 93–97
  Responsible Energy Action (REA) 84–85, 89–90, 96
  Wheeler review panel 91–93
Nova Scotia Fracking Research and Advocacy Coalition (NOFRAC) 84–85
Novelli, N. 30
Nunes, M. 142

O

occupational and environmental health 189–209
 activists 190–191
 context 192–195
  community development and organising 193–194
  global political economy 192–193
  health and safety 193
  relationship between occupational and environmental justice struggles 195
 findings 195–208
  barriers and solutions 206–208
  external organisers 200–202
  tactics 202–204
  work and community boundaries 195–197
  workers' organisations 197–204
 global context 191
oil 15–16, 18
 see also fracking; Shell to Sea
oil extraction 174–175
oil refining 174
oppositional community development 25
oppositional consciousness 46–47
organisation 47–48

P

Palestine 117
 al Nakba (the Catastrophe) 120
 Apartheid Wall 127–129
 colonisation 117–119, 153–154
  and environmental justice 154–155

community development 156–157
 and international solidarity 166–167
 as normalisation 163–166
 as popular struggle 157–163
Environmental Education Center (EEC) 129–131
environmental exploitation 119–120
illegal Israeli settlements 122–126
Israeli occupation 120–121
Palestinian loss of land, 1917-2012 *119*
Palmer, Hilda 190
Pandita, Sanjiv 191, 193, 196, 209
Panimbang, F. 192, 195, 200
participatory democracy 4–5
passive revolution 175
Paul, D. 95
Peace and Friendship Treaties, Mi'kma'ki 87–88, 88–89, 90
perseverance 47
Peters, Molly 93, 94
Petroleum, Chemicals and Petrochemicals Investment Region (PCPIR) 174–175
Petroworth Resources 89
philanthrocapitalism 180–184, 185
Philippines 199
Piterberg, G. 154
Plank, K. 180, 181
planning system 75–76, 78–79, 80
plastic waste 181–182
pluralism 96, 97
Polchies, Amanda 88
police violence 17, 18, 23–24, 40–44, 87
 see also state violence
political violence 33
 see also state violence
politicians 15, 17, 23
politics and praxis 113–115
pollution 124–126
Pontin, B. 126
Popple, K. 9
popular resistance 157–163
poverty
 Asia 192
 Buenaventura, Colombia 33
 Roma, Slovakia 62, 67
 South Africa 108, 110, 138, 142
Powell, F. 9
power 86, 113–115, 139–140, 142, 175–176, 181, 215
power plants 53–54, 103, 104
 development 54–56
 map *55*
 public resistance to 57–58
 and social class 59–61

praxis 113–115, 143–144
pressure on government 204
privatisation 32, 33–34, 55, 138
Procesco de Communidades Negras (PCN) 34
professional activists 25–26
puntos de encuentos (Roadblocks) 37–38

Q

Qasrawi, Jawad 190
Qato, D.M. 126
Qumsiyeh, M.B. 157, 157–158

R

racism
  Colombia 44
  Nova Scotia 84, 86, 88, 93
  Slovakia 60–61, 63, 67
radical self-education 23
rainforests 32
Ramaphosa, Cyril 137
Rancière, Jacques 8
recycling 69, 71–72, 73, 74
Regional Public Health Authority (RÚVZ), Laborov 58
renewable energy 181
Renewable Obligation Scotland Order Act 2006 72
repression 18, 50
resistance 2, 8, 9
Responsible Energy Action (REA) 84–85, 89–90, 96
road accidents 197
roadblocks (*puntos de encuentro*) 37–38
Robillard, C.-E. 165
Roma 53, 54, 57, 59–60, 60–61, 61–62, 63, 65–67
Rosenfeld, M. 157
Ross, S. 93
Rossport Five 16, 20
Rossport struggle 19
Royal Canadian Mounted Police (RCMP) 87
Rustomjee, Z. 145

S

Safi, A.S. 155
Samsung 196, 200
Scandrett, E. 4, 73, 157, 159, 174
Scheffel, D. 61
Schneider, K. 106
Schugurensky, D. 90
Scotland
  anti-incineration movement 73–79, 80
  Better than Zero 190, 200, 202, 205–206
  Challenge Breast Cancer Scotland 199–200
  Circular Economy Strategy 79
  Energy from Waste 69–70
  Fair Hospitality 204
  National Waste Strategy 70–72
  planning system 75–76, 78–79, 80
  Renewable Obligation Scotland Order Act 2006 72
  Zero Waste Plan 2010 73
Scottish Waste Awareness Group 71
second nature 1
segregation 54, 61–62
Seikaly, S. 156
Sekukuneland Environmental Justice Network 147
selective hegemony 174, 176, 181
self-education 21–22, 23, 24, 90
settler-colonisation, Palestine 117–119, 153–154
  and community development 156–157
  and international solidarity 166–167
  as normalisation 163–166
  as popular struggle 157–163
  and environmental justice 154–155
Seven Weeks for Water 131
Shaw, M. 166, 215
Shell to Sea 15–18
  campaign goals 21–22, 24
  cohesion among activists 20–21
  counter-expertise 22
  impact on radical politics 19–20
  knowledge transfer 24
  police violence 17, 18, 23–24
  professional activists 25–26
  radical self-education 23
Silicon Valley 203
Simpson, Bryan 190
Sklair, Lesley 4
Skobla, D. 62
Šládek, J. 58, 62
Slovakia
  coal-burning power plant 53–54
  development 54–56
  map 55
  public resistance to 57–58
  and social class 59–61
  Roma population 53, 54, 57, 59–60, 60–61, 61
  waste management 62–66
Smart Cities 181
Smith, H. 87, 88
Smith, Ted 191
social class 59–61, 77, 96, 215
social home-care workers 196
social justice 141

social media 202, 208
social movement learning (SML) 85–86
social movement process 180
social movements 22, 29
social partnership 19, 25
Solidar Suisse 191
solidarity 10, 26, 213, 214, 215–216
  Buenaventura civic strike 46, 47–48
  occupational and environmental health 204–206
  Palestine 166–167
South Africa
  accumulation by dispossession 137–138
  colonialism 102–103, 140
  Constitution of 1996 141
  development 137
  environmental justice movements 141
  extractive industry 101
    community resistance 105, 106, 107–113, 113–115, 147–148
    history 102–105
    licensing 137
    present day 105–107
  groundWork 141–142
    Environmental Justice School (EJS) 135–136, 142–146
      challenges 149–150
      participants' evaluations 146, 150
      participants' struggles 146–148
  neoliberalism 139
  power 139–140
South Korea 199, 200
Special Economic Zones 174
Sports Direct 200, 201, 208
state violence 40–44, 50, 51
  see also police violence; political violence
Steger, T. 62
Steingraber, Sandra 83, 84
Stewart, P. 103
strike see Civic Strike to Live with Dignity in Buenaventura
sub-contracting 208
supply chains 208
Supporters for the Health and Rights of People in the Semiconductors Industry (SHARPS) 199
sustainable development 3–5
SWN Energy Co. 87, 88

T

Tal, A. 163
Taula Catalana por los Derechos Humanos en Colombia 32
technology 202
televised debates 49–50

territory see land rights
testimony 203
Thobejane, Mmathopelo 147, 150
trade deals 32, 33, 208
trade unions 207–208
traffic accidents 197
Tulkarm region, Palestine 124–126
Turkey 197

U

Union Carbide insecticide factory 173
Union of Agricultural Works Committees (UAWC) 160–161
unionisation 207–208
Unite the Union 201
United Nations Conference on Environment and Development (UNCED) 3, 4
unity 46, 47
US
  day labourers 196–197
  environmental justice movements 5–6
  National Council for Occupational Safety and Health (COSH) 198, 203, 204, 206

V

Varley, T. 25
Veracini, L. 153
Vietnam 196
violence see police violence; political violence; state violence
Voortrekkers 102

W

Wacquant, Loïc 54, 62
Walia, H. 88, 94
Waste Framework Directive (EU) 72–73, 75
waste hierarchy 69, 72–73
waste industry 69–70, 71, 72–73
  anti-incineration movement 73–79, 80
waste management
  Laborov 53, 61, 62–66, 64, 66
  marine litter 181–182
  Renewable Obligation Scotland Order Act 2006 72
  Scottish National Waste Strategy 70–72
  Zero Waste Cities 182
  Zero Waste Plan 2010 Scotland 73
water 121, 128, 131, 139, 148, 155, 165, 166–167
West Bank 121, 122, 124, 127, 154–155
Wheeler review panel 91–93
Whitehead, J. 174, 175, 176, 179

Whitelaw, G. 102
Williams, A. 88
women 2, 161–163, 199–200
  labour market 196–197
  women's march, Colombia *48*
Women's Environment Network 199
work and community boundaries
    195–197
workers' organisations 197–204
workplace *see* occupational and
    environmental health
World Council of Churches (WCC)
    131

Y

young people 200
youth centres 159–160
Ytterstad, A. 24

Z

Zeitoun, M. 120, 165
zero waste 70–73, 74, 75, 79
Zero Waste Cities 182
Zikode, S'bu 114
Zionist movement 117–118, 118–119
  see also settler-colonisation, Palestine
Zohary, T. 120
Zuma, Jacob 139
Zwahre, M. 157, 159, 162